Private International Law in China

Guangjian Tu

Private International Law in China

Springer

Guangjian Tu
School of Law
University of Macau
Macau
People's Republic of China

ISBN 978-981-10-0675-3 ISBN 978-981-287-993-6 (eBook)
DOI 10.1007/978-981-287-993-6

Springer Singapore Heidelberg New York Dordrecht London

Softcover re-print of the Hardcover 1st edition 2016

Printed on acid-free paper

Springer Science+Business Media Singapore Pte Ltd. is part of Springer Science+Business Media (www.springer.com)

Contents

About the Author

Prof. Dr. Guangjian Tu is currently an associate professor of Law in the University of Macau, a life member of Clare Hall (Cambridge University), an elected associate member of the International Academy of Comparative Law, and a standing member of the Chinese Society of Private International Law. Although his first major was not law but medical science, his strong interests in law came to surface when he was still an undergraduate student in the Science and Technology University of Central China (Wuhan, PRC). After graduation from that university, he obtained a diploma on law from Zhejiang University (Hangzhou, PRC) and was qualified to be a lawyer and a judge, respectively, by sitting national examinations of the PRC. Having served in the Intermediate Court of Ningbo (Zhejiang Province, PRC) for a while, he left for UK to pursue his LLM and Ph.D. in the University of Aberdeen. He formally started his academic career at the University of Macau in September 2007. Since then, he has been teaching and researching in the field of Private International Law. So far, he has published two monographs and many academic articles extensively on Chinese Private International Law in widely circulated and internationally recognized journals.

Abbreviations

CCL	Chinese Contract Law
CPL	Chinese Civil Procedure Law
CSPIL	Chinese Society of Private International Law
EC	European Community
GPCL	General Principles on Civil Law
HCCH	Hague Conference on Private International Law
IP	Intellectual Property
LAL	Law on the Application of Law for Foreign-related Civil Legal Relationships
NPC	The National People's Congress
PIL	Private International Law
PRC	The People's Republic of China
SCNPC	The Standing Committee of the National People's Congress
SPC	The Supreme People's Court
UK	The United Kingdom
US	The United States of America
WTO	World Trade Organization

Chapter 1
Introduction

1.1 Historical Development of Private International Law in China

1.1.1 The Period Before 1978

1. Back in 600–700 years A.D. when ancient China was still in Tang Dynasty, there seemingly appeared the earliest Chinese conflict of law rules which says, 'If foreigners from the same country offend each other, their own law shall apply; if foreigners from different countries offend each other, this law [the then Chinese law] shall apply'.[1] Due to the fact that in ancient China, criminal law and civil law were not strictly separated, these conflict rules applied to both criminal law and civil law cases.[2] Later on, these conflict rules had been followed until Ming and Qing Dynasties when the Chinese stance came back to adopt the principle of 'strict territoriality' i.e. any foreign-related case shall be decided according to Chinese law.[3] Since the Opium War broke out in 1840, China had lost much of its sovereignty including judicial sovereignty. As far as foreign-related cases were concerned, Chinese judges normally had no power to try so that Private International Law (PIL) was not developed at that time at all.[4] After the establishment of the Republic of China in 1911, an 'Act on Application of Foreign Law' was adopted in 1918, modeled on the 1896 German counterpart and 1898 Japanese counterpart.[5] This Act was, however, not so useful and applied so much in practice because it was not really compatible with the then Chinese society.[6]

---

[1]See Li (2000, p. 89).

[2]See Huang (2005, p. 162).

[3]Ibid.

[4]See Han (2003, 59).

[5]See Zhao (2007, p. 47).

[6]Ibid.

G. Tu, *Private International Law in China*, DOI 10.1007/978-981-287-993-6_1

2. Ever since the People's Republic of China (PRC) was founded in 1949, it abolished all the unequal treaties imposed by the imperialism countries during the late Qing Dynasty and abrogated the privileges of foreigners in China and became a country with a unitary socialist legal system.[7] This provided the political conditions for China to develop its external relationships independently and its own conflict of laws. However, owing to the America's 'embargo' and 'blockade' policies following the 'Korean War', China was impeded from developing diplomatic relationships with western countries. Although China successfully established diplomatic relationships with some other socialist countries, it mainly remained closed or semi-closed.[8] Foreign-related civil relationships only happened occasionally, and under the circumstances at that time, the lawsuits or legal problems with foreign elements were basically decided or resolved according to Chinese law. Therefore, the legislative body did not pay much attention to PIL.[9] Except for the only conflict rule made in the <Sino-Soviet Consular Treaty> in 1959, one could not find any other until after 1978.[10] The domestic legislation regarding PIL was, therefore, totally a blank during this period.

1.1.2 The Period After 1978–Up to Now

3. After 1978, China began to implement the 'opening up' policy. With the increasing integration between China and the global market and the broad interactions between China and foreign countries, the need for legislation on PIL has become more and more acute. The fast-growing Chinese economy has contributed a lot to the development of Chinese PIL in various aspects. It is in this period that China made most of its PIL laws that are currently applicable. Over the past three decades, together with other laws, China has extensively and intensively enacted in the field of PIL including rules on the legal status of foreigners,[11] choice of law rules, international jurisdiction rules, rules of service of documents abroad, rules of taking of evidence abroad and rules of international commercial arbitration.[12]

[7]Generally see MacFarquhar and Fairbank (1987, p. 5).

[8]See Huang (2005, p. 120).

[9]Ibid.

[10]See Art. 16, para. 1, sub-para. 3 of the Sino-Soviet Consular Treaty signed on 10 September 1986 which entered into force on 16 April 1987, which says, 'Under the circumstances that do not interfere with the power of the recipient country's authority, it shall be governed by the laws and regulations of the sending state to solve the dispute between the captain and sailor, including the dispute on salary and labor contract'.

[11]Generally, foreigners in China can enjoy equal civil legal status as Chinese citizens, see Arts. 18 and 32 of the Constitution of PRC; Art. 8, para. 2 and Art. 48 of General Principles on Civil Law of the People's Republic of China; Arts. 6 and 24 of Foreign Trade Law of the People's Republic of China; Arts. 193, 196 and 197 of Company Law of the People's Republic of China.

[12]These rules will be discussed in details in the following respective parts of this book.

In the meantime, China has become more and more active in participating in international conventions and negotiations respecting PIL, following its growing importance in the international arena.[13]

1.2 The Chinese Political Structure, Court System and Legal Sources of PIL

1.2.1 The Chinese Political Structure

4. Unlike a federal country such as the US, Canada or Australia, China is a highly centralized one in which there is only one unified constitution for the whole land, a strong central government with all powers if not being devolved to local governments and a set of laws including private laws applicable to the whole territory.[14] Basically, the governmental machinery includes the people's congress, the administrative government, the people's court and the people's procuratorate, the latter three of which are produced by and answerable to the first one.[15]

5. The National People's Congress (NPC) and its Standing Committee (SCNPC) are the most important legislature in the central government. They enjoy most power of legislation. The Constitution and basic laws such as Criminal law, Criminal Procedure Law, General Principles on Civil Law, Civil Procedure Law all must be made or revised by them.[16] The SCNPC also enjoys the power of 'Legislative Interpretation' on the laws made by the NPC and itself, which shall prevail over the interpretations given in judicial practice by the Supreme People's Court or the Supreme People's Procuratorate if there is any conflict.[17]

---

[13]See infra Sect. 1.4 of this chapter.

[14]See Zhang (2004, pp. 261–286). However, with the return of Hong Kong and Macau, this statement should be qualified, see infra Sect. 1.3 of this chapter. Hereinafter, in this book, when the Chinese situation is discussed, Hong Kong and Macau are not included in unless specifically indicated otherwise.

[15]See Arts. 3, 85, 105, 123 and 129 of the Constitution of PRC.

[16]See Art. 57 of the Constitution of PRC, which says, 'Its [National People's Congress] permanent body is the Standing Committee of the National People's Congress'; Art. 62, para. 3 [NPC's functions and powers], which says, 'To enact and amend basic statutes concerning criminal offences, civil affairs, the State organs and other Matters'; Art. 67, para. 2 [SCNPC's functions and powers], which says, 'To enact and amend statutes with the exception of those which should be enacted by the National People's Congress'.

[17]See Art. 67, para. 4 of the Constitution of PRC [SCNPC's functions and powers], which says, 'To interpret statutes'. Also see Wu (2005, p. 60).

1.2.2 The Chinese Court System

6. In China, there are basically four levels of courts in ascending order i.e. the court at county (or district) level, the intermediate court at a middle-size city (or prefecture) level, the high court at province (or autonomous region or municipality) level and the Supreme People's Court (SPC, the only highest court) for the whole country.[18] A case normally can have two instances if it is not initiated in the SPC.[19]

1.2.2.1 The Supreme People's Court and Its Documents

7. Although it is said that the SPC itself can try cases, the SPC seldom performs this function and the main role actually played by the SPC is to supervise and provide guidance for judicial practice in lower courts.[20] The guidance of the SPC is usually given in the documentations of 'Judicial Interpretations',[21] which may be made in four different forms, namely, 'Interpretation (*Jieshi*)', 'Provision (*Guiding*)', 'Reply (*Pifu*)' and 'Decision (*Jueding*)'.[22] These four forms of Interpretations are all legally binding.[23] As will be seen in the following text of this book, the SPC's Interpretations actually occupy a very important position in Chinese legal system, without knowledge of which one cannot really understand and have a full picture for Chinese law including private international law. The

[18]Apart from the normal courts, there are also some special courts in China such as martial courts, maritime courts, railway courts etc., see Art. 2 of Organic Law of the People's Courts of the People's Republic of China; also see Claker (1996, pp. 6–7).

[19]See Art. 11 of Organic Law of the People's Courts of the People's Republic of China; Art. 164 of Chinese Civil Procedure Law. If a case is initiated in the Supreme People's Court, there will be only one instance allowed, see Art. 155 of Chinese Civil Procedure Law. In China, there is, however, the trial-supervision procedure that could be launched to correct the mistakes of normal trials, see Arts. 198 and 199 of Chinese Civil Procedure Law. Also see Zhong and Yu (2004, p. 398).

[20]See Art. 127 of the Constitution of PRC, which says, 'The Supreme People's Court supervises the administration of justice by the local people's courts at different levels and by the special people's courts'.

[21]See Art. 32 of Organic Law of the People's Courts of the People's Republic of China, which says, 'The Supreme People's Court gives interpretation on questions concerning specific application of laws and decrees in judicial proceedings'; Resolution of SCNPC Providing an Improved Interpretation of the Law, Art. 2, which says, 'Interpretation of questions involving the specific application of laws and decrees in court trials shall be provided by the Supreme People's Court.' The Supreme People's Procuratorate can also give 'Judicial Interpretation' but its Interpretations are mainly about criminal and criminal procedure laws, which are not so relevant to this book.

[22]See Art. 6 of 'Provisions on Judicial Interpretation Work by the Supreme People's Court' which was issued on 23 March 2007 by the SPC and came into force on 1 April 2007.

[23]See Art. 5, ibid.

large amount of Judicial Interpretations made by the Supreme People's Court is, on the one hand, the culmination of judicial experiences by Chinese courts; on the other hand, aimed at the new situations and problems to be encountered in judicial practice. This is, of course, also attributable to the reality that in China, laws have only been developed quite recently on the whole and many laws have been made quite abstract, crude and unworkable in practice with details left to be filled in by judicial practice, for which the SPC is assigned the task.

8. As said, the power of 'Legislative Interpretation' is exclusively conferred upon the Standing Committee of the NPC and 'Legislative Interpretation' shall prevail over 'Judicial Interpretation' where there is a conflict.[24] Theoretically, the Supreme People's Court can make judicial interpretations only on the matters arising out of the application of laws in adjudicatory practices.[25] In reality, however, the Standing Committee of NPC has not fully performed its function of construing the laws. This has left much room for the SPC which has been playing an even more important role in interpreting laws than the Standing Committee of the NPC and de facto almost has the exclusive power of interpreting laws.[26] In particular, since 1980s, the Chinese policy of reform and opening-up has brought about great changes for and strong impact on Chinese judicial system. Laws have been consecutively laid out and cases of international civil litigation before Chinese courts have been increasing by a large scale. However, the Chinese laws were still found increasingly inadequate to meet the drastic social and economic changes.[27] Under such circumstances, the Supreme People's Court has to undertake even more of the task of interpreting laws to provide guidance for lower courts to deal with real cases in practice.[28]

9. The SPC may also issue other kinds of legal documents like 'Notice (*Tongzhi*)' or 'Answer (*Jieda*)', which, theoretically, are not legally binding but only have persuasive effects on lower courts' practice.[29] The issuance of Notices (or Circulars) by the Supreme People's Court also accounts for a large portion of the SPC's work of supervising and guiding. Some Notices issued by Supreme People's Court do interpret laws although they are not given the status of Judicial Interpretations.[30] It is well understood that lower courts also treat these documents as de facto legally binding.[31]

---

[24]See supra para. 5.

[25]See Art. 32 of Organic Law of the People's Courts of the People's Republic of China.

[26]See Liu (1989–1990, p. 278).

[27]See Finder (1993, p. 165).

[28]Ibid.

[29]See Zhang (1997, pp. 102–103).

[30]See Finder (1993, p. 180). Also see Article 6 of Provisions on Judicial Interpretation Work by the Supreme People's Court which was issued on 23 March 2007 by the SPC and came into force on 1 April 2007.

[31]See Folsom et al. (1992, p. 129).

10. Owing to this unique phenomenon in Chinese legal landscape, some even say that the SPC enjoys de facto quasi-legislative power although it is not a legislature but judicature.[32] Undoubtedly, to give detailed guidance on the application of law in judicial practice for lower courts by issuing documents is an important and meaningful job especially when the Chinese legislations are not yet designed delicately enough. However, it does not fully conform to the role the SPC shall perform as a judicature rather than a legislature. In addition, too many Interpretations could be confusing and may cause conflicts with the laws or each other and this obviously should not be the long-term strategy.

1.2.2.2 The Effects of the SPC's Judgments and Higher Courts' Judgments

11. Traditionally, China is a country of civil law family[33] and theoretically an earlier judgment, even a judgment rendered by the SPC, does not have any legally binding effect as a precedent in a common law jurisdiction.[34] Therefore, Chinese judges in lower levels of courts are generally not bound by the judgments made by judges in higher levels of courts.

12. Nevertheless, since 1985, the SPC has begun to publicize more and more cases decided by itself in its Gazette. Apart from its own judgments, the SPC has also collected cases from lower levels of courts which it thought as typical and representative, re-written the reasoning of the judgments and made the cases open to the public. The publicized cases were supposed to only serve as guidance for the judges in the lower levels' courts and 'models to help less experienced judges learn methods of legal reasoning'.[35] The official statement of the Supreme People's Court did say that the publicized cases in the Gazette do not mean to be precedents.[36] Indeed, there were no Chinese judges that invoked other judgments as basis for making decisions.

13. However, shortly after the publication of decided cases by the SPC in its Gazette, it was argued that the real situation might have been changing subtly. Although it is not convincing that the Supreme People's Court intends to make these cases as precedents, by editing and re-writing the reasoning in the reported cases to guide the lower levels of courts, the Supreme People's Court actually is imitating the case-law method.[37] Especially, when viewed from the perspective of judges in lower levels of courts, the 'guidance' in their minds does not merely embrace the literal meaning. They are more likely to follow the reasoning in the

[32]See Huang (1998, pp. 188–207).

[33]See Wang (2006, p. 77).

[34]See Robertson (1968, p. 78).

[35]See Hsia and Zeldin (1987, pp. 258–259).

[36]See Liu (1991, p. 114).

[37]See Liu (1991, p. 118).

publicized cases due to their capacity of applying law and the ambiguities existing in legislations. As a matter of fact, not only the cases publicized in the SPC's Gazette, but also all the cases decided by higher levels of courts may have a certain value of precedent, given that lower court judgments may be reversed and lower court judges even may lose their career if they do not follow. Therefore, Chinese judges will generally follow the track of the judgments rendered by higher levels of courts. Accordingly, as argued, the cases publicized by the SPC (and also cases decided in higher levels' courts) do have 'regulatory effects' on later judgments.[38]

14. Nowadays, Chinese courts are more and more encouraged and required to publicize their cases online with the technology development of communication.[39] For the purpose of PIL, there is a website specifically designed for publicizing foreign-related civil, commercial and maritime cases where one can find a lot of cases of different kinds.[40]

15. To sum up, it can be said that court cases in China are not legally binding but do have influence or persuasive effects, especially those cases decided or publicized by the SPC or higher levels' courts. Therefore, to know the law in practice, in some following parts of this book, court cases will be studied to demonstrate the real situation in China.[41]

1.2.2.3 Chinese Judges

16. In China, the reputation of judges was generally unsatisfactory if not notorious. The situation, however, has seemingly been changing for better in recent years because more and more graduates from law schools with some years' experience of judicial practice are replacing their senior colleagues, most of whom are veterans, as Chinese judges. Moreover, on top of a law degree, the new generation of Chinese judges must have passed the National Judicial Examination before they can become a judge, compared to their elder colleagues who could be a judge without sitting any professional exam and any degree, let alone a degree of law.[42] Given this trend, the general quality of personnel in Chinese courts is, therefore, improving.

17. This is true especially as far as judges dealing with international civil and commercial cases are concerned. In China, judges for foreign-related cases are often specially chosen, with emphasis on professionalism, and they are already at

---

[38]Ibid.

[39]See 'Decisions of the Supreme People's Court about the Judicial Publicity (6 Items)' issued on 8 December 2009, available at http://www.court.gov.cn/qwfb/sfwj/jd/201003/t20100331_3593.htm (last visited on 8 August 2015).

[40]See the Chinese website of Trials on Foreign-related Commercial and Maritime Cases, http://www.ccmt.org.cn/.

[41]See infra paras. 94 and 217.

[42]See Lubman (2000, p. 396), Avino (2003, p. 380) and Hung (2008, p. 223).

the higher level than others. According to a report delivered by the then vice-president of the Supreme People's Court in 2005, 'there are totally 2142 judges exclusively dealing with international commercial and maritime case, 93 % of whom are above the educational level of bachelor degree, 32 % of whom are above master degree and 3 % have doctorate degree'.[43] Although this data is not enough to prove how professional this group of Chinese judges is, one can see that they had reached a reasonable standard, at least in terms of educational background.

18. Nevertheless, the overall political environment for Chinese judges is undesirable, not only because of the administrative nature of Chinese court system, but also the lack of judicial independence to some extent.[44] In China, judges are viewed as government employees. In terms of applying law, the role of judges has been limited to 'the straightforward and mechanical application of the law to identify the correct solutions'.[45] Moreover, within the court system, the working method is that each decision made by a judge has to be approved by his/er superior. Sometimes, even external interference or pressure from other departments of the government or the organs of the communist party may occur. Problems may also come from the special features of Chinese culture in which people used to and still believe more in 'rule by people' rather than 'rule by law' and in which Confucian morality to maintain social relations ('*guan xi*') lead to a 'harmonious outcome, rather than a predictable and "legally proper" outcome'.[46] Therefore, it is still difficult for Chinese judges to be free from these factors in dealing with cases including international civil and commercial cases.

1.2.2.4 Chinese Judgments

19. In almost all cases, the statement of reasoning in a Chinese judgment is usually quite short, sometimes even no much reasoning is provided. It is difficult for one to figure out what the judges are really thinking of the case from the text of the judgment. Unlike the judgments in common law countries or some civil law countries where one can see a lot of reasoning on why and how the judges have applied the law to the case, Chinese judgments lay out long length of the facts, short length of laws applicable and even shorter length to fit the facts into the law which is the most important part to render the judgment for the case.[47] Therefore, if one

---

[43]See the speech delivered in the Second Country-wide Conference on Trial Work of Foreign-related Commercial and Maritime Cases by the then Vice President of the Supreme People's Court, Wan Erxiang, which can still be accessed at http://www.ccmt.org.cn/shownews.php?id=6354 (last visited on 8 August 2015).

[44]See Peerenboom (2002, p. 318), in which it is said, 'courts have been viewed as party/state organs and judges as government administrators or bureaucrats. Within the bureaucracy, the stature of the judiciary and judges has been low'.

[45]See Chow (2003, p. 204).

[46]See Heye (2003–2004, pp. 546, 548–549).

[47]See Chow (2003, p. 211).

wants to study Chinese cases, as done in some of the following parts by the current author, s/he should be quite able to summarize and extract the essence from those cases to explore what the real Chinese law in practice is.

1.2.3 Legal Sources of Chinese PIL

20. From the above introduction, one can see that in China, the laws legislated by the NPC (or SCNPC) are the foremost important sources for PIL such as the Law on the Application of Law for Foreign-related Civil Legal Relationship, General Principles on Civil Law and Chinese Civil Procedure Law.[48] However, the prominent position of the SPC in providing guidance for lower courts' judicial practice in China dictates that the study of the relevant documents (Interpretations and others) issued by the SPC is necessary if one really wants to know the full picture of Chinese law. Although no 'precedent' is recognized in Chinese law, the SPC has increasingly drawn lower courts' attention to the cases decided or selected to be publicized by it and has also increasingly encouraged, or even commanded lower courts to publicize their judgments online. Indeed, if one wants to study the real law in practice, rather than the law in the statute, one can now find many reported Chinese cases although the judgments, especially the reasoning of the judgments for those cases might be rather short. Therefore, Chinese court cases, especially those publicized or decided by the SPC, at least have persuasive force and could be regarded as legal source for Chinese PIL, too. Apart from the sources derived from domestic laws, any international convention on private international law, of course, can become source of Chinese PIL if China has ratified/acceded to it.[49] However, it seems unclear whether scholars' treatises or scholarly doctrine can be some kind of source for Chinese PIL. According to the current author's observation, they have not become legal sources yet at this stage of Chinese legal development.

1.3 Inter-regional Conflict of Laws Within China

1.3.1 The Emergence of Chinese Inter-regional Conflict of Laws

21. As said, China is a highly-centralized country in which the basic laws like civil law and civil procedure law should be applicable to the whole territory and there

[48]These laws will be discussed in more detail later on in this book.

[49]See infra Sect. 1.4 of this chapter.

thus should not be the problem of conflict of laws within China.[50] This situation, however, has changed with the return of Hong Kong from the UK and Macau from Portugal to the motherland respectively in 1997 and 1999 under the policy of 'One Country, Two Systems'.[51] Since then, China has become a country with multiple legal systems and inter-regional conflict of laws has come into exist within China.[52] This is because according to the Hong Kong and Macau Basic Laws, both of the two Special Administrative Region (SAR)s can enjoy very high autonomy,[53] based upon which both Hong Kong and Macau can have most their own laws including private laws that are different from those applicable in the mainland China.[54] The current situation is, therefore, that the so-called Chinese law, on most occasions, refers to the laws in the mainland China only and the laws applicable in Hong Kong SAR and Macau SAR are those different ones largely inherited from their colonizers respectively i.e. England and Portugal.[55]

---

[50]See supra para. 4.

[51]The policy of 'one country, two systems' was first conceived in late 1978 when Deng Xiaoping formulated his policy for the peaceful settlement of the Issue of Taiwan. See 'Deng Xiaoping's Talk with Yang Liyu', in Deng (1993, p. 230). Later on, this policy was incorporated into two joint declarations. One was concluded between the PRC and the United Kingdom for the return of Hong Kong in 1997 i.e. Joint Declaration on the Question of Hong Kong, Sept. 26, 1984, U.K.—P.R.C., 23 I.L.M. 1371 [hereinafter, the Sino-British Joint Declaration]. For comments, see Davis (1988, p. 145) (saying that, 'The Joint Declaration reveals a prominent commitment to autonomy, self-determination, stability, capitalist economy, and human rights in a common law framework. These concepts collectively provide the outline of a pluralist, liberal capitalist system'); see also Chiu et al. (1987) (discussing the political, legal, economic and social aspects of the Sino-British Joint Declaration on Hong Kong); Palumbo (1990–1991, p. 667) and Corwin (1987, p. 505). Another was concluded between the PRC and Portugal for the return of Macau in 1999 i.e. Joint Declaration on the Question of Macau, Mar. 26, 1987, P.R.C.-Port., Beijing Review, April 6, 1987 [hereinafter the Sino-Portuguese Joint Declaration]. For more discussion on the policy of 'one country, two systems', see 'A Reliable Guarantee for Hong Kong's Long-Term Stability and Prosperity', *Hongqi* [*Red Flag*] (Beijing), 21 October 1984, 21–22, which was reprinted by *Foreign Broadcast Information Service* (United States), 10 December 1984, 34; see also Chang (1988, p. 99), Hansell et al. (1986, p. 348) and Turkel (1986–1987, p. 471).

[52]This part will not touch upon the conflict of laws issues related to Taiwan because the political landscape is different as far as Taiwan is concerned.

[53]See Art. 2 of the Basic Law of the Hong Kong Special Administrative Region of the People's Republic of China (hereinafter, Hong Kong Basic Law) and the Basic Law of the Macau Special Administrative Region of the People's Republic of China (hereinafter, Macau Basic Law), which says, 'The National People's Congress authorizes Hong Kong (Macau) Special Administrative Region to exercise a high degree of autonomy …'. Compared with a state or a province in a federal country such as the US or Canada, Hong Kong and Macau can actually enjoy more autonomy, see Ding and Zhidong (2005, p. 326). The two Basic Laws serve as a mini-constitution for the two SARs.

[54]See Art. 8 of Hong Kong Basic Law and Macau Basic Law. The laws that can apply to the whole territory of China including Hong Kong and Macau are mainly those related to foreign diplomatic affairs and national security, see Annex III of the Hong Kong Basic Law and Macau Basic Law.

[55]See Luke (2000, p. 717) and Edmonds and Yee (1999, pp. 801, 801–817).

1.3.2 The Features of Chinese Inter-regional Conflict of Laws

22. In contrast with the situation in a federal country or other countries with multiple legal systems, the Chinese inter-regional conflict of laws has its own special features because of the unique political status of the two SARs.

First, in the mainland China, although market economy is introduced, it is still the socialism regime that is being implemented while in the two SARs, the society is of capitalism.[56] This means that the big societal differences would still exist between the mainland China and the two SARs, which will contribute to the difficulty in harmonizing private laws between them to some extent.

23. Secondly, although there is the so-called Constitution of the People's Republic of China, this Constitution is, again, only applicable to the mainland China except one Article [applicable to Hong Kong SAR and Macau SAR] which says, 'The State may establish Special Administrative Regions when necessary. The systems to be instituted in Special Administrative Regions shall be prescribed by law enacted by the National People's Congress in the light of specific conditions.'[57] Due to the lack of a common constitutional basis, it would be relatively more difficult to take any action in unifying or harmonizing private laws among them.[58]

24. Thirdly, Hong Kong SAR and Macau SAR can enjoy highly independent legislative power for a broad scope of matters including criminal law, administrative law, civil law and commercial law etc.[59] The laws made by the central government can apply in Hong Kong and Macau usually only when issues of foreign diplomacy or national security are concerned.[60] Thus, there is no legislature in China that can make any uniform private law that is applicable to all the three regions, due to which it was argued that Chinese inter-regional conflict of laws is essentially or almost like international conflict of laws.[61]

25. Fourthly, according to the Basic Laws, Hong Kong and Macau can enjoy final adjudicatory power.[62] The Supreme People's Court in Beijing is only the highest court for the mainland China and not for the two SARs. Hong Kong and Macau have their own Court of Final Appeal.[63] Therefore, there is actually no one court that can give a judgment for all the three regions. Otherwise, a common supreme court might be able to harmonize private laws by giving judgments for the whole land.[64]

---

[56]See Art. 5 of Hong Kong Basic Law and Macau Basic Law.

[57]See Art. 31 of the Constitution of PRC.

[58]Cf. in the US, inter-state conflict of laws has been harmonized on the basis of clauses in the Constitution such as 'due process' and 'full faith and credit', see Symeonides (2008, pp. 46–47).

[59]See Art. 17 of Hong Kong Basic Law and Macau Basic Law.

[60]See Annex III of Hong Kong Basic Law and Macau Basic Law.

[61]See Ding and Chen (2005, p. 326).

[62]See Article 19 of Hong Kong Basic Law and Macau Basic Law.

[63]See Article 82 of Hong Kong Basic Law and Article 84 of Macau Basic Law.

[64]Cf. the situation in the US where the Supreme Court has harmonized conflict of laws by a series of cases, see Symeonides (2008, pp. 26–34, 327–333). Also see Han (2003, p. 327).

26. Fifthly, the Chinese inter-regional conflict of laws occurs between different legal traditions. The mainland China, as said, is basically a jurisdiction of civil law tradition.[65] Macau has closely followed Portuguese law, which belongs to the civil law family as well. However, Hong Kong has inherited the approaches and methodologies of the English legal system. It, thus, seems natural that there would be more difficulties in achieving harmonization between the mainland China and Hong Kong but less between mainland China and Macau.[66]

27. Sixthly, owing to the high autonomy the SARs can enjoy, the international treaties between mainland China and other countries are not directly applicable to Hong Kong and Macau and the applicability of those treaties may extend to the two SARs only after requested and agreed by the SARs[67]; the international conventions (agreements) that were previously applicable in the SARs can continue to apply after the handover even if those treaties have not been accepted by the mainland China.[68] Therefore, each of the three regions may be a member of/join an international agreement (convention) without the others. This could make the situation even more complicated. On the one hand, there are the conflicts among the domestic private laws of the three regions; on the other hand, the private laws of one region may have conflict with the international agreement that has come into effect in the other region and an international agreement applicable in one region may have conflict with an international agreement applicable in the other.[69]

28. As can be seen, the Chinese inter-regional conflict of laws does have its own distinctive features even if one cannot say it is necessarily more complicated than its counterparts in other places. These features dictate the possible solutions and the achievements that have been obtained so far.

1.3.3 Possible Solutions for Chinese Inter-regional Conflict of Laws

29. As early as in 1995, before Hong Kong and Macau's handover, some Chinese scholars had already noticed the issue of Chinese inter-regional conflict laws and proposed alternative solutions to it:

---

[65]See Wang (2006, p. 77).

[66]See infra para. 39.

[67]See Article 153 of Hong Kong Basic Law and Article 138 of Macau Basic Law (Zhang 1998, p. 364). According to Article 138 of the Macau Basic Law, China has extended the applicability of 1958 New York Convention on Recognition and Enforcement of Foreign Arbitral Award to Macau SAR in 2005.

[68]See Article 153 of Hong Kong Basic Law and Article 138 of Macau Basic Law.

[69]See Zhao (2007, p. 433).

(1) unifying the different substantive laws;
(2) adopting uniform conflict rules; or
(3) providing a general framework.[70]

30. They also analyzed the feasibility of the different possible solutions according to the different stages of development.[71] Later on, the issue attracted more attentions from Chinese lawyers and a few more suggestions have been added.[72] All the proposals that have been debated by Chinese lawyers can succinctly be summarized as in the immediately following text.

1.3.3.1 Uniform Substantive Law Approach

31. This approach intends to resolve Chinese inter-regional conflict of laws by unifying the substantive private laws in the three regions. It is the most ideal and also the most effective if it could be implemented. However, as mentioned earlier, there is no legislature in China that can legislate uniformly for the three regions respecting private laws.[73] It is, therefore, idealistic and unrealistic. In addition, this approach might also go against the policy of 'One Country, Two Systems' under which the different laws in the different regions should be maintained at least for fifty years after the handover.[74]

1.3.3.2 Uniform Conflict Rules Approach

32. This approach intends to prescribe a uniform set of conflict rules for the three regions that could be uniformly applied by the three regions. This is not a bad idea and has actually been implemented in other regions with success.[75] However, to

---

[70]See Huang and Qian (1995, pp. 289–328).

[71]According to Huang and Qian, in the short run, the different regions would have to maintain their own respective existing conflict rules or could respectively formulate a new set of rules to deal with inter-regional cases; as an intermediate step, the mainland China and SARs need to negotiate a set of unified conflict rules that could be applied by all the three regions; after the 50 years as promulgated in the Joint Declarations and Basic Laws, the mainland China and SARs should eventually be able to be fully integrated, thereafter unified substantive laws may possibly be enacted for all the three regions, see Huang and Qian (1995, pp. 289–328).

[72]See Xiao (2002, p. 182), Xiao and Du (1998, p. 358), Zhu (2002, p. 637) and Zhang and Smart (2006, p. 568).

[73]See supra para. 24.

[74]See supra para. 21.

[75]For example, in the EU, see Regulation (EC) No 593/2008 of the European Parliament and of the Council of 17 June 2008 on the law applicable to contractual obligations (Rome I); Regulation (EC) No 864/2007 of the European Parliament and of the Council of 11 July 2007 on the law applicable to non-contractual obligations (Rome II); Council Regulation (EU) No 1259/2010 of 20 December 2010 implementing enhanced cooperation in the area of the law applicable to divorce and legal separation.

unify conflict rules within China is not easier than to unify substantive laws because conflict rules normally exist in the civil code if there were one in the concerned jurisdiction or a place that regulate matters which should belong to the civil code. As mentioned, there is no uniform legislature in China which could take action for this approach.[76] Meanwhile, the momentum for adopting this approach by multi-lateral agreement among the three regions is still insufficiently strong at this stage.

1.3.3.3 Respective Conflict Rules Dealing with Inter-regional Cases Approach

33. This approach intends to ask the three regions to specifically legislate their own conflict rules dealing with inter-regional cases that are different from those conflict rules dealing with private international cases. This approach recognizes the differences between inter-regional private law cases and international private cases. Of course, the respective conflict rules dealing with inter-regional cases might be able to move towards the same trend and can be harmonized to a certain extent in the process. However, as said by Prof. Han, the late founding father of PIL in China, it is 'feasible but undesirable' and could add another layer of complexity to the laws of the three regions because it could cause conflicts of inter-regional conflict rules.[77]

1.3.3.4 Quasi-private International Law Approach

34. This approach intends to allow the three regions to deal with inter-regional private cases in the same or a quite similar way as with international private cases. The three regions can actually borrow or refer to their respective laws and rules for international private cases when they come across inter-regional private cases. This approach might be the easiest one to be applied and accepted. However, it ignores the differences between international private cases and inter-regional private cases and actually makes no progress at all for the problem.[78]

1.3.3.5 Model Law Approach

35. This approach intends to provide uniform model laws for the three regions. If all the three regions could move towards the model laws, eventually the laws in the three regions would be harmonized. One can see that this approach has been

[76] See supra paras. 21 and 24.

[77] See Han (2003, p. 329).

[78] See Ding and Chen (2005, p. 329).

employed successfully in other countries such as the US.[79] However, on the one hand, the model laws are not legally binding and it takes quite a while before the model laws really exercise effects on the respective domestic legislations; on the other hand, there must be an active organization that can draft and provide the model laws, which does not exist yet within China.

1.3.3.6 Piece-Meal Approach

36. This approach intends to resolve the problem step by step and item by item. In the area where unification is urgently needed or possible, the uniform substantive law approach or the uniform conflict rules approach as discussed above will be adopted. Indeed, this approach is quite a realistic and useful one and it has been successfully relied on to obtain the achievements over the past decade.[80]

37. As a matter of fact, no any single approach discussed above can resolve the whole problem.[81] Realistically, one has to take into account all the approaches and can utilize them flexibly when encountered with the issue of Chinese inter-regional conflict of laws. Indeed, over the past decade, by this way, some achievements have been made in the field.

1.3.4 Achievements Made So Far and the Way Forward

38. Although there is no clause in the Chinese Constitution that can provide a sound common legal basis for the harmonization of inter-regional conflict of laws,[82] one can find such a clause for inter-regional judicial assistance in the mini-Constitutions of the SARs which says, 'The Hong Kong (Macau) Special Administrative Region may, through consultations and in accordance with law, maintain juridical relations with the judicial organs of other parts of the country, and they may render assistance to each other'.[83]

39. According to this clause and by a piece-meal approach, the achievements made over the past decade through the form of bilateral arrangement are as follows:

(1) Arrangement for Mutual Service of Judicial Documents in Civil and Commercial Proceedings between the Mainland and Hong Kong Courts, which was signed in Shenzhen on 14 Jan 1999 and came into force on 30 Mar 1999;

---

[79]E.g. the Uniform Commercial Code proposed by the American Law Institute has been broadly accepted by the States in the US.

[80]See Wong (1999, pp. 67–70) and Zhu (2002, p. 674).

[81]See Xiao (2006, p. 85).

[82]See supra para. 23.

[83]See Article 95 of Hong Kong Basic Law and Article 93 of Macau Basic Law.

(2) Arrangement Concerning Mutual Recognition and Enforcement of Arbitral Awards between the Mainland and the Hong Kong Special Administrative Region, which was signed in Shenzhen on 21 Jun 1999 and came into force on 1 Feb 2000;
(3) Arrangement for Mutual Service of Judicial Documents and Taking of Evidence in Civil and Commercial Proceedings between the Mainland and the Macau Special Administrative Region, which was signed in Macau on 15 Aug 2001 and came into force on 15 Sept 2001;
(4) Arrangement on Reciprocal Recognition and Enforcement of Judgments in Civil and Commercial Matters by the Courts of the Mainland and of the Macau Special Administrative Region, which was signed in Macau SAR on 28 Feb 2006 and came into force on 1 Apr 2006;
(5) Arrangement Concerning Reciprocal Recognition and Enforcement of Arbitral Awards between the Mainland and Macau Courts, which was signed in Beijing on 30 Oct 2007 and came into force on 1 Jan 2008;
(6) Arrangement on Reciprocal Recognition and Enforcement of Judgments in Civil and Commercial Matters by the Courts of the Mainland and of the Hong Kong Special Administrative Region Pursuant to Choice of Court Agreements between Parties Concerned, which was signed in Hong Kong on 14 Jul 2006 and came into force on 1 Aug 2008;
(7) Arrangement Concerning Reciprocal Recognition and Enforcement of Arbitral Awards between the Hong Kong Special Administrative Region and the Macau Special Administrative Region, which was signed in Macau on 7 Jan 2013 (and this Arrangement shall come into force on the date designated by both sides on consensus).

40. One still has to wait to see and more research needs to be done on how these Arrangements have been implemented and can be further improved.[84]

41. It has been wondered if the concept of 'judicial assistance' in the clause of the mini-Constitutions could be expanded to cover jurisdiction, choice of law and other issues, whereby these areas can also be harmonized on the legal basis provided by the clause in the future. This has been heatedly debated and is still a pending question.[85] Anyway, except the above Arrangements, each region is still treating the other as a foreign country and dealing with the cases related to the other in the same or pretty much the same way as related to a foreign country.[86] It is, however, the author's belief that more actions would and could be taken on Chinese inter-regional conflict of laws once it catches the attention of Chinese politicians although this might not be able to happen in the near future.

[84]For one of such papers, see Tu (2013, pp. 349–376).

[85]See Zhu (2002, p. 557).

[86]Ibid, p. 560.

1.4 International Participation by China

42. With the rapid development of Chinese economy and the increasing importance of China in the international arena especially in recent years, China has been more and more active in international participation for many matters including private international law, which can be reflected by the international activities for PIL China has engaged in and the international conventions (agreements) for PIL China has ratified or acceded to.[87]

1.4.1 International Activities Regarding PIL

43. Ever since 1981, China had been invited to send representatives as observers to attend the Special Committee Meeting of the Hague Conference on Private international Law for several times and indeed Chinese delegates had attended those meetings. In October 1986, China formally submitted its application to join the Hague Conference on Private international Law and became an official member on 3 July 1987. In October 1988, China sent its first delegation to attend the 16th Diplomatic Session of the Hague Conference. Thereafter, China has begun to participate in the activities of the Hague Conference on Private International Law more and more regularly.[88]

44. As well known, the International Institute for the Unification of Private Laws (UNIDROIT) headquartered in Rome, Italy, is another important inter-governmental organization for the harmonization of private laws, inter alia, through making draft conventions and model laws. In early 1983, Chinese government was invited by UNIDROIT to send delegation to attend the diplomatic conference discussing the <Convention on Agency in the International Sale of Goods> in Geneva. It was the first contact between China and the organization. In June 1985, China officially joined UNIDROIT and has played an increasingly active role in the Institute's activities since then.[89]

45. To sum up, against the backdrop of globalization, international trade and opening-up policy, China has been trying to integrate itself with the western developed countries and the general outside world. China realized the importance of participating in international activities (organizations) including those related to PIL, whereby it could have more communication with the outside and express its concerns in international fora. The international experience, of course, would on the one hand enhance the understanding between China and other countries and on the other hand be beneficial to Chinese domestic legislations.

---

[87]For an overview of this issue, see Xu (2008, p. 407).

[88]See Xu (2008, p. 407).

[89]See Yan and Wang (1984).

1.4.2 International Conventions (Agreements) Regarding PIL

46. In the field of PIL, the main multi-lateral international conventions (agreements) China has ratified/acceded to so far include:

(1) 1883.3.20 <Paris Convention for the Protection of industrial Property> (It was signed by China on 14 Nov 1984 and came into force in China on 15 Mar 1989);
(2) 1886.9.9 <Berne Convention for the Protection of Literary and Artistic Works> (It was signed by China on 1 Jul 1992 and came into force in China on 15 Oct 1992);
(3) 1891.4.14 <Madrid Agreement Concerning the International Registration of Marks> (It was signed by China on 1 Jul 1989 and came into force in China on 4 Oct 1989);
(4) 1958.6.10 <Convention on the Recognition and Enforcement of Foreign Arbitral Wards> (It was signed by China on 22 Jan 1987 and came into force in China on 22 Apr 1987);
(5) 1965.11.15 <Convention on the Service abroad of Judicial and Extra-judicial Documents in Civil or Commercial matters> (It was signed by China on 2 Mar 1991 and came into force in China on 1 Jan 1992);
(6) 1970.3.18 <Convention on the Taking of Evidence Abroad in Civil or Commercial Matters> (It was signed by China on 8 Dec 1997 and came into force in China on 8 Feb 1998);
(7) 1980.1.1 <United Nations Convention on Contracts for the International Sale of Goods> (It was signed by China on 30 Sept 1981 and came into force in China on 11 Dec 1986);
(8) 1989.6.27 <Protocol relating to the Madrid Agreement Concerning International Registration of marks> (It was signed by China on 1 Sept 1995 and came into force in China on 1 Apr 1996);
(9) 1993.5.29 <Convention on the Protection of Children and Co-operation in Respect of Inter-country Adoption> (It was signed by China on 1 May 2000 and came into force in China on 27 Apr 2005).

47. For the purpose of international judicial assistance in civil and commercial matters, China has also signed quite a lot of bi-lateral agreements, for instance, the <Agreement between the People's Republic of China and the Republic of France on Mutual Judicial Assistance in Civil and Commercial Matters> (signed on 4 May 1987 and came into force on 8 February 1988), the <Agreement between the People's Republic of China and the Republic of Poland on Mutual Judicial Assistance in Civil and Criminal Matters> (signed on 5 June 1987 and came into force on 13 February 1988) and the <Treaty between the People's Republic of China and the Republic of Italy on Mutual Judicial Assistance in Civil Matters> (signed on 20 May 1991 and came into force on 1 January 1995).[90]

---

[90]So far, China has signed more than 30 bilateral agreements respecting international judicial assistance in civil and commercial matters, see http://www.cnarb.com/algy/conventions/chinabjas/201101/15349.html (last visited on 8 August 2015).

48. It is gratifying to see that China has participated in some of the most important conventions in the field such as CISG, the Hague Service Convention and the Hague Evidence Convention. It is, however, regretful to see that China has not yet joined many other important conventions although it could have done so.[91] By the large quantity of bi-lateral agreements, judicial assistance between China and the concerned countries would undoubtedly be facilitated but this could make international judicial assistance work in Chinese courts practice rather complicated. Looking to the future, China should join more of the Hague multi-lateral conventions, especially for the issues of jurisdiction, choice of law and recognition and enforcement of judgments in specific areas.[92]

1.5 Chinese Scholarly Doctrines on PIL

49. As mentioned, although the People's Republic of China was founded in 1949, law had not been formally developed in general and PIL in particular until after 1978.[93] Although the course of PIL appeared in few law schools' curriculum for undergraduate students in 1950s,[94] the first doctorate degree on PIL was not granted until 1988 in China.[95] Since 1990s, there have been more and more scholars teaching and researching in this area.[96] Two general theories advocated by Chinese PIL lawyers might be worth mentioning here.

1.5.1 Depei Han's Theory on the Scope of PIL

50. For a while, what the scope of PIL should be had been heatedly debated in the circle of Chinese PIL lawyers. Prof. Han, who is the founding father of Chinese PIL has a unique view on this problem. He invented the famous theory of 'One Plane Body, Two Wings'. According to this theory, PIL is like a plane. The main body of the plane shall include conflict rules and uniform substantive rules, even mandatory rules; one wing refers to nationality and legal status of foreigners, which is the premise for resolving PIL cases; another wing refers to the procedural issues of international civil litigation and international commercial arbitration,

[91]E.g. the <Hague Convention on the Civil Aspects of International Child Abduction> which was adopted on 25 Oct 1980 and entered into force on 1 Dec 1983 and now has 90 Contracting States as of 1 Mar 2013; the <Convention of 30 June 2005 on Choice of Court Agreements>. Also see Tu (2007, pp. 347–366).

[92]See Huang (2005, p. 104).

[93]Ibid.

[94]See Zhang (1999, p. 30).

[95]The recipient is Prof. Huang Jin whose theory on PIL will be discussed shortly.

[96]See He (2010, p. 118).

which covers jurisdiction, judicial assistance, recognition and enforcement of foreign judgments etc.[97] This theory has been broadly accepted by the mainland China scholars.

1.5.2 Jin Huang's Theory on the Application of Foreign Law

51. Influenced by the Former Soviet Union's theory of 'Necessity of Foreign Policy', Prof. Huang, the first doctorate degree holder for PIL educated in China and the current president of the Chinese Society of PIL advocated the theory of 'Mutual Benefits for International Exchange'.[98] The core of this theory is that the reason why a domestic court can apply a foreign law in deciding an international private case is the necessity of international exchange based on equality and reciprocity.[99] Although this theory sounds like a political slogan, it is also broadly accepted in the mainland China.

1.6 Scope and Coverage of This Book

52. Due to that the issue of inter-regional conflict of laws has already been briefly discussed and the general stance is that mainland China will treat inter-regional conflict cases in pretty much the same way as international cases, the following text of this book will not specifically touch upon the issue of Chinese inter-regional conflict of laws unless necessary. As mentioned, Hong Kong SAR and Macau SAR have their own respective independent legal systems including respective independent PILs, it is not the aim of this book to have the PIL systems in the two SARs included into be discussed. Therefore, this book is focused on the PIL in mainland China only. Generally, Part I of this book will explore the general themes (issues) of PIL in mainland China, and Part II will examine the specific choice of law rules for different areas in the Chinese PIL while Part III will explore Chinese foreign-related civil procedure rules including rules for international commercial arbitration.

[97]See Han (1997, pp. 8–9).

[98]See Huang (2005, p. 16).

[99]Ibid.

Part I
General Principles: Choice of Law Technique

53. In this part, the general principles and issues of conflict of laws in China will be examined. Before doing that, legal sources of PIL in China will be systematically reviewed. The general principles will be stated in Chap. 3, whereas general issues will be discussed in Chap. 4.

Chapter 2
Legal Sources of PIL in PRC

2.1 Domestic Legislations

54. In recent times, the earliest domestic legislations in which some modern choice of law rules could be found in the world were probably the <The Bavarian Code> enacted in 1756 and the <The Prussian General Code> enacted in 1794.[1] Thereafter, the influential civil code i.e. the <French Civil Code> enacted in 1804 prescribed some rules for general issues of PIL, apart from choice of law rules.[2] Nowadays, countries in the world normally regulate conflict issues in the following four different manners:

(1) put relevant conflict rules in the different chapters of a civil code[3];
(2) draw up a specific chapter or section in a civil code regulating conflict issues[4];
(3) lay down some special conflict rules in special laws[5]; or
(4) make a comprehensive conflict code regulating conflict issues systematically.[6]

The last one represents the modern trend of PIL evolution.[7]

55. In China, no specific code on private international law was compiled until 28 October 2010 when the <Law on the Application of Law for Foreign-Related Civil Legal Relationships of the People's Republic of China> (hereinafter, LAL) was adopted by the Standing Committee of the National People's Congress.[8] Before LAL, conflict rules were largely scattered in different laws. While the <Constitution of the People's Republic of China> confirmed the generally equal

[1]See Huang (2005, p. 78)

[2]Ibid.

[3]E.g. see 1978 <Italian Civil Code>.

[4]E.g. see 1948 <Egyptian Civil Code>; 1999 <Macau Civil Code>.

[5]E.g. see 1882 <Bills of Exchange Act> in the UK.

[6]E.g. see 1987 <Switzerland's Federal Code on Private International Law>.

[7]See Huang (2005, pp. 95–105).

[8]For detailed discussion of this code, see infra Chaps. 3 and 4 of this Part and Part II of this book.

G. Tu, *Private International Law in China*, DOI 10.1007/978-981-287-993-6_2

legal status of foreigners,[9] China promulgated a series of laws during the past decades in which one could find some conflict rules, i.e. <Law of the People's Republic of China on Economic Contracts Involving Foreign Interest> (hereinafter, FECL),[10] <Law of Succession of the People's Republic of China>,[11] <Regulations of the People's Republic of China on the Administration of Contracts Introducing Technology>,[12] <Detailed Rules For the Implementation of the Law of the People's Republic of China on Wholly Foreign-Owned Enterprises in China>,[13] <Adoption Law of the People's Republic of China>,[14] <Maritime

[9]See Article 32, which says: 'The People's Republic of China protects the lawful rights and interests of foreigners within the Chinese territory…'; Article 18, Paragraph 2, which says: 'All foreign enterprises, other foreign economic organizations as well as Chinese-foreign joint ventures within Chinese territory shall abide by the laws of the People's Republic of China. Their lawful rights and interests are protected by the laws of the People's Republic of China'.

[10]This law was enacted by the Standing Committee of the National People's Congress on 21 Mar 1985 and repealed on 1 Oct 1999, Article 5 of which says: 'The parties to a contract may choose the proper law applicable to the settlement of contract disputes. In the absence of such a choice by the parties, the law of the country which has the closest connection with the contract shall apply. The law of the People's Republic of China shall apply to contracts that are to be performed within the territory of the People's Republic of China, namely contracts for Chinese-foreign equity joint ventures, Chinese-foreign contractual joint ventures and Chinese-foreign cooperative exploration and development of natural resources. For matters that are not covered in the law of the People's Republic of China, international practice shall be followed'.

[11]This law was enacted by National People's Congress on 10 Apr 1985, Article 36 of which says: 'For inheritance by a Chinese citizen of an estate outside the People's Republic of China or of an estate of a foreigner within the People's Republic of China, the law of the place of domicile of the decedent shall apply in the case of movable property; in the case of immovable property, the law of the place where the property is located shall apply. For inheritance by a foreigner of an estate within the People's Republic of China or of an estate of a Chinese citizen outside the People's Republic of China, the law of the place of domicile of the decedent shall apply in the case of movable property; in the case of immovable property, the law of the place where the property is located shall apply. Where treaties or agreements exist between the People's Republic of China and foreign countries, matters of inheritance shall be handled in accordance with such treaties or agreements'.

[12]This law was enacted by the State Council on 24 May 1985 and repealed on 1 Jan 2002, Article 5, Paragraph 1 of which says: 'The conclusion of technology import contracts must conform to the relevant provisions of the "Foreign Economic Contract Law" and other laws of the People's Republic of China'.

[13]This law was enacted by the Ministry of Foreign Trade and Economic Cooperation (now the Ministry of Commerce, formerly the Ministry of Foreign Economy and Trade) on 12 Dec 1990 and amended by the State Council on 12 Apr 2001, Article 81 of which says: 'All contracts between a foreign-funded enterprise and any other [Chinese] company, enterprise or economic organization and individual shall be governed by the Contract Law of the People's Republic of China'.

[14]This law was enacted by the Standing Committee of the National People's Congress on 29 Dec. 1991 and amended on 4 Nov. 1998, Article 21 of which says: 'A foreigner may, in accordance with this Law, adopt a child (male or female) in the People's Republic of China. Where a foreigner wishes to adopt a child in the People's Republic of China, the matter shall be subject to examination and approval of the competent authorities of the adopter's residence country in accordance with the law of that country …'.

Law of the People's Republic of China>,[15] <Law of the People's Republic of China on Negotiable Instruments>,[16] <Civil Aviation Law of the People's

[15]This law was enacted by the Standing Committee of the National People's Congress on 7 Nov. 1992, Chapter XIV of which is titled 'Application of Law in Relation to Foreign-related Matters'. This chapter contains Articles 268 through to 276, which prescribe choice of law rules for foreign-related maritime matters. Article 268 says: 'If any international treaty concluded or acceded to by the People's Republic of China contains provisions differing from those contained in this Law, the provisions of the relevant international treaty shall apply, unless the provisions are those on which the People's Republic of China has announced reservations. International practice may be applied to matters for which neither the relevant laws of the People's Republic of China nor any international treaty concluded or acceded to by the People's Republic of China contain any relevant provisions'; Article 269 says: 'The parties to a contract may choose the law applicable to such contract unless the law provides otherwise. Where the parties to a contract have not made a choice, the law of the country having the closest connection with the contract shall apply'; Article 270 says: 'The law of the flag State of the ship shall apply to the acquisition, transfer and extinction of the ownership of the ship'; Article 271 says: 'The law of the flag State of the ship shall apply to the mortgage of the ship. The law of the original country of registry of a ship shall apply to the mortgage of the ship if its mortgage is established before or during its bareboat charter period'; Article 272 says: 'The law of the place where the court hearing the case is located shall apply to matters pertaining to maritime liens'; Article 273 says: 'The law of the place where the infringing act is committed shall apply to claims for damages arising from collision of ships. The law of the place where the court hearing the case is located shall apply to claims for damages arising from collision of ships on the high sea. If the colliding ships belong to the same country, no matter where the collision occurs, the law of the flag State shall apply to claims against one another for damages arising from such collision'; Article 274 says: 'The law where the adjustment of general average is made shall apply to the adjustment of general average'; Article 275 says: 'The law of the place where the court hearing the case is located shall apply to the limitation of liability for maritime claims'; Article 276 says: 'The application of foreign laws or international practices pursuant to the provisions of this chapter shall not jeopardize the public interests of the People's Republic of China'.

[16]This law was enacted on 10 May 1995 and amended on 28 Aug 2004 by the Standing Committee of the National People's Congress, Chapter V of which is titled 'Application of Law on Foreign-related Negotiable Instruments'. This chapter contains Articles 94 through to 101, which prescribe rules related to or choice of law rules for foreign-related negotiable instruments. Article 94 says: 'The application of law concerning foreign-related negotiable instruments shall follow the provisions of this chapter. The term "foreign-related negotiable instruments" used in the preceding paragraph refers to instruments whose draft, endorsement, acceptance, guaranty or payment occur both within and outside the territory of the People's Republic of China'; Article 95 says: 'In the case when the provisions of the international treaties to which the People's Republic of China is a signatory party or in which the People's Republic of China has joined differ from the provisions of this law, the provisions of the international treaties apply, except those articles on which the People's Republic of China has declared to have reservations. For cases where there are no provisions in this law or in the international treaties to which the People's Republic of China is a signatory party or in which the People's Republic of China has joined, the common international practice shall apply'; Article 96 says: 'For the capability of civil acts of debtors of negotiable instruments, the domestic law shall apply. In the case when a debtor is regarded as being incapable of civil act by the domestic law or whose civil act is restricted but the debtor is regarded as having the capability of civil act by the law of the place of act, the law of the place of act shall apply'; Article 97 says: 'For recordings on the draft and promissory notes when drafting, the law of the place of draft shall apply. For the recordings on the checks, the law of the place of issue shall apply. But the law of the place of payment may also apply if the parties concerned so agree'; Article 98 says: 'For acts of endorsement, acceptance, payment and

Republic of China>,[17] <Contract Law of the People's Republic of China> (hereinafter, CCL)[18] and <General Principles on Civil Law of the People's Republic of China> (hereinafter, GPCL).[19]

Footnote 16 (continued)

guaranty for negotiable instruments, the law of the place of act shall apply'; Article 99 says: 'For the time limit for exercising the right of recourse concerning negotiable instruments, the law of the place of draft shall apply'; Article 100 says: 'For the time limit for presentation of negotiable instruments, the method of certificates of dis-honor and the time limit for producing certificates of dis-honor, the law of the place of payment shall apply'; Article 101 says: 'For the procedures for applying for protection of negotiable instruments by a holder who has lost negotiable instruments, the law of the place of payment shall apply'.

[17]This law was enacted by the Standing Committee of the National People's Congress on 30 Oct. 1995, Chapter XIII of which is titled 'Special Provisions for Foreign Civil Aircraft' containing Articles 173 through to 183 and Chapter XIV of which is titled 'Applications of Foreign-related Laws and Regulations' containing Articles 184 through to 190. Quite a few Articles in the two chapters prescribe choice of law rules for foreign-related aviation matters. Article 173 says: 'The operation of civil aviation by foreign nationals using foreign civil aircraft inside PRC territories should be undertaken in accordance with provisions in this chapter as well as other relevant provisions in this law where this chapter does not cover'; Article 174 says: 'Foreign civil aircraft can only fly into or out of PRC territorial air and fly and land inside PRC territories by dint of accords or agreements signed between the government of the country of the aircraft registration and the PRC government, or approval or consent from CAA …'; Article 184 says: 'Where contradiction appears, provisions of international treaties to which PRC is a signatory party shall prevail over those of this law except those on which PRC has made reservations. Where PRC laws and international treaties to which PRC is a signatory party make no provisions, international practices can be referred to'; Article 185 says: 'Laws of the country of registration of civil aircraft apply to the securement, transfer and loss of the ownership of civil aircraft'; Article 186 says: 'Laws of the country of registration of civil aircraft apply to the mortgage of civil aircraft'; Article 187 says: 'The law of the seat of the court which accepts the cases involved shall apply to the priority of civil aircraft concerned'; Article 188 says: 'Parties to civil air transport contracts can choose the law to apply to the contracts, except otherwise stipulated by law. Where the parties to contracts make no choices, the law of the country mostly involved in the contract applies'; Article 189 says: 'The law of the tort location where the tort concerned happens applies to liabilities for injuries or damage to the third party on the ground by civil aircraft. The law of the seat of the court which accepts the cases involved should apply to liabilities for injuries or damage to a third party above the surface of open sea in a civil aircraft'; Article 190 says: 'The application of foreign laws or international practices in accordance with provisions of this chapter should not violate the public interest of PRC'.

[18]This law was enacted by the National People's Congress on 15 Mar. 1999, Article 126 of which says: 'Parties to a foreign-related contract may select the applicable law for resolution of a contractual dispute, except as otherwise provided by law. Where parties to the foreign-related contract fail to select the applicable law, the contract shall be governed by the law of the country with the closest connection thereto; For a Chinese-foreign equity joint venture contract, Chinese-foreign contractual joint venture contract, or a contract for Chinese-foreign joint exploration and development of natural resources which is performed within the territory of the People's Republic of China, the law of the People's Republic of China shall be applied'.

[19]This law was enacted by National People's Congress on 12 Apr. 1986, Chapter VIII of which is titled 'Application of Law in Civil Relations with Foreign Elements' composed of Articles 142–150. For more detailed discussion on this Chapter and choice of law rules therein, see infra paras. 56 and 57.

56. Prior to LAL, the last-cited one i.e. GPCL was the most important source of domestic law for conflict rules at the time although all the statutes just mentioned, as a matter of fact, played a role as a part of PIL in China to a more or less extent. Therefore, the development of conflict rules in the GPCL deserves a bit more elaboration here. Back in 1979 when attempting to draw up a comprehensive Chinese Civil Law, the legislative body initially considered drafting a specific chapter with comprehensive conflict rules to be included therein. In early 1985, some Chinese PIL lawyers made proposals on conflict rules for the drafting of a comprehensive Chinese Civil Law. In August of the same year, Chinese PIL lawyers, throughout the country, gathered together for the first time in Guiyang, the capital city of Guizhou Province to have a heated discussion, inter alia, on the draft conflict rules provisionally made in the draft Chinese Civil Law and came up with some more suggestions to supplement and modify those rules.[20] In November of the same year, more than 300 governmental officials, scholars and practitioners made further suggestions on the draft of a comprehensive Chinese Civil Law at a seminar hosted by the Standing Committee of the National People's Congress including further suggestions for conflict rules. During the whole course of legislation, conflict rules in the draft Chinese Civil Law were amended for a few times. In the draft of June 1985, there were 28 articles and 42 paragraphs for PIL while 21 articles and 33 paragraphs in the draft of November 1985. The final version submitted to the National People's Congress for readings had 14 articles and 25 paragraphs.[21] In the ultimate version of the scaled-down Chinese Civil Law i.e. the GPCL which was adopted on 12 April 1986, there are 9 articles and 13 paragraphs only for conflict issues. The main reason for the constant simplification and reduction of contents and clauses for Chinese Civil Law in general and for PIL issues in particular was that some thought the conditions were not mature enough for China to make relatively comprehensive civil law and conflict of laws system. Chapter 8 of GPCL was probably the best one could get at the time for PIL.[22] Anyway, Chapter 8 of the GPCL initiated the PRC's history of regulating conflict of laws issues in a specific chapter in its legislation of general civil law and it was the first

---

[20]See 'China's First Private International Law Colloquium Held in Huaxi, Guiyang', *Journal of Guizhou University* 4 (1985) (Social Sciences edition), p. 44.

[21]See Huang (2005, p. 128).

[22]See Yang, (1986, p. 8).

attempt of PRC to regulate conflict rules in its crude civil code, being a milestone for PIL's development in PRC.[23]

57. Due to the fact that GPCL enjoyed the status of civil code in China, the conflict rules in it constituted a sketch of Chinese conflict of laws at the time. Simple and easy as those rules looked, the legislation of them, like China's economic development, had gone through a tortuous path.[24] The then development of PIL in China was in conformity with its then economic development and societal development. Constructing a comprehensive civil code with a comprehensive conflict of laws system included therein was an extraordinary time-consuming task, which might take years or even decades and could not be finished in a short while. In addition, China was lack of experience in law-making, especially for private international law, it was thus simply impossible to draw up a complete conflicts code at the very beginning.[25] However, the developing judicial reality going along with the increasing economic reform and openness in China pressed for immediate conflict rules available for Chinese courts to apply to resolve urgent problems. To meet this requirement, China had to, as an expedient measure, prescribe conflict

[23]As said, before LAL, Chapter 8 of GPCL was the most important place where one could find conflict rules in Chinese law. In Chapter 8 of GPCL, Article 142 says: 'The application of law in civil relations with foreign elements shall be determined by the provisions in this chapter. If any international treaty concluded or acceded to by the People's Republic of China contains provisions differing from those in the civil laws of the People's Republic of China, the provisions of the international treaty shall apply, unless the provisions are ones on which the People's Republic of China has announced reservations. International practice may be applied on matters for which neither the law of the People's Republic of China nor any international treaty concluded or acceded to by the People's Republic of China has any provisions'; Article 143 says: 'If a citizen of the People's Republic of China settles in a foreign country, the law of that country may be applicable as regards his capacity for civil conduct'; Article 144 says: 'The ownership of immovable property shall be bound by the law of the place where it is situated'; Article 145 says: 'The parties to a contract involving foreign interests may choose the law applicable to settlement of their contractual disputes, except as otherwise stipulated by law. If the parties to a contract involving foreign interests have not made a choice, the law of the country to which the contract is most closely connected shall be applied'; Article 146 says: 'The law of the place where an infringing act is committed shall apply in handling compensation claims for any damage caused by the act. If both parties are citizens of the same country or have established domicile in another country, the law of their own country or the country of domicile may be applied. An act committed outside the People's Republic of China shall not be treated as an infringing act if under the law of the People's Republic of China it is not considered an infringing act'; Article 147 says: 'The marriage of a citizen of the People's Republic of China to a foreigner shall be bound by the law of the place where they get married, while a divorce shall be bound by the law of the place where a court accepts the case'; Article 148 says: 'Maintenance of a spouse after divorce shall be bound by the law of the country to which the spouse is most closely connected'; Article 149 says: 'In the statutory succession of an estate, movable property shall be bound by the law of the decedent's last place of residence, and immovable property shall be bound by the law of the place where the property is situated'; Article 150 says: 'The application of foreign laws or international practice in accordance with the provisions of this chapter shall not violate the public interest of the People's Republic of China'.

[24]See Tong et al. (1988, p. 20).

[25]See Ding (2001, p. 127).

rules by a piece-meal approach, which led China to, as illustrated above, put special conflict rules regulating special foreign-related civil relationships in quite a few special laws with the most common ones in its general civil law i.e. GPCL.

2.2 Interpretations of the SPC

58. In China, a Judicial Interpretation is an explanation given by the competent judicial authority on certain issues of law arising out of judicial practice. It provides detailed guidance for lower courts to apply the laws properly and is legally binding. As stated in the 'General Introduction' of this book, the Supreme People's Court is the authority in China to draw up the broadly-existing Judicial Interpretations.[26]

59. As far as PIL is concerned, corresponding to the laws mentioned earlier, the Supreme People's Court has released a considerable amount of Judicial Interpretations in sequence plus Replies, Notices and Opinions on different matters. The most important ones are:

(1) <Opinions of the Supreme People's Court on Certain Issues Concerning the Implementation of the 'Law of Succession of the People's Republic of China'>[27];
(2) <Replies of the Supreme People's Court on Certain Issues Concerning the Application of the 'Law of the People's Republic of China on Economic Contracts Involving Foreign Interest'> (hereinafter, 1987 Interpretation on FECL)[28];

[26]See supra paras. 7–10.

[27]This Interpretation was issued by the SPC on 11 Sept 1986, Article 63 of which says: 'For inheritance by a Chinese citizen of an estate outside the People's Republic of China or of an estate of a foreigner within the People's Republic of China, the law of the place of domicile of the decedent shall apply in the case of movable property; in other words, the law of the place of the last domicile of the decedent shall apply'.

[28]This Interpretation was issued by the SPC on 19 Oct 1987 and repealed on 13 Jul 2000. It prescribed quite a few conflict rules for dealing with foreign-related contractual disputes, in which Part 2 titled 'The Question of the Application of Law to Resolve Disputes involving Foreign Economic Contracts' says:

(1) The term 'disputes arising out of the contract' as stated in Article 5 of the Foreign Economic Contract Law shall be understood in the general sense. All disputes between the two parties to a contract over matters such as the existence of a contract, the time of its establishment, interpretation of the contents of a contract, implementation of a contract, liability for breach of contract, as well as disputes over the amendment, suspension, assignment, dissolution or termination of a contract shall be included under this term.
(2) The parties to a contract shall have the right to choose the law applicable to the settlement of disputes arising from the contract at the time of the signing of the contract or after a

Footnote 28 (continued)

dispute arises and the People's Court shall act in accordance with the law chosen by the parties concerned when hearing the contract dispute case. The law selected by the parties to a contract may be the law of the People's Republic of China or it may be the law of the District of Hong Kong or Macao or the law of a foreign country. However, the law selected by the parties concerned shall be unanimously and unequivocally agreed on following consultation between both parties.

(3) Contracts for Sino-foreign joint equity enterprise and Sino-foreign co-operative enterprise projects and for Sino-foreign co-operative exploration and exploitation of natural resources to be implemented within Chinese territory shall be governed by the law of the People's Republic of China. A clause in a contract which states that the parties to the contract agree to the choice of foreign law shall be invalid.

(4) In the absence, at the time of the signing of a contract or after a dispute has arisen, of the selection of the type of law to apply in a dispute, the People's Court, after agreeing to accept and hear a case, shall allow the parties to the contract to select the law to be applied before the court session is opened and the case is heard. If, after consultation, the parties concerned still fail to reach unanimous agreement on their selection of the applicable law, the People's Court shall determine the applicable law in accordance with the principle of using that with the closest relationship.

(5) The law chosen to apply to the settlement of disputes arising from a contract, either through consultation by the parties concerned or through determination by the People's Court in accordance with the principle of the closest relationship shall be actual law currently in effect and shall not include conflicts of law or procedural law.

(6) If the parties to a contract fail to select the law to apply to the contract, in normal circumstances the People's Court shall determine the applicable law in accordance with the principle of the closest relationship for the following types of foreign economic contracts:

(a) In the case of an international commodity trade contract, the law of the region where the seller has its operational base at the time of the signing of the contract shall apply. If a contract is negotiated and signed at the operational base of the buyer, or if the main terms and conditions of a contract are determined by the buyer and the contract is concluded after the buyer has called for tenders, or if a contract clearly states that the seller shall fulfil its delivery obligations at the operational base of the buyer, the law of the region where the buyer has its operational base at the time of the signing of the contract shall prevail.

(b) In the case of a bank loan contract or a contract of guarantee, the law of the region of the bank which is supplying the loan or guarantee shall apply.

(c) In the case of an insurance contract, the law of the region where the insurer has its operational base shall apply.

(d) In the case of a processing contract of work, the law of the region where the processor has its operational base shall apply.

(e) In the case of a technology transfer contract, the law of the region where the assignee has its operational base shall apply.

(f) In the case of a project tender contract, the law of the region where the project is being implemented shall apply.

(g) In the case of a contract for scientific or technical consultancy or for design services, the law of the region where the client has its operational base shall apply.

(h) In the case of a labour contract, the law of the region where the labour services are to be performed shall apply.

(i) In the case of a contract for the supply of complete sets of equipment, the law of the region where the equipment is to be installed and transported shall apply.

(j) In the case of an agency contract, the law of the region where the agent has its operational base shall apply.

(k) In the case of a contract for the leasing, purchase or sale or mortgage of real estate, the law of the region where the real estate is located shall apply.

(3) <Provisions of the Supreme People's Court on Certain Issues Concerning the Application of Law in the Trial of Cases Involving Disputes over Foreign-related Civil or Commercial Contracts> (hereinafter, 2007 Interpretation)[29];
(4) <Opinions of the Supreme People's Court on Certain Issues Concerning the Implementation of the 'General Principles on the Civil Law of the People's Republic of China' (Trial)> (hereinafter, 1988 Interpretation on GPCL).[30]

Footnote 28 (continued)

(l) In the case of a contract for the leasing of movable property, the law of the region where the lessor has its operational base shall apply.
(m) In the case of a storage and custody contract, the law of the region where the storage and custody unit has its operational base shall apply.

If, however, a contract is obviously closely related to the law of another country or region, the People's Court shall deal with a contract dispute in accordance with the law of the other country or region.

(7) If the party concerned has more than one operational base, the operational base which is most closely related to the contract in question shall apply. If the party concerned is without an operational base, its place of domicile or actual residence shall apply.
(8) If an international treaty which the People's Republic of China has concluded or participated in has provisions that differ from its foreign economic contract law or other laws related to foreign economic contracts, the provisions of the international treaty shall prevail, with the exception of clauses to which the People's Republic of China has declared reservation.
(9) International practice may be applied in a case where Chinese law should apply, but where the law lacks relevant provisions to make a ruling in a particular contract dispute.
(10) In a case where foreign law should apply, but application of such law would violate the fundamental principles of Chinese law and the public interest of society, it shall not be permitted to be applied and corresponding Chinese law shall apply instead.
(11) If the People's Court is unable to determine the content of a law in a case where foreign law should apply, it may ascertain the facts via:

(a) supply of details by the parties concerned;
(b) supply of details by the Chinese embassy or consulate stationed in the relevant country;
(c) supply of details by the embassy or consulate of the relevant country stationed in China;
(d) supply of details by an expert in Sino-foreign law.

If details of the law in question are still unable to be ascertained after use of the above-mentioned clauses, the case may be deal with in accordance with corresponding Chinese law.

[29]This interpretation was issued by the SPC on 23 Jul 2007 and given specifically for contractual matters and replaced the 1987 Interpretation on FECL mentioned just now. It will be discussed in detail in Part II of this book.

[30]This Interpretation was given by the SPC on 26 Jan 1988, in which Part VII titled 'Application of Law for Foreign-related Civil Relations' says:

(178) Where either party or both parties in a civil legal relationship is an alien, a stateless person or a foreign legal person, and the object of the civil legal relationship is within the territory of a foreign country, and the legal facts that produce, alter or annihilate the civil relations of rights and obligations occur in a foreign country, such relationship shall be called foreign-related civil relations. When hearing a foreign civil relationship, the people's court shall apply the substantive law in accordance with the provisions of Chapter VIII of the General Principles on Civil Law.

Footnote 30 (continued)

(179) For the capacity for civil conduct of any citizen of our country who settles down overseas, the law of our country shall apply if his act is conducted in the territory of China; if the act is conducted in the country he settles down, the law of the country he settles down may be applied.

(180) In case an alien conducts civil legal activities within the territory of our country, and if he is a person without capacity for civil conduct according to his domestic law, but he is a person with capacity for civil conduct according to the Chinese law, he shall be determined as a person having capacity for civil conduct.

(181) For the capacity for civil conduct of a stateless person, the law of the country where he settles down shall apply in general; if he does not settle down in the country, the law of the country of his residence may be applied.

(182) For an alien who has double or multi-nationalities, the law of the country of his residence or the country of closest connection shall be deemed as his domestic law.

(183) In case the residence of a party is not clear or cannot be determined, his habitual abode shall be his residence. If a party has several abodes, the abode that has closest connection with the civil relationship in dispute shall be his residence.

(184) For a foreign legal person, the law of its registration country shall be deemed as its domestic law, and the capacity for civil conduct of a legal person shall be determined according to its domestic law.

In case any foreign legal person carries out civil activities within the territory of China, it shall comply with the law provisions of our country.

(185) Where a party has two or more business places, the business place that has closest connection with the civil relationship in dispute shall be followed; if a party has no business place, his residence place or habitual residence shall be taken instead.

(186) Land, appurtenant easements, and the appertaining equipments of other appurtenant and construction shall be real estates. The law of the place where a real property is located shall apply to such civil relationships as the property right, sales, tenancy, mortgage and use of a real property.

(187) The lex delicti (law of the place where a tort is committed) shall include the lex loci delicti commissi (law of the place where a tort is committed) and the law of the place where the result of a tort took place. If the two laws are inconsistent with each other, the people's court may choose to apply either of them.

(188) The law of our country may be applied in the acceptance of foreign related divorce cases. For the divorces and the property divisions arising from divorce, the laws of our country shall apply. The law of the place where the marriage is concluded shall be applicable to the determination of the validity of a marriage.

(189) The law of the country that has the closest connection with the person being supported shall be applicable to the support between parents and children, husband and wife, and other person having relationship of support. The nationalities and residence of the supporter and the person being supported and the place where the property for the support of the person being supported shall all be regarded as having the closest connection with the person being supported.

(190) The domestic law of the person under guardianship shall apply to the establishment, alteration and termination of a guardianship. But the law of our country shall be applied if the person under guardianship has residence within the territory of China.

60. As can be seen, these Interpretations not only interpret the relevant clauses in the relevant laws but also create more rules to supplement the laws quite often. To know the real Chinese situation, the Chinese laws thus shall be read together with the Interpretations given for them respectively by the SPC. In the past decades, these Interpretations have played an important role in guiding Chinese judges to make decisions for foreign-related cases. Therefore, in the following discussion of this book, wherever a provision in an effective relevant Interpretation on the law is applicable, it will also be taken into account and examined. Among the Interpretations mentioned, the last one was the most important at the time because it interpreted the most common and important law in this field i.e. GPCL. Actually, it also provided quite a few rules for common conflict issues and, together with GPCL, served as the general law in this field before the promulgation of LAL.

2.3 The Currently Most Important Legal Source: The New Chinese Conflicts Code and Interpretation I On It

61. Following the entry into the World Trade Organization (WTO) in 2001, the need for a comprehensive conflict of laws code in the People's Republic of China has become increasingly acute. For this reason, in 2000 the Chinese Society of Private International Law (CSPIL) produced a model code which was drafted by

Footnote 30 (continued)

(191) Where a foreigner dies within the territory of China, his property left within the territory of China shall be handled according to the Chinese law if no one inherits it or accepts bequeath, unless it is otherwise specified by the international conventions concluded or joined in by the two countries.

(192) Where the law of a foreign country shall be applied according to law, and if different laws are implemented in different regions of the foreign country, the applicable law shall be determined according to the provisions of the law of the foreign country on adjusting domestic legal conflict. If there are no provisions in the law of the country, the law that has the closest connection with the civil relation shall be applied directly.

(193) The applicable foreign law may be found out through the following ways: a. Provided by the parties; b. Provided by the central organ of the opposite party who has concluded judicial assistant convention; c. Provided by our embassy or consulate in the foreign country; d. Provided by the embassy of the foreign country in China; e. Provided by both Chinese and foreign legal experts. If the applicable foreign law still cannot be determined through the above method, the law of the people's republic of China may be applied.

(194) In case any party has any act of evading the compulsory or prohibitive legal criterions of our country, the foreign law shall not be applied.

(195) The statute of limitations for foreign related civil juristic relations shall be determined according to the governing law for civil juristic relations determined by conflicting rules.

PIL scholars.[31] Book Nine of the 2002 Chinese Draft Civil Code was the formal legislative attempt to codify a comprehensive Chinese conflict of laws system.[32] Yet, for many reasons the idea of a comprehensive Chinese civil code was dropped again, and it was decided that laws that might have been included in such a code should be enacted on an individual basis. Recent years have witnessed the completion of various such statutes such as the Chinese Property Law and the Chinese Tort Liabilities Law.[33] The latest in this series is the Law on the Application of Law for Foreign-Related Civil Legal Relationships of the People's Republic of China (LAL). As said, this legislation was adopted by the Standing Committee of the National People's Congress on 28 Oct 2010 and it has entered into force since 1 Apr 2011.[34] The LAL is not only supposed to have summed up the trial experience of foreign-related civil cases since the reform and opening up of the PRC, but also tightly followed the development of contemporary private international law techniques in the world. It is the culmination of efforts made by many concerned parties over the past decade and the first-ever legislation in the history of China systematically dealing with conflict of laws issues.[35]

62. As the codification of conflict of laws in many other jurisdictions, the Chinese exercise has also produced a comprehensive rule-based system for conflict of laws issues.[36] The new Chinese conflicts code comprises a general part dealing with general themes of conflict of laws and several specific parts designing choice of law rules for the respective areas, namely civil parties, marriage and family relations, succession, property, obligations and intellectual property (IP) rights.[37]

63. For LAL to be applied, one fundamental question to be asked is the scope of LAL. LAL will be applicable only if a civil legal relationship can be classified as a 'foreign-related' one. The concept of foreign-related civil legal relationship is, therefore, crucial to the whole law and the whole conflict of laws system.

---

[31]The Chinese Society of Private International Law was established in 1987 and it now convenes a country-wide conference every year in which scholars come together to discuss topical issues in the field i.e. the Annual Conference of Private International Law in China. After a few such conferences in 1990s, a model law on Chinese PIL was produced in 2000. Apart from rules on general issues of conflict of laws and choice of law rules, this model law also has provisions regarding international jurisdiction and recognition and enforcement of foreign judgments, on file with the author.

[32]See generally Zhu (2007, p. 283).

[33]Chinese Property Law was passed on 16 March 2007 and Chinese Tort Liability Law was passed on 26 December 2009.

[34]See Article 52 of LAL.

[35]As has been seen, before LAL, one could mainly find conflict of laws rules in the GPCL and the 1988 Interpretation on GPCL and conflict of laws rules were not systematic in them. Some sporadic conflict of laws rules also existed in other special laws such as Chinese Maritime Law and Chinese Civil Aviation Law and various Interpretations of the SPC. See supra paras. 55–59.

[36]See Zhu (2007, p. 283) and Fiorini (2005, p. 499).

[37]There are altogether 52 Articles in LAL. Choice of law rules are given for these areas one after another in the sequence as enumerated from Chapters 2 to 7. Chapter 8 has two final clauses.

However, no provision in LAL has touched upon and given a definition for this important concept of the law. Previously, there was a definition for it in the 1988 Interpretation on GPCL, the first paragraph of Part 7 of which said:

> Foreign-related civil legal relationships are those civil legal relationships in which one or both parties are foreign, a stateless person or a foreign legal person; or the subject matter of the concerned civil legal relationship is located outside the territory of China; or any legal fact that caused the formation, alteration or extinguishment of the concerned legal relationship occurred outside the territory of China.[38]

64. Accordingly, for a civil legal relationship to be 'foreign-related' in China, that civil legal relationship, therefore, must have at least one foreign element i.e. one of the parties or the subject matter of the civil legal relationship or one of the legal facts underlying the civil legal relationship.

As can be seen, Paragraph 178 of the 1988 Interpretation on GPCL seemed to measure the 'foreignness' of parties only according to their nationalities whether it is a legal person or natural person.[39] In many private international law cases, however, the domicile or habitual residence or the place of business of the parties is a far more important and meaningful connecting factor than nationality. Indeed, it has been reported that in practice, lower courts have decided that if only one or both parties had a foreign domicile, or habitual residence or place of business in a case, that case could be treated as a foreign-related case.[40]

65. In the reading of the drafts of LAL, some members of the Standing Committee of the NPC did call for a new definition for this concept in the new law and suggested the expansion of the concept.[41] Unfortunately, their proposal was not accepted. Regretfully, one could not yet have a new definition for this important concept in the new law. However, this has been remedied by the latest Interpretation of the SPC on LAL, Article 1 of which says:

> A civil legal relationship can be classified as a foreign-related one if it can satisfy one of the following conditions:
>
> (1) if one or both parties are foreign, a stateless person or a foreign legal person;
> (2) if one or both parties have their habitual residences outside the territory of China;
> (3) if the subject matter of the concerned civil legal relationship is located outside the territory of China;
> (4) if any legal fact that caused the formation, alteration or extinguishment of the concerned legal relationship has occurred outside the territory of China;
> (5) if it is a case that is suitable to be so regarded.[42]

---

[38]See para. 178 of the 1988 Interpretation on GPCL.

[39]See Guo and Xu (2008, pp. 122, 135).

[40]Ibid, 135–136.

[41]See the speech of Mr. Chunyao Shen in the conference reading the draft of LAL, on file with the author.

[42]See Article 1 of the Supreme People's Court's Interpretation I on Some Questions in the Application of the Law on the Application of Law for Foreign-related Civil Legal Relationships of PRC which was issued on 28 Dec 2012 and came into force on 7 Jan 2013 (hereinafter, Interpretation I on LAL).

66. Compared with the previous definition in the 1988 Interpretation on GPCL, progress has been made and this new one has indeed expanded the scope by taking into account habitual residence of the parties and providing a flexible open-ended clause to meet the demand in practice.

67. Based on the general principle that 'new law prevails over old law', the LAL supersedes the GPCL and conflicts rules in the LAL supersede those in previous laws if there is any conflict.[43] More specifically, to resolve the potential problems, LAL in its final clauses declares that Articles 146 and 147 of GPCL and Article 36 of the Law of Succession shall give way to the rules in LAL where they are contradictory.[44] On the other hand, the LAL, however, acknowledges that some special laws may have special previsions for special matters. If this is the case, those special previsions of conflict rules shall be applied.[45] This idea corresponds to the principle that specific matter should be subject to a specific law specifically designed for it if there is one, rather than the general law. The current general situation is, therefore, that LAL has become the main legal source of Chinese conflict of laws while the conflict rules in other laws are still effective if they do not contradict with those in LAL or they are 'special' in the eyes of LAL.[46] This sounds reasonable but it could lead to conflict and incongruity between the application of the new law and the old laws and the general law and special laws in practice.[47]

68. Undoubtedly, the promulgation of LAL and Interpretation I on LAL helps protect the legal rights and interests of parties engaging in foreign-related civil relationships and promotes the efficiency of civil and commercial activities. It can also effectively direct Chinese courts, administrative organs and arbitration institutions to quickly find the applicable law for foreign-related civil legal relationships. However, some provisions included in the LAL are not operable and call for clarification. Although the Supreme People's Court has recently given the

[43]See Article 83 of the Law on Legislation of the People's Republic of China, which says: 'With regard to laws, administrative regulations, local regulations, autonomous regulations, separate regulations or rules, if they are formulated by one and same organ and if there is inconsistency between special provisions and general provisions, the special provisions shall prevail; if there is inconsistency between the new provisions and the old provisions, the new provisions shall prevail'; Article 3 of Interpretation I on LAL.

[44]See Article 51 of LAL, which says: 'If the provisions in Article 146 and Article 147 of the General Principles on Civil Law of the People's Republic of China and Article 36 of the Law of Succession of the People's Republic of China do not conform to the provisions in this Law, the provisions in this Law shall prevail'; supra para. 55.

[45]See Article 2 of LAL, which says: 'The application of laws concerning foreign-related civil relations shall be determined in accordance with this Law. However, if there are other special provisions in other special laws on the application of laws concerning other special foreign-related civil relations, such provisions shall prevail …'; for examples of the special conflict rules in the special laws, see Article 3 of Interpretation I on LAL; supra para. 55.

[46]See Article 3 of Interpretation I on LAL.

[47]Generally Xiao (2011, p. 48); Huang (2011, p. 12).

Interpretation I on LAL, this Interpretation touches upon some general issues in the Law only. Therefore, more Judicial Interpretations are still needed to make LAL effectively workable. It is to be hoped that the SPC could do more research and work out more Interpretations for the application of LAL in the future.

As has been said, LAL is now the most important source for PIL in China. In the following chapters of this Part and Part II of this book, it is, therefore, the conflict rules in the LAL that will be examined in more detail.[48] Of course, the relevant rules in Interpretation I on LAL and other laws and Interpretations applicable will also be covered wherever necessary.

[48]LAL is equally applicable to cases related to Hong Kong and Macau, see Article 19 of Interpretation I on LAL; supra para. 41. Due to the fact that China has almost not joined any international convention dealing with choice of law issues, in the following text where choice of law rules for different areas are examined, generally no international convention will be touched upon, see supra paras. 46–48.

Chapter 3
Modern Doctrines Accepted in the New Chinese Conflicts Code

3.1 The Closest Connection Principle

69. One of the most important innovations by LAL for Chinese conflict of laws system is that the closest connection test has now been expressly established as a salient principle for the whole system. Initially, there was a provision in the general part of the draft of the second reading which said: 'The applicable law for a foreign-related civil legal relationship shall have the closest connection with that legal relationship',[1] whereby all choice of law rules shall be based on the closest connection principle.[2] Although this provision was eventually deleted, one can still see that throughout the whole system, the closest connection principle has not only been directly and explicitly employed in some areas[3] but also it has served as the basis for building up the fixed traditional style choice of law rules in many others.[4] More importantly, this principle becomes the default choice of law rule for all kinds of foreign-related civil legal relationships, for which Article 2 of LAL says:

> If there is no choice of law rule for a foreign-related civil legal relationship in this law and in any other law, that foreign-related civil legal relationship shall be governed by the law of the place which has the closest connection with it.[5]

70. While it might be true, as many said in the reading of the drafts, that to introduce the closest connection principle as a basic one for the whole system is the modern trend, one may have the worry how effectively this test can be applied

---

[1]See Paragraph 1 of Article 3 of the draft for the second reading, on file with the author.

[2]With the exception of party autonomy, see Article 4 of the draft.

[3]See Article 6 dealing with multiple-legal systems, infra para. 78; Article 19 dealing with multiple-nationalities, infra para. 98; Article 41 dealing with contract, infra para. 130; Article 39 dealing with securities, infra para. 120.

[4]See e.g. Articles 16, 17, 23 and 40 of LAL.

[5]See Article 2 of LAL.

G. Tu, *Private International Law in China*, DOI 10.1007/978-981-287-993-6_3

by courts in practice.[6] Given that Chinese judges are normally not experienced in dealing with foreign-related cases,[7] it was argued and actually has been negatively proved that this test has been applied unsatisfactorily in the context of contract where China first introduced it.[8] The expansion of this open-ended test would surely be a challenge for many un-experienced Chinese judges when confronted with foreign-related cases.

3.2 The Principle of Party Autonomy

71. It was believed that on the conflicts level, party autonomy could mirror the substantive principle of freedom in many areas of private law.[9] In addition, to accept the doctrine of party autonomy can bring about certainty and efficiency because it is relatively easy for the parties and the court to know which law is applicable and the rights and obligations of the parties under the applicable law. Some Chinese scholars have observed that the doctrine of party autonomy had been applied by Chinese courts in practice even in areas other than contract such as tort, property and unjust enrichment before there was a formal authorization.[10]

72. Consequently, another innovation by LAL is that the doctrine of party autonomy is now put in a prominent place in the system, for which Article 3 of LAL says:

> The parties, according to law, can choose the governing law for their foreign-related civil legal relationships in an explicit manner.[11]

73. It, however, has to be noted that this Article does not mean that the parties can choose the governing law whatever the foreign-related civil legal relationship is. The limitation is: the parties must do that 'according to law' which is further confirmed by Article 6 of Interpretation I on LAL.[12] Therefore, the parties can choose the governing law for a foreign-related legal relationship only in a situation where the law allows them to do so. As a result, this principle seemingly cannot have as broad application as the principle of the closest connection which is the default rule for the whole system and all kinds of foreign-related civil legal relationships.[13]

---

[6]See the discussions and reports, on file with the author.

[7]See Huang (2005, p. 314) and Xu (1989, pp. 648, 650).

[8]See Guo and Xu (2008, pp. 122, 145–147, 149).

[9]See the reports and discussions, on file with the author; Juenger (1995).

[10]See Guo and Xu (2008, pp. 122, 131, 140–142).

[11]See Article 3 of LAL.

[12]See Article 6 of Interpretation I on LAL, which says: 'The choice of law made by the parties for their foreign-related civil legal relationship shall be regarded as invalid if no law in the People's Republic of China has explicitly allowed them to do so'.

[13]See supra para. 69.

Nevertheless, if one checks through LAL, one will immediately find out that the doctrine of party autonomy has broadly been accepted for many matters and is often the first resort for determining the applicable law for those matters such as agency,[14] trust,[15] arbitral agreements,[16] matrimonial property relationships,[17] divorce by mutual consent,[18] movables,[19] general contracts,[20] consumer contracts,[21] post-tort disputes,[22] unjust enrichment and gestio negotiorum,[23] the transfer and license of IP rights,[24] and post-infringement disputes arising out of IP rights.[25]

74. For the purpose of easier and uniform application of the law,[26] another limitation is imposed on party autonomy that the parties' choice must be made 'in an explicit manner'.[27] However, the truth is that the parties' real choice can be explicit or implicit. Take contract as an example, even if the parties did not make an explicit choice of law by a clause in their contract, it is still possible to reasonably infer that they have made an implicit choice according to the terms of the contract or the circumstances of the case.[28] The expansion of the doctrine of party autonomy without recognizing implicit choices will amplify the tension between the law and reality.

---

[14]See Article 16, which says: 'Agency shall be governed by the law of the place of where the act of agency took place; however, the civil relationship between the principal and the agent shall be governed by the law of the place where the agency relationship happened. The principal and the agent can choose the governing law for the agency relationship between them'.

[15]See Article 17, which says: 'The parties can choose the governing law for trust; failing which, trust shall be governed by the law of the place where the trusted property is located or where the relationship of trust took place'.

[16]See Article 18, which says: 'The parties can choose the governing law for their arbitral agreements; failing which, the law of the place where the arbitral institution is located or where the arbitration takes place shall apply'.

[17]See Article 24; infra para. 104.

[18]See Article 26, infra para. 105.

[19]See Article 37, infra para. 118.

[20]See Article 41, infra para. 130.

[21]See Article 42, infra para. 193.

[22]See Article 44, infra para. 197.

[23]See Article 47, infra para. 216.

[24]See Article 49, infra para. 124.

[25]See Article 50, infra para. 127.

[26]See Huang (2005, p. 314) and Xu (1989, pp. 648, 650).

[27]See Art. 3 of LAL. For limitation on party autonomy respecting consumer contracts and employment contracts, see infra paras. 193–194.

[28]For some typical situations where an implicit choice can be inferred, see Cheshire et al. (2008, pp. 700–705) and Dicey et al. (2000, pp. 1573–1574). Cf. Article 3 (1) of Regulation (EC) No 539/2008 of the European Parliament and of the Council of 17 June 2008 on the law applicable to contractual obligations (hereinafter, Rome I Regulation) and its predecessor i.e. 1980 Rome Convention on the law applicable to contractual obligations (hereinafter, Rome Convention).

3.3 The Principle of Protecting the Weaker Parties

75. The third innovation by LAL for the new Chinese conflict of laws system is that it accepted the principle of protecting the supposedly weaker parties. This policy might be drawn from the ideology that when pursing conflicts justice, conflict of laws should also have the goal of material justice.[29]

76. To protect the supposedly weaker parties by conflicts method has long been a policy in the legislations of the European Community (EC) in this field. In the EC, the weaker parties such as consumers, employees and the insured have been singled out and given special protection in terms of not only choice of law[30] but also jurisdiction.[31] Back in 2007 when the Supreme People's Court's Interpretation on contractual choice of law was issued,[32] some argued that contracts related to weaker parties such as consumers and employees should be differentiated from other contracts and the weaker parties should deserve special protection.[33] This policy was not adopted in the 2007 Interpretation but now in the LAL. In this new law, consumer contracts and employment contracts are detached from other contracts and given choice of laws rules independently.[34] In addition, one can also see this policy in product liability cases[35] and family matters where the protection of the weaker party could always be a concern such as maintenance,[36] custody[37] and the relationship between parent(s) and child (children).[38]

[29]See Symeonides (2000, pp. 36–37, 43–45).

[30]See Arts 6, 7 and 8 of Rome I Regulation; Arts 5 and 6 of Rome Convention.

[31]See sections 3, 4 and 5 of Chapter II of Council Regulation (EC) No. 44/2001 of 22 December 2000 on jurisdiction and the recognition and enforcement of judgments in civil and commercial matters (hereinafter, Brussels I Regulation); sections 3 and 4 of Title II of its predecessor i.e. 1968 Brussels Convention on jurisdiction and the enforcement of judgments in civil and commercial matters (hereinafter, Brussels Convention).

[32]See 2007 Interpretation, supra para. 59.

[33]See Huang et al. (2008, pp. 443, 440).

[34]See Arts 42 and 43 of LAL; infra paras. 193–194.

[35]See infra paras. 205–208. Cases of infringing personality rights could probably be also included, see infra paras. 209–210.

[36]See Art. 29; infra para. 107.

[37]See Art. 30; infra para. 108.

[38]See Art. 25; infra para. 106.

Chapter 4
Basic Terms

4.1 Public Policy and Mandatory Rules

77. The device of 'public policy' in conflict of laws can work as a 'safety valve' that can prevent the application of a foreign law which is repugnant to the fundamental principles or moral standards of the local forum.[1] Although this omnipotent antidote should be exercised defensively rather than aggressively or else the purpose of conflicts of law would be frustrated, it is necessary and exists in almost every conflict of laws system.[2] This device in the new Chinese system finds its place in Article 5 of LAL, according to which if the application of a foreign law will damage the public interests of China, that foreign law will be discarded and Chinese law shall apply instead.[3] On the other side of the coin, Chinese mandatory rules shall directly be applicable to a case if there are such rules in Chinese law, regardless of whether there is a foreign law that is applicable.[4] To give further practical guidance, six situations have been enumerated in Interpretation I on LAL as where Chinese mandatory rules shall be directly applicable:

(1) where the case is concerned with the protection of employee's interests;
(2) where the safety of foods or public health is at stake;
(3) where the safety of environment is involved;
(4) where the safety of finance is at risk;
(5) where anti-monopoly or anti-dumping is related;
(6) where it is suitable only if concerned rules in Chinese law shall be regarded as mandatory.[5]

---

[1]See Mills (2008, pp. 201, 202) and Chong (2006, pp. 27, 30).

[2]See Cheshire et al. (2008, pp. 700–705) and Dicey et al. (2000, p. 81).

[3]See Article 5 of LAL, which says: 'If the application of foreign law will damage the public interests of the People's Republic of China, Chinese law shall apply'.

[4]See Article 4 of LAL, which says: 'If there are mandatory rules in Chinese law for a foreign-related civil legal relationship, the Chinese mandatory rules shall directly be applicable'.

[5]See Article 10 of Interpretation I on LAL.

G. Tu, *Private International Law in China*, DOI 10.1007/978-981-287-993-6_4

4.2 Multiple Legal Systems

78. What if a choice of law rule in LAL point to a country which has more than one legal unit whose private laws are different from each other (one another) such as the US and UK? In different conflict of laws systems, there are different approaches dealing with this problem. Some systems decide the issue of which legal unit's law in the designated country should be applicable according to the intra-conflict of laws system in that country if there is such an intra-system; others decide according to which legal unit the concerned person is domiciled or has his habitual residence in.[6] There is a third group deciding according to the closest connection test[7] that is followed by the Chinese system in the new law, Article 6 of which says:

> Where a foreign-related civil legal relationship is subject to the law of a foreign country which has more than one legal unit whose private laws are different from each other (one another), the applicable law shall be the one of the legal unit which has the closest connection with the foreign-related civil legal relationship.[8]

To the present author, this is a reasonable approach and it also conforms to the closest connection principle established in Article 2.[9]

4.3 Substance/Procedure

79. The delimitation between substance and procedure is a tough issue in conflict of laws. Although the demarcation between substance and procedure is difficult to be made and still unclear in many areas,[10] it is a broadly-accepted principle, whether in common law countries or in civil law countries, that substantive issues should be governed by *lex causae* whereas procedural issues should be governed by *lex fori.*[11]

80. While several conflict of laws systems have a general rule recognizing this principle, there is no provision explicitly prescribing this principle in the new Chinese system.[12] An exception, however, does exist that as far as the issue of 'limitation period' is concerned, Article 7 of LAL confirms that it should be classified as being of substance rather than procedure.[13]

---

[6]See Huang and Guo (1997, pp. 67–68).

[7]Ibid.

[8]See Article 6 of LAL.

[9]See supra para. 69.

[10]See Cheshire et al. (2008, pp. 80–109), Dicey et al. (2000, pp. 158–181) and Carruthers (2005, p. 323).

[11]See Panagopoulos (2005, p. 69), Cheshire et al. (2008, p. 75) and Dicey et al. (2000, p. 157).

[12]See Panagopoulos (2005, p. 69).

[13]See Article 7 of LAL, which says 'Limitation period shall be governed by the law that governs the foreign-related civil legal relationship out of which the dispute on limitation period arises'.

4.4 Characterization

81. Characterization is another important issue in conflict of laws. It is generally agreed that there are two main alternatives by which characterization can be done; one is *lex fori* and the other *lex causae*.[14] It seems that the parochial attitude that characterization can be made only according to lex fori must be, at least, reconciled with some 'international spirit' in the modern age.[15] The combination of the two main alternatives have become more and more popular in the process of characterization with some putting more premiums on *lex fori* while others on *lex causae*.[16]

82. The issue of characterization in the new Chinese conflict of laws system is dealt with by Article 8 of LAL, which says: 'Characterization for foreign-related civil legal relationships shall be subject to *lex fori*.'[17] According to this Article, characterization by Chinese courts will be done only according to *lex fori* in the future, which might be too arbitrary to the present author and leave Chinese law behind the modern trend in the world.

4.5 Renvoi

83. *Renvoi* is of questionable value and need in conflict of laws.[18] The persuasive justification for the existence of *renvoi* is that its application can facilitate international decisional uniformity and bring about desirable results in some circumstances.[19] However, a high price has to be paid when enjoying the possible benefits offered by this doctrine such as unpredictability of result, *circulus inextricabilis* and non-accordance with the reasonable expectations of the parties.[20] The current trend in the world seems to be that *renvoi* is only accepted in limited areas or/and has only limited utilization in the areas where it has been accepted.[21]

---

[14]See Dicey et al. (2000, p. 35).

[15]See Cheshire et al. (2008, p. 44–45).

[16]See Christopher (2006, pp. 425, 430–431).

[17]See Article 8 of LAL.

[18]See Dicey et al. (2000, pp. 72–79) and Huang (2005, pp. 196–197).

[19]See Cheshire et al. (2008, p. 71) and Mortensen (2006, pp. 1, 22–26).

[20]See Dicey et al. (2000, pp. 76–78), Huang (2005, pp. 196–197) and Lee and Lu (2005, pp. 35, 66).

[21]See Lee and Lu (2005, pp. 35, 36), Dicey et al. (2000, pp. 71–79) and Cheshire et al. (2008, pp. 71–73).

84. Article 9 of LAL says:

> The applicable law for a foreign-related civil legal relationship shall not include the conflict of laws rules in that law.[22]

85. *Renvoi*, therefore, has generally been rejected by the new Chinese conflict of laws system. While this attitude can make the application of foreign law more certain and easier, an absolute rejection of this mechanism might not be proper because there are cases where this mechanism could still be useful.[23]

4.6 Evasion of Law

86. Evasion of law refers to the situation where one party has deliberately changed the connecting factor for the purpose of avoiding the application of the law that should have been applied if the connecting factor had not been so changed by that party.[24] This phenomenon used to happen in the area of family matters. It, however, has gained more popularity in the area of commercial law in the modern age of globalization.[25] To such behavior of the parties, some countries totally deny the legal effects whether foreign law or domestic law has been evaded while other countries are only concerned with the evasion of their domestic laws.[26]

87. In LAL, one cannot find a provision dealing with this issue. In Interpretation I on LAL, one, however, can find a clause declaring that the evasion of Chinese law is invalid, which says:

> If one of the parties has purposefully changed the connecting factor for a foreign-related civil legal relationship to avoid the application of mandatory rules in the laws or administrative regulations of the People's Republic of China, People's Court shall deny the effects resulting from the change of the connecting factor and the application of foreign law.[27]

4.7 *Dépeçage*

88. With the increasing complexity of modern life, a traditional choice of law rule that is designed to cover a broad category of legal relationships cannot be suitable to all legal relationships of that category, let alone all issues or aspects of that kind

[22]See Article 9 of LAL.

[23]See supra para. 83; Cheshire et al. (2008, p. 1201).

[24]See Han (2000, p. 132).

[25]Ibid.

[26]Ibid, pp. 133–135.

[27]See Article 11 of Interpretation I on LAL.

of legal relationships.[28] It is observed that more individualized choice of law rules can bring about more nuanced fairness though with more uncertainties and difficulties in the application.[29] Detailed choice of law rules are therefore recommended for further classified legal relationships or even different aspects or issues of those relationships, which can be evidenced in the American Restatement (Second) and the possible Restatement (Third).[30] In other jurisdictions, this phenomenon of issue-by-issue choice or *dépeçage* can also be seen more or less, at least in the area of contract.[31] It is arguable that due to individual fairness is historically emphasized in common law countries, *dépeçage* is easier to be accepted in common law jurisdictions than in civil law jurisdictions, for the latter of which China stands as an example.

89. The Chinese conflict of laws system usually does not provide different choice of law rules for different issues or aspects of one legal relationship and *Dépeçage* is, thus, not favored in LAL on the whole. However, the situation might have changed subtly because now one can find a provision in the Interpretation I on LAL, which says: 'If a case is concerned with more than one foreign-related civil legal relationship, People's court shall find the applicable substantive laws for them respectively'.[32]

4.8 Preliminary Question

90. Preliminary question could be a difficult issue to be handled in a PIL case.[33] In LAL, there is no provision for such an issue one might have to face from time to time. In the Interpretation I on LAL, Article 12 says:

> Where a foreign-related civil legal relationship has to be determined on the premise of the determination of another foreign-related civil legal relationship [a preliminary question], People's Court shall determine the applicable law for the preliminary question [another foreign-related civil legal relationship] according to its own nature.[34]

91. As can be seen, although Article 12 of Interpretation I on LAL recognizes the issue and differentiates preliminary question from the main question of a case,

[28]See Xiao (2007, pp. 18–19) and Cheshire et al. (2008, pp. 54–55).

[29]Ibid.

[30]See Symeonides (2009, pp. 383, 388, 409–410).

[31]Eg. Article 4 of Rome Convention allows *dépeçage*; For national practices on *dépeçage*, see Symeonides (2000, pp. 105–106, 142, 162, 276, 316, 345, 407, 440–441, 458, 477). Also see infra para. 145.

[32]See Article 13 of Interpretation I on LAL.

[33]See Cheshire et al. (2008, pp. 51–53).

[34]See Article 12 of Interpretation I on LAL.

it, however, does not indicate clearly according to which jurisdiction's conflict rule the applicable law for a preliminary question shall be found, which has to be answered by Chinese court's practice in the future.[35]

4.9 Proof of Foreign Law

92. Compared with the situation in common law jurisdictions where foreign law is normally treated as a matter of fact and applicable only if it has been pleaded and proved by the parties, judges in civil law jurisdictions are usually required to take judicial notice of foreign law ex officio.[36] As mentioned, historically, China is a country of civil law tradition.[37] Accordingly, as far as proof of foreign law is concerned, the responsibility normally does not lie with the parties but the court. Although during the reading of the drafts of LAL, it was proposed that the parties could play a more active role,[38] the traditional stance is re-confirmed in the new law but with the exception that the parties themselves shall provide the foreign applicable law where the application of that law is because of their choice. Now, Article 10 of LAL says:

> The applicable foreign law for a foreign-related civil legal relationship shall be ascertained by the concerned court, arbitration tribunal or administrative organ; where the applicable law is the one chosen by the parties, the parties shall provide the applicable law. However, Chinese law shall apply if the applicable foreign law cannot be ascertained or there are no relevant applicable rules in that law.[39]

93. To avoid Chinese judges' *lex fori* favoritism at the excuse of foreign law being unascertainable, Article 17 of Interpretation I on LAL commands Chinese judges to try as possible means as they can to find the applicable law.[40] To make the application of foreign law more workable and realistic, if the parties could reach consensus on the contents and understanding of the concerned foreign law between themselves, Article 18 of Interpretation I on LAL allows Chinese courts to directly accept their opinions.[41]

---

[35]See Cheshire et al. (2008, pp. 51–53).

[36]See Geeroms (2004, pp. 13–39).

[37]See Chen (2010, p. 159).

[38]See Article 11 of the draft for the seconding reading, which said: 'If the applicable foreign law is chosen by the *parties*, the parties shall provide that law; if it is not chosen by the parties, the concerned court or arbitration tribunal or administrative organ can either ascertain ex officio or require the parties to provide the applicable foreign law …', on file with the author.

[39]Cf. Article 11 of the draft for the second reading, ibid.

[40]See Article 17 of Interpretation I on LAL.

[41]See Article 18 of Interpretation I on LAL.

Part II
Rules of Choice of Law

94. In this part, choice of law rules in LAL will be examined one by one in detail for the different areas, while the relevant applicable rules in other laws or SPC's Interpretations will also be explored where necessary. Due to the importance of the issue of contractual conflicts against the background of globalization and international trade, emphasis will be put on contractual choice of law rules in the following discussion, especially those for general contracts. Therefore, in Chap. 10 where the law of obligations in China is explored, court cases will also be studied to reveal the detailed application of the relevant contractual choice of law rules. In particular, the closest connection test will be examined by taking into account the judicial practice in Chinese courts.

Chapter 5
Personal Law

95. Personal law is the linchpin to a conflict of laws system and especially important to the areas of marriage, family relations and succession therein.[1] Immediately following the rules on general issues in Chapter 1, rules regarding personal law are given in Chapter 2 of LAL.

5.1 Personal Law for Natural Persons

96. It is generally agreed that personal law should govern the matters closely related to a person such as the status and capacity of the person and family relations concerning that person and should always govern those matters wherever he goes.[2] However, the exact scope of those matters can differ from country to country.[3] Historically, there were mainly two alternative connecting factors for personal law i.e. domicile and nationality.[4] While the former was often and is still utilized in English law and those jurisdictions following the English law tradition, the latter was normally and is still employed by Continental European countries and those jurisdictions following their suit.[5] An English style of domicile might be able to ensure more meaningful connections between the person and his personal law and avoid the difficulty arising out of multiple legal systems but it could be very complicated and difficult to be identified.[6] While the concept of nationality can usually be easy to be understood and confirmed, it could have the problem of leading to tenuous or no real ties between the person and his personal law or even the application of a law, from the country of which he has fled, as his personal law

[1]See Zhu (2007, pp. 283, 291) and Cheshire et al. (2008, p. 154).

[2]See Huang and Guo (1997, p. 91) and Dicey et al. (2006, pp. 172–173).

[3]See Cheshire et al. (2008, pp. 154).

[4]See Huang and Guo (1997, p. 91) and Dicey et al. (2006, pp. 172–173).

[5]Ibid. Cheshire et al. (2008, p. 180).

[6]See Cheshire et al. (2008, pp. 154–183).

G. Tu, *Private International Law in China*, DOI 10.1007/978-981-287-993-6_5

against his wish.[7] Furthermore, the standard of nationality for personal law can be meaningless when facing a country of multiple legal systems.[8] In addition, a person could be stateless or a citizen of more than one country.[9] The modern trend seems to be that internationally and domestically, a compromised concept, habitual residence has gained more and more ground as an alternative for personal law.[10]

97. Although Chapter 2 of LAL does not explicitly say which connecting factor should be the one for personal law in Chinese conflict of laws system, it can be read out from the whole Chapter and the whole law that it is the law of habitual residence that mainly serves as personal law. Under the Chinese system, this law governs the entitlement of legal rights of a natural person as a civil party,[11] the declaration of disappearance and death of a natural person[12] and the contents of personality rights.[13] It also normally governs the legal capacity of a natural person although for the purpose of protecting the security of local commercial transactions, even if a person does not have legal capacity according to the law of his own habitual residence, that person can still be regarded as having legal capacity if he has legal capacity according to the law of the place where he performs legal acts other than those related to family, marriage and succession matters.[14] Beyond Chapter 2 of LAL, it can be seen from the whole LAL that the law of the civil party's habitual residence or the common habitual residence of both parties could broadly govern many issues in the areas of marriage, family relations and succession.[15] Nevertheless, the situation is not monolithic. The law of nationality or common nationality can come to play as an alternative in some issues[16] or as a secondary choice in others.[17]

---

[7]Ibid; Dicey et al. (2006, pp. 173–174).

[8]Ibid.

[9]Ibid.

[10]Ibid.

[11]See Article 11 of LAL, which says: 'The entitlement of a natural person's civil legal rights shall be governed by the law of his habitual residence'.

[12]See Article 13 of LAL, which says: 'The declaration of disappearance and death of a natural person shall be governed by the law of that person's habitual residence'.

[13]See Article 15 of LAL, which says: 'The contents of personality rights shall be governed by the law of the rights holder's habitual residence.'

[14]See Article 12 of LAL, which says: 'The legal capacity of a natural person shall be governed by the law of that person's habitual residence; however, when a natural person performs legal acts, if according to the law of his habitual residence he has no legal capacity but according to the law of the place where he performs legal acts he has, the latter law shall apply with the exception of marriage, family relations and succession matters'.

[15]See Chapters 3 and 4 of LAL; with the exception of divorce by litigation in which case *lex fori* shall apply, see Article 27 of LAL and the exception of intestate succession to immovables, see infra paras. 105, 110.

[16]See e.g. Articles 22, 24, 26, 29, 30, 32 and 33 of LAL.

[17]See e.g. Articles 21, 23, 24, 25 and 26 of LAL.

98. In LAL, there is, however, no definition for the key concept of habitual residence although it is said that where the habitual residence of a natural person is unclear, the law of the place where he currently resides shall take the place.[18] There used to be no reliable legal authority on this concept for the purpose of choice of law in China. However, in the context of jurisdiction, the SPC once said that the place of habitual residence of a natural person meant the place where he had continuously resided for more than a year.[19] It was argued that this definition might be able to be adopted in practice before there was another authority. Indeed, in the latest Interpretation on LAL given by the SPC, it is confirmed that the place of habitual residence is the one where a person has resided for more than a year inclusive.[20] As to nationality, the definitional problem might not arise because a person's nationality can easily be known e.g. simply by checking his passport. However, as mentioned above, a person could be stateless or a citizen of more than one country. According to Article 19 of LAL, if it is the former case, the law of his habitual residence shall apply instead; if it is the latter case, the law of the nationality of the country where the concerned person has his habitual residence shall prevail, failing which the law of the nationality of the country which has the closest connection with him shall apply.[21]

5.2 Personal Law for Legal Persons

99. In LAL, one can also find an Article dealing with personal law for legal persons. According to Article 14, personal law of a legal person shall normally be the law of the place where the legal person is registered and this law shall govern the issues of civil legal rights, legal capacity and organization of that legal person and the rights and obligations of shareholders etc.[22] Nevertheless, if the place of registration is different from the principal business place, those issues governed by the law of the place of registration mentioned above can be governed by the law of the principal business place which should often be the place of the legal person's habitual residence.[23] There is, however, no definition for a legal person's habitual residence in LAL.[24]

---

[18]See Article 20 of LAL.

[19]See paragraph 5 of the Opinions of the Supreme People's Court on Some Issues Concerning the Application of the Civil Procedure Law of the People's Republic of China (hereinafter, 1992 Interpretation on CPL); infra para. 222.

[20]See Article 15 of Interpretation I on LAL.

[21]See Article 19 of LAL.

[22]See Article 14 (1) of LAL.

[23]See Article 14 (2) of LAL.

[24]For more knowledge of personal law in Chinese PIL, see He (2013, pp. 137–157).

Chapter 6
Family Law

100. Before LAL, there were only few sporadic choice of law rules in Chinese law respecting family matters which were unsystematic and inconsistent in the eyes of Chinese PIL lawyers.[1] It was, therefore, expected that in the new Chinese conflicts code, conflicts rules could be more comprehensive and better designed for this field.[2] Chapter 3 in the LAL now is the specific chapter dealing with family matters in which one can find choice of law rules for marriage, spousal relationship, relationship between parent/s and child/ren, adoption, maintenance and custody.

6.1 Rules for Marital Issues

6.1.1 Rules for Marriage

101. It is generally agreed that the formal validity and essential validity of a marriage should be handled separately in PIL and governed by different laws.[3] Following the old doctrine of *locus regit actum*, it is broadly accepted that the formal validity of a marriage shall be governed by the law of the place where the marriage is celebrated.[4] As to the governing law for the essential validity of a marriage, there are different alternatives which might be dual personal law of the parties because personal law shall govern the important issues related to a person including marriage, the law of the intended matrimonial home because that place has a reasonable policy claim over the marriage or sometimes even the law of the place of celebration because of the same doctrine employed to justify the governing law for formal validity.[5]

[1]See supra paras. 55 and 59; Huo (2011, pp. 1065, 1079).

[2]See Huo, ibid.

[3]See Cheshire et al. (2008, pp. 878–916) and Huang (2005, pp. 347–349).

[4]See Cheshire et al. (2008, p. 878) and Huang (2005, pp. 348–349).

[5]See Cheshire et al. (2008, p. 896) and Huang (2005, pp. 347–348).

G. Tu, *Private International Law in China*, DOI 10.1007/978-981-287-993-6_6

102. According to LAL, if the formality of a marriage can satisfy the law of the place of celebration, the marriage is certainly formally valid. Furthermore, a marriage can also be formally valid if only it can satisfy the requirement of the law of the habitual residence or nationality of one of the parties.[6] LAL, obviously, has followed the international trend of *favour matrimonii.*[7] As far as the essential validity of a marriage is concerned, Article 21 of LAL says: 'The essential validity of a marriage shall be governed by the law of the parties' common habitual residence; failing which by the law of the parties' common nationality; failing which by the law of the place of celebration provided that the place of celebration is the habitual residence of one of the parties or the country of nationality of one of the parties'.[8] Although there are a few alternatives, as pointed out, if none of the conditions can be satisfied, the essential validity of a marriage would probably have to be subject to the closest connection principle.[9]

6.1.2 Rules for Spousal Relationship

103. There are mainly two aspects of spousal relationship i.e. personal relationship and property relationship. According to Article 23 of LAL, personal relationship between husband and wife shall primarily be governed by the law of their common habitual residence. This rule may be justifiable on the ground that on the one hand the couple normally should have a common habitual residence and they are familiar with local laws; on the other hand, their behaviors should conform to local norms and local laws have reasonable claims in regulating their conducts. Article 23 goes on to state if the couple do not have a common habitual residence, the law of their common nationality shall apply.[10] Difficulties, however, will arise where the couple neither have common habitual residence nor common nationality.[11]

104. For property relationship, according to Article 24, the couple have the freedom to choose the applicable law by mutual agreement from among the law of the habitual residence of one of the parties, the law of the country of nationality of one of the parties and the law of the place where the couple have their main property. If they did not make a choice, the same conflict rules as for personal

[6]See Article 22 of LAL, which says: 'The formality of a marriage is valid if it can satisfy the law of the place of celebration, or the law of the habitual residence or nationality of one of the parties'.

[7]See Huo (2011, pp. 1065, 1080).

[8]See Article 21 of LAL.

[9]See Huo (2011 pp. 1065, 1080); supra para. 69.

[10]See Article 23 of LAL, which says: 'Personal relationship between husband and wife shall be governed by the law of their common habitual residence; failing which the law of their common nationality'.

[11]See Huo (2011, pp. 1065, 1081).

relationship shall apply.[12] It is good to see that this Article has followed the general trend in the world that party autonomy has been expanded from commercial law to family law and from substantive private law to international private law. However, if the parties did not make a choice, the same difficulty of application with the conflict rules for personal relationship will also arise in practice.[13]

6.1.3 Rules for Divorce

105. LAL prescribes conflict rules for divorce by litigation and divorce by mutual consent respectively. For the former, *lex fori* shall be the governing law[14]; for the latter, there are quite a few alternatives. First of all, the parties can choose the law of the habitual residence of one of the parties or the law of the country of nationality of one of the parties as the governing law for their divorce by mutual consent; if they did not make a choice, the law of their common habitual residence shall apply; if they do not have common habitual residence but common nationality, the law of their common nationality shall apply; the last resort is the law of the place where their divorce is registered.[15]

6.2 Rules for Relationship Between Parent/s and Child/ren

106. The relationship between parent/s and child/ren also covers two aspects i.e. personal and property. However, LAL does not distinguish them when giving choice of law rules. Both personal relationship and property relationship between parent/s and child/ren shall be governed by the law of their common habitual residence if there is one. Where the parent/s and child/ren do not have a common habitual residence, the principle of protecting the weaker party, as mentioned already, is vividly reflected in the conflict rules which commands the application of the law of habitual residence of one of the parties or the law of the country of

[12]See Article 24 of LAL, which says: 'The parties can choose the law of the habitual residence of one of the parties, or the law of country of nationality of one of the parties or the law of the place where the parties have their main property as the governing law for their property relationship. If the parties did not make a choice, the law of their common habitual residence shall apply; failing which the law of their common nationality shall apply'.

[13]See supra para. 103.

[14]See Article 27 of LAL, which says: 'Divorce by litigation shall be governed by the law of the forum'.

[15]See Article 26 of LAL, which says: 'The parties can choose the law of the habitual residence of one of the parties or the law of the country of nationality of one of the parties as the governing law for their divorce by mutual consent. Where the parties did not make a choice, the law of their common habitual residence shall apply; failing which the law of their common nationality shall apply; failing which the law of the place where their divorce is registered shall apply'.

nationality of one of the parties, whichever is more favorable to the weaker party.[16]

6.3 Rules for Adoption, Maintenance and Custody

107. Both the formal validity and essential validity of adoption shall be governed by both the law of the adopter's habitual residence and the law of the adoptee's habitual residence.[17] While the non-differentiation of formal validity and essential validity is unusual, the double application of both laws of the parties' habitual residences can make international adoption related to China much more difficult although it might provide more protection in the meantime.[18] To encourage adoption and for the benefits of the adopter, the effect of adoption shall be governed by the law of the adopter's habitual residence at the time of adoption.[19] To protect the adoptee or the possibly-concerned public policy of the forum, the termination of adoption shall be governed by the law of the adoptee's habitual residence at the time of adoption or *lex fori*.[20] The maintenance creditor is supposedly a weaker party so that the relationship of maintenance shall be governed by the law of the habitual residence of one of the parties, or the law of country of nationality of one of the parties or the law of the place where the main property is located, whichever is more favorable to the maintenance creditor.[21]

108. The ward is also supposedly a weaker party so that the relationship of guardianship shall be governed by the law of the habitual residence of one of the parties or the law of country of nationality of one of the parties, whichever is more favorable to the ward.[22]

---

[16]See Article 25 of LAL, which says: 'Personal and property relationships between parent(s) and child (children) shall be governed by the law of their common habitual residence; where there is no common habitual residence, the relationship shall be governed by the law of the place where one of the parties has his/her habitual residence, or the law of the nationality of one of the parties, whichever is more beneficial to the weaker party'; supra para. 76.

[17]See Article 28 of LAL, which says: 'The formal validity and essential validity of adoption shall be governed by the law of the adopter's habitual residence and the law of the adoptee's habitual residence …'.

[18]See Huang (2005, pp. 359–360) and Huo (2011, pp. 1065, 1081–1082).

[19]See Article 28 of LAL, which says: 'the effect of adoption shall be governed by the law of the adopter's habitual residence at the time of adoption …'.

[20]See Article 28 of LAL, which says: 'the termination of adoption shall be governed by the law of the adoptee's habitual residence at the time of adoption or the law of the forum'.

[21]See Article 29 of LAL, which says: 'Maintenance shall be governed by the law of the place where one of the parties has his/her habitual residence, or the law of the nationality of one of the parties, or the law of the place where the main property is located, whichever is more beneficial to the person who claims maintenance'; supra para. 76.

[22]See Article 30 of LAL, which says: 'Custody shall be governed by the law of the place where one of the parties has his/her habitual residence, or the law of the nationality of one of the parties, whichever is more beneficial to the rights of the person who needs custody'; supra para. 76.

Chapter 7
Law of Succession

109. Compared with the previous situation in Chinese law where there were only sporadic and inconsistent conflict rules respecting succession, LAL has now designed a comprehensive and coherent conflict of laws system for succession which include conflict rules for intestate succession, testate succession, succession of vacant estate and the administration of estate.[1]

7.1 Rules for Intestate Succession

110. Unlike the unitary approach, LAL followed the approach of scission according to which the succession of movables and that of immovables shall be subject to different laws respectively.[2] According to Article 31 of LAL, intestate succession of movables shall be governed by the law of the deceased's habitual residence at the time of his/er death whereas intestate succession of immovables shall be governed by the law of the place where the immovables are located.[3]

7.2 Rules for Testate Succession

111. As with the issues of marriage and adoption, testate succession also has the problems of formal validity and essential validity. LAL obviously follows the doctrine of *favour testamenti* as far as the formal validity of testate succession is concerned because under LAL, the formality of testate succession is satisfied if only it

---

[1]See supra para. 55; Huo (2011, pp. 1065, 1082).

[2]See Huang (2005, p. 367).

[3]See Article 31 of LAL, which says: 'Intestate succession shall be governed by the law of the deceased's habitual residence at the time of his/er death. However, intestate succession of immovables shall be governed by the law of the place where the immovables are located'.

G. Tu, *Private International Law in China*, DOI 10.1007/978-981-287-993-6_7

can meet the requirement of the law of the habitual residence or nationality of the deceased at the time of death or making the will or the law of the place where the will was made.[4] The essential validity including the effect of a will is governed by the law of habitual residence or nationality of the deceased at the time of making the will or his/er death.[5]

7.3 Rules for Succession of Vacant Estate and The Administration of Estate

112. According to LAL, succession of vacant estate shall be governed by the law of the place where the estate is located at the time of the deceased's death while the administration of estate shall be governed by the law of the place where the estate is situated.[6] These rules sound reasonable because they may bring about convenience and make relevant judgments more enforceable.[7]

[4]See Article 32 of LAL, which says: 'The form of a will is valid if only it can satisfy the law of the habitual residence or nationality of the deceased at the time of his/er death or making the will or the law of the place where the will was made.'

[5]See Article 33 of LAL, which says: 'The effect of a will is subject to the law of habitual residence or nationality of the deceased at the time of making the will or his/er death.'

[6]See Articles 34 and 35 of LAL.

[7]See Huang (2005, pp. 368–369).

Chapter 8
Law of Property

113. Choice of law rules for immovables and movables can be found in Chapter 5 of LAL. However, before being able to apply these rules to ascertain the applicable law for them respectively, one has to resolve the problem of which law shall be applied to make the distinction between immovables and movables i.e. how properties should be classified. Despite the problem of general classification has been dealt with by Article 8, it might be inappropriate to classify immovables and movables by the same approach.[1] The modern trend in the world is that the law of the *situs* shall determine whether a property is immovable or movable,[2] which, in the present author's view, should and could be followed by Chinese courts as well although there is no specific provision on this issue in LAL.[3]

8.1 Rules for Immovables

114. Due to strong national interests possibly involved in immovables within the territory such as land,[4] it is said to be almost a universal rule that 'the law of the *situs* is the governing law for all questions that arise with regard to immovable property'.[5] As done before,[6] this rule is also re-confirmed in Article 36 of LAL, which says:

> Rights over immovables shall be governed by the law of the place where the immovables are located.[7]

115. While the Chinese wording in Article 36 is nebulous, the wording of 'all questions that arise with regard to immovable property', to the present author, might be a little bit exaggerating and needs to be delimited to some extent. It is

---

[1]See supra para. 82.

[2]See Cheshire et al. (2008, pp. 1193–1194) and Huang (2005, p. 269).

[3]See Huang ibid.

[4]See Huang (2005, p. 267).

[5]See Cheshire et al. (2008, p. 1199).

[6]See Article 144 of GPCL and Paragraph 186 of the 1988 Interpretation on GPCL.

[7]See Article 36 of LAL.

G. Tu, *Private International Law in China*, DOI 10.1007/978-981-287-993-6_8

true that issues such as the legal capacity to take and transfer immovables, the formal validity of a transfer of immovables and the essential validity of transfer shall normally be governed by the law of the *situs*.[8] However, issues in a contract related to immovables such as the formal and essential validity of the contract and the legal capacity of the parties for the contract could be governed by the law chosen by the parties or another different law.[9]

116. No arrangement has been made for subtleties with respect to the applicable law for immovables in LAL and they have to be spelled out by the practice of Chinese courts in the future.[10]

8.2 Rules for Movables

117. Historically, there were mainly two theories regarding the applicable law for movables that recommended the law of the domicile and the law of the *situs* respectively.[11] The theory of the law of the domicile was advocated because it was thought that 'goods follow the person', 'personal property has no locality' and rights over movables had to be governed by the law of the domicile of their owner.[12] The theory of the law of the *situs* was advanced on the grounds that the country of the *situs* should be able to exercise effective power by the application of its law over the property located within its territory; it is natural for a reasonable man to expect that the transaction will be subject to the law of the place where the subject matter of the transaction is currently situated; and the application of the law of the *situs* can also bring about certainty for the transaction of property.[13] It seems that the latter theory has been broadly accepted in the modern world.[14]

118. The novelty with the new Chinese system is that LAL has introduced the doctrine of party autonomy into the conflict rules for tangible movables, irrespective of whether the movables are being in transit or not.[15] If the parties did not

[8]See Cheshire et al. (2008, pp. 1202–1204) and Huang (2005, pp. 269–270).

[9]See Point (4) of Paragraph 2 of Article 5 of the 2007 Interpretation, infra para. 150; Cf. Articles 3, 4, 10, 11 and 13 of Rome I Regulation; Cheshire et al. (2008, pp. 1205–1206).

[10]Cf. Zhu (2007, pp. 283, 292–293). However, Article 31 says the law of the *situs* shall also apply to intestate succession to immovables, supra para. 110.

[11]See Huang (2005, pp. 265–267). In English law, there were also the theories recommending the law of the place of acting and the law governing the transfer, see Cheshire (2008, pp. 1208–1211).

[12]See Huang (2005, pp. 265–267) and Cheshire et al. (2008, p. 1208).

[13]See Huang (2005, p. 267) and Cheshire et al. (2008, pp. 1209–1210).

[14]See Huang (2005, pp. 266–267) and Cheshire et al. (2008, p. 1212).

[15]See Article 37 of LAL, which says: 'The parties can choose the governing law for the rights over movables; where the parties did not make a choice, the applicable law shall be the law of the place where the concerned movable property was located when the relevant legal act occurred'; Article 38 of LAL, which says: 'The parties can choose the governing law for the transfer of a movable property that is being in transit; where the parties did not make a choice, the applicable law shall be the law of the destination of the concerned property in transit'.

make a choice, the theory of the law of the *situs* has been accepted as the leading one i.e. normally the law of the *situs* shall be the governing law for rights over movables.[16] However, the problem is that a movable property can be moving and change places during the course of events leading up to litigation so that it is difficult to say where the locality of a movable property is without pinpointing the relevant timing.[17] Therefore, Article 37 further says that the determinative locality of a movable property for the purpose of choice of law is the place where it was located when the relevant legal act such as transfer took place.[18] If the parties did not make a choice of governing law for the transfer of a movable property that is being in transit, Article 38 says that the law of the stipulated place of destination, rather than the law of the *situs*, shall apply because it is unrealistic to identify the locality of a continuously moving property being in transit.[19] Nevertheless, Article 38 does not say what if the stipulated destination is altered during the course of the transit, which could frequently happen in international business practices.[20]

119. Further considerations could have been given to the nature of the disputes respecting movables. While a dispute related to movables that is of proprietary character should normally be governed by the law designated by the rules analyzed above in Articles 37 and 38, a dispute of contractual character could properly be governed by the applicable law of the contract.[21] Moreover, what if it is a more complicated situation where disputes having both characters can happen?[22]

120. In LAL, following those choice of law rules regarding tangible movables, simply-made choice of law rules are also provided for securities and rights over pledge. For the former, Article 39 says: 'Securities shall be governed by the law of the place where the rights regarding the securities were realized or the law of another place which has the closest connection with the securities in dispute'.[23] For the latter, Article 40 says: 'Rights over pledge shall be governed by the law of the place where the pledge was created'.[24]

---

[16]See Article 37. However, Article 31 says intestate succession to movables shall be governed by the law of the decedent's habitual residence i.e. the decedent's personal law when he died, see supra para. 110.

[17]See Huang (2005, p. 268) and Cheshire et al. (2008, p. 1210).

[18]See Article 37 of LAL.

[19]See Article 38 of LAL.

[20]See Cheshire et al. (2008, p. 1221).

[21]See Cheshire et al. (2008, pp. 1208, 1211–1213).

[22]Ibid.

[23]See Article 39 of LAL; Cf. Cheshire et al. (2008, pp. 1244–1252).

[24]See Article 40 of LAL.

Chapter 9
Law of IP Rights

121. Given the huge and continuously increasing volume of contemporary international trade related to IP, how to effectively protect cross-border private IP rights in practice has become a topical issue and the interaction between IP law and PIL has attracted much attention in the past years. As far as choice of law for IP rights is concerned, generally speaking, there are three main aspects that need to be regulated i.e. matters pertaining to IP rights themselves such as the existence, initial ownership, scope, limitation, duration and transferability of IP rights, the exploitation of IP rights such as transfer and license and the infringement of IP rights. Due to the special nature of IP rights, an independent chapter is devoted to this area by LAL i.e. Chapter 7.[1]

9.1 Rule for Matters Pertaining to IP Rights Themselves

122. Historically, the principle of territoriality is the cornerstone of IP rights.[2] At conflict level, it is thus natural that matters regarding IP rights themselves should normally be governed by the law of the country where (the IP rights are granted and) the protection is claimed (*lex loci protectionis*), more exactly in the case of registered IP rights, the law of the country of registration.[3] It, however, has been argued that in some fields of IP rights, the territoriality principle might be of no relevance, whereby the issue of initial ownership, especially regarding copyright works and employees' inventions could be governed by a law other than *lex loci protectionis*, namely the law of the country of origin for the former; the law

[1]See Chapter 7 of LAL.

[2]See generally Basedow (2010, p. 5).

[3]See Fawcett and Torremans (1998, pp. 455 et seq.).

G. Tu, *Private International Law in China*, DOI 10.1007/978-981-287-993-6_9

governing the employment contract for the latter.[4] Initially, in the draft of LAL, it was said that [matters regarding] IP rights [themselves] should be governed by the law of the country where the protection was claimed or the law of the country of origin of the concerned IP rights.[5] Nevertheless, the ultimate rule in Article 48 of LAL reads:

> The [initial] ownership and contents of IP rights shall be governed by the law of the country where the protection is claimed.[6]

123. One can see that the Chinese legislation has now followed the strict territoriality principle. While the issues of initial ownership and contents of IP rights have been dealt with, other matters such as existence, duration and transferability, however, have been left unregulated, which, to the present author, seems to be an omission of the legislators. It is the author's belief that these matters will also be governed by *lex loci protectionis* in Chinese practice, given the Chinese preference of strict territoriality principle as demonstrated by this Article.

9.2 Rules for Transfer and License of IP Rights

124. With respect to transfer and license of IP rights, Article 49 of LAL says:

> The parties can, by mutual agreement, choose the governing law for transfer or license of intellectual property rights; if the parties did not make a choice, the relevant choice of law rules for contract in this law shall be applicable.[7]

125. To understand this Article correctly, it is the current author's opinion that 'transfer' in the context of this Article, as can be seen from the wording, should refer to the contractual matters of transfer of IP rights rather than matters of proprietary nature of transfer, namely 'transferability' which should, as said above, be governed by Article 48 of LAL. Contracts regarding transfer or license of IP rights, according to Article 49, should be subject to the general choice of law rules as analyzed below.[8] In the case where the parties did not make a choice of the governing law for a contract of transfer or license, however, there is no reliable

[4]See sections 311–313 of 'Intellectual Property: Principles Governing Jurisdiction, Choice of Law and Judgments in Transnational Disputes' proposed by the American Law Institute (ALI Publishers, 2008) (hereinafter, ALI Principles); section 2 of Part 3 of 'Principles for Conflict of Laws in Intellectual Property' prepared by the European Max Planck Group on Conflict of Laws in Intellectual Property and publicized on Sept. 1, 2010 (hereinafter, CLIP Principles), which can be found at http://www.ip.mpg.de/ww/de/pub/mikroseiten/cl_ip_eu/ (last visited on 17 Jul 2013), and Dessemontet (2005, pp. 849, 861–863).

[5]See Article 51 of the draft of LAL for the seconding reading, on file with the author.

[6]See Article 48 of LAL.

[7]See Article 49 of LAL.

[8]See infra Sect. 10.1 of this Part.

specific fixed choice of law rule in the prescribed list of Article 5 (2) of the 2007 Interpretation for these two kinds of contracts respectively.[9] Therefore, the applicable law for them has to be determined according to the closest connection test with characteristic obligation being particularly emphasized and taken into account.[10] While in typically simple cases, it might be easy to find the characteristic performer for a contract of transfer or license, namely the transferor or licensor, thereby the applicable law, it could be quite difficult to do so in cases where complicated contracts concerning transfer or license are involved.[11] One has to face the same problems as those related to finding the applicable law in the absence of choice for other general contracts.[12]

9.3 Rules for Infringement of IP Rights

126. Owing to the special nature and territoriality principle of IP rights, infringement of IP rights has to be distinguished from other torts[13] and it should also normally be governed by the law of the country where the protection is sought.[14] However, it has been suggested that the consequences of infringement could be governed by the law chosen by the parties[15] and in a case of ubiquitous infringement, a law other than *lex loci protectionis* might be more suitable to resolve the problems for the whole case.[16]

127. Chinese choice of law rules for infringement of IP rights can be found in Article 50 of LAL, which says:

> Liabilities arising out of infringement of intellectual property rights shall be governed by the law of the place where the protection is claimed; after the infringement, the parties can choose *lex fori* as the governing law for their disputes.[17]

128. Once again, the principle of territoriality has been followed to establish the basic rule. In contrast with other jurisdictions where this principle must be strictly followed in cases of infringement of IP rights,[18] Chinese law allows the parties to choose the applicable law after the infringement but the choice is limited to

[9]See infra para. 150. Cf. in Rome I Regulation, although there is no fixed rule for contracts of IP rights, either, a specific choice of law rule for franchise contract is given, see Article 4 (1) (e) of Rome I Regulation.

[10]See infra para. 130.

[11]See generally De Miguel Asensio (2008, p. 199).

[12]See infra paras. 149–191.

[13]See infra Sect. 10.2 of this Part.

[14]See Cheshire et al. (2008, pp. 815–816).

[15]See Article 3: 605 of CLIP Principles.

[16]See Sect. 321 of the ALI Principles; Article 3: 603 of CLIP Principles.

[17]See Article 50 of LAL.

[18]See Cheshire et al. (2008, pp. 816–817).

lex fori only which should be Chinese law.[19] This approach might be helpful for ubiquitous infringement or resolving the disputes respecting the consequences of infringement but it could be doubtful, to the present author, when it is not a case of ubiquitous infringement and the dispute is about whether certain acts could constitute an infringement rather than the damages resulting from the infringement.

[19]Cf. Article 8 (3) of Rome II Regulation which explicitly forbids the parties to make a choice of law for infringement of IP rights.

Chapter 10
Law of Obligations

10.1 Contract

129. Contractual choice of law, due to its practical importance,[1] has long been regarded by Chinese lawyers as the pioneer of Chinese Private International Law, to which particular attention has continuously been paid.[2] Back in 1985 after the opening-up policy was adopted, choice of law rules for contractual matters were first provided in the legislation regulating foreign contractual businesses i.e. Foreign Economic Contract Law (FECL).[3] To give sense to the relatively abstract provisions in FECL, the Supreme People's Court issued an Interpretation in 1987 containing some sophisticated clauses dealing with contractual conflicts and interpreting the contractual choice of law rules in FECL.[4] The contractual choice of law rules in FECL, therefore, came into being even earlier than the choice of law rules in the General Principles on Civil Law (GPCL) that were made in 1986 in which most choice of law rules in Chinese PIL could be found before LAL.[5]

---

[1]According to statistics issued by the Supreme People's Court, there were more than 28,000 foreign cases tried in Chinese courts each year, three samples of which indicated that more than 80 % of the cases were contractual. The number of foreign cases has, for sure, been rising year by year. These figures covered cases related to Hong Kong, Macau and Taiwan because cases related to Hong Kong, Macau and Taiwan were treated in the same way as 'foreign' cases in Chinese courts, see supra para. 41. Also see Guo and Xu (2008, pp. 122, 125–126) and Huang et al. (2008, pp. 433, 441–453, 2009, pp. 415, 425–440).

[2]See Zhang (2006, pp. 289, 312–313) and Huang (2005, p. 313).

[3]As has been cited, choice of law rules for contractual matters were given in Article 5 of this law, see supra para. 55. For a general introduction to and the significance of this law at the time, see Zhang and McLean (1987, p. 120).

[4]For this Interpretation, see supra para. 59. For general knowledge of the choice of law rules in the FECL and the more detailed choice of law rules in the 1987 Interpretation on FECL, see supra paras. 55, 59; Xu (1989, p. 648).

[5]See supra paras. 56–57.

G. Tu, *Private International Law in China*, DOI 10.1007/978-981-287-993-6_10

GPCL did not provide anything new for contractual conflicts and just reiterated the provisions in FECL.[6] There was no specific provision on contractual conflicts in the 1988 Interpretation on GPCL, either.[7] The reason might be that GPCL was in the position of 'general' law while FECL was a 'special' law which should enjoy priority in application. Now that there were specific provisions on contractual conflicts in the 'special' law of FECL and the supporting Interpretation for it, all the 'general' law of GPCL needs to do is to acknowledge and reconfirm the basic principles established in the 'special law' and leave those specific issues with the 'special' law. [8] Nevertheless, when the Chinese Contract Law (CCL) that is also a 'special' law in nature came into force on 1 October 1999 and replaced the FECL,[9] Article 126, the only Article on contractual choice of law in CCL is basically, again, a repetition of Article 5 of FECL.[10] Worse yet, the SPC's Interpretation on CCL did not say anything on contractual conflicts.[11] Theoretically, with the repeal of FECL, the 1987 Interpretation on FECL should also be repealed,[12] which meant that the much more sophisticated contractual choice of law rules in the latter would have no legal effects although those simpler rules in the former have survived in GPCL and CCL. A legal vacuum for contractual choice of law thus appeared though some argued that the 1987 Interpretation on FECL should still be applicable or at least be able to give judges some guidance in practice until there was another similar Interpretation given by the SPC.[13] Fortunately, this legal vacuum was eventually filled in 2007. Based on the previous 1987 Interpretation on FECL, the SPC issued a new Interpretation which was said to be given in accordance with the relevant Articles in GPCL and CCL i.e. Article 145 of GPCL and Article 126 of CCL.[14] Compared with the previous one that not only dealt with contractual choice of law issues but also many other issues related to foreign economic contracts, this new Interpretation is specifically designed to deal with contractual choice of law issues only (2007 Interpretation), whereby the SPC publicized modern Chinese conflict of laws rules regarding contractual disputes.[15] In LAL which is supposed to establish a complete conflict of laws system for

[6]Contractual choice of law rules can be found in Article 145 of the GPCL. This Article is almost the same as Article 5 of FECL. see supra para. 56.

[7]For this Interpretation, see supra para. 59.

[8]See Zhang (2007, pp. 141–142).

[9]See Article 428 of the CCL which states that the Foreign Economic Contract Law is repealed when the Chinese Contract Law comes into force.

[10]See Article 126 of CCL.

[11]This Interpretation came into force on 1 December 1999.

[12]Indeed, as indicated, this Interpretation was repealed on 13 July 2000; Huang et al. (2008, pp. 433, 434–435).

[13]See Zhang (2006, pp. 289, 315). This had actually been proved by the courts' practice, see infra paras. 157–159.

[14]See preamble of this Interpretation.

[15]For this Interpretation, see supra para. 59.

China, there are, however, only three Articles specifically touching upon contractual conflicts.[16] While Articles 42 and 43 of LAL have prescribed choice of law rules for special contracts i.e. consumer contracts and employment contracts, Article 41 providing choice of law rules for general contracts has, once again, basically re-confirmed the doctrine of party autonomy and the closest connection principle that had already been established in the previous Article 5 of FECL, Article 145 of GPCL and Article 126 of CCL.

10.1.1 General Contracts

10.1.1.1 The Relationship Between the Rules in LAL and Those in the 2007 Interpretation of SPC

130. The general rules for contractual choice of law can be found in Article 41 of LAL, which says:

> The parties, by agreement, can choose the governing law for their contract; if the parties did not make a choice, the applicable law shall be the law of the place where the party who is to effect the characteristic obligation for the contract has his habitual residence or the law of another place which has the closest connection with the contract.[17]

131. While it is clear that the doctrine of party autonomy is established as the leading principle for contractual choice of law as in many other jurisdictions, it might be unclear about how to apply this Article in practice.[18]

132. As mentioned above, in 2007, the SPC issued an Interpretation specifically dealing with contractual choice of law issues that has much more detailed rules than this Article.[19] Now that LAL has come into effect, will this Interpretation still be applicable? If 'yes', can the 2007 Interpretation be comfortably accommodated by LAL which surely shall prevail over the former in terms of the hierarchy of the legal instruments?[20] A systematic check by the present author found that no essential conflicts exist between the new law, LAL and the 2007 Interpretation,[21] which might be attributable to the fact that the SPC was consulted in the making of LAL

---

[16]See Articles 41, 42 and 43 of LAL.

[17]See Article 41 of LAL.

[18]See Zhang (2006, pp. 289, 292).

[19]See supra para. 59.

[20]The hierarchy of legal instruments in China is: the law made by the NPC; the law made by the Standing Committee of the NPC; ……; the Interpretation of the Supreme People's Court, generally see supra paras. 4–5.

[21]There is one exception with proof of foreign law for which the 2007 Interpretation adopted the approach of the draft in the second reading of LAL, see Article 9 of the 2007 Interpretation; supra para. 92.

and the legislators of NPC and judges of SPC might have already taken into consideration the questions raised above. It is, therefore, the present author's belief that it will still be the 2007 Interpretation of SPC that mainly governs the contractual conflicts issues in future for a while. In the latest Interpretation given by the SPC on LAL i.e. Interpretation I on LAL, one can also find some Articles that are relevant to contractual choice of law, which will also be taken into account in the following discussion.[22]

10.1.1.2 The Doctrine of Party Autonomy in Chinese Contractual Choice of Law

133. As far as the parties' choice is concerned, although explicit choice is required by both LAL and the 2007 Interpretation,[23] there are some other issues that are regulated by the latter but no provisions for which are applicable in the former such as the timing and alteration of choice[24] and the choice made by both parties invoking the same law in the proceedings.[25] In the following text where specific issues of contractual choice of law regarding party autonomy are discussed, the rules in LAL, Interpretation I on LAL and the 2007 Interpretation will all be put together to see what the Chinese situation is. Before doing that, it, however, might be necessary to make some general remarks on the doctrine of party autonomy respecting contractual choice of law.

Some General Remarks

134. Nowadays, it seems self-evident that party autonomy should be the leading principle for contractual choice of law i.e. an international contract should be governed by the law chosen by the parties if the parties have made such a valid choice for their contract.[26] This doctrine, however, has been controversial and, at least, not accepted in the US, some other American countries and China until recently although it has as long a history as back in sixteenth century.[27] The growing

---

[22]See supra para. 68.

[23]See Article 3 of LAL and the 2007 Interpretation.

[24]See Article 4 (1) of the 2007 Interpretation. Also see Article 8 of Interpretation I on LAL.

[25]See Article 4 (2) of the 2007 Interpretation. Also see Article 8 of Interpretation I on LAL.

[26]See Zhang (2006, p. 551). For the broad acceptance of this doctrine in the world, see Preliminary Document No. 22 B of March 2007 Feasibility Study on the Choice of Law in International Contracts-Overview and Analysis of Existing Instruments-Note prepared by Thalia Kruger for the Permanent Bureau (hereinafter, Kruger Note), pp. 5–8, 19. This document can be found at the official website of the Hague Conference on Private International Law.

[27]See Juenger (1997, p. 195); Zhang, ibid, 551, 516–518.

strength of this doctrine may have been grounded on two bases. First, in substantive sense, 'the will of the parties is sovereign [in contract law]',[28] parties can make to each other whatever promises they want to make and are bound by their own promises; contract law is supplementary in nature, and if the parties did not specify their obligations in their contract, contract law can come to fill in[29]; now that the parties have the rights to set their obligations whatsoever in their contract, they should also, of course, be allowed to choose the law that they want to supplement (govern) their contract so that the expectations of the parties can be met by the application of the chosen law.[30] It was, therefore, said that 'party autonomy mirrors, on the conflicts level, the substantive principle of freedom of contract'.[31] Secondly, in technical sense, to accept the doctrine of party autonomy for contractual choice of law can bring about certainty because it is relatively easy for the parties and the court to know which law is applicable to the contract and the rights and obligations of the contract under the applicable law[32]; if this doctrine is broadly accepted by countries, international uniformity will certainly be promoted, and efficiency for the conduct of international trade and commerce would be enhanced because problems caused by legal and judicial divergences might be alleviated.[33]

135. In China, owing to the fear of influence from 'Western Capitalism' and the belief that 'judicial sovereignty is absolute [in the territory]', extra-territorial effects of foreign civil and commercial law were not acceptable and there was almost no application of foreign law in Chinese courts at all before the opening-up policy was adopted, let alone the doctrine of party autonomy for contractual choice of law.[34] This doctrine, however, immediately gained recognition in Chinese law once China decided to move towards the mainstream of the world economy.[35] In the 1985 Foreign Economic Contract Law (FECL), paragraph 1 of Article 5 said:

> [Foreign] Contractual parties can choose the law to resolve their contractual disputes ...[36]

136. This principle was almost verbatim re-confirmed in both Paragraph 1 of Article 145 of General Principles on Contract Law (GPCL) and Article 126 of

---

[28]See Lorenzen (1921, pp. 565, 573).

[29]See Kruger Note, 8.

[30]See Zhang (2006, pp. 512, 552–553); Kruger Note, 8.

[31]See Juenger (1995, pp. 445, 449).

[32]See Zhang (2006, pp. 512, 553).

[33]See Juenger (1997, pp. 195, 196); Zhang, ibid.

[34]See Zhang (2006, pp. 289, 300–301); supra paras. 1–2.

[35]See Zhang, ibid, 290, 301.

[36]See Article 5 (1) of FECL; supra para. 55.

Chinese Contract Law (CCL).[37] Although once among Chinese scholars there was debate on what the scope of 'contractual disputes' exactly was and doubt if this paragraph meant the same as the doctrine of party autonomy,[38] it had been settled that this sentence was indeed a statement of the doctrine of party autonomy for contractual choice of law in China,[39] which led to the eventual acceptance by LAL for the area of contract and beyond.[40]

137. Despite the fact that party autonomy is broadly accepted by countries for contractual choice of law, differences lie in the details of how this doctrine is applied in different legal systems.[41] Chinese version of this doctrine has its own features.

The Scope of Choice: What Law Can Be Chosen?

138. Traditionally, the parties were only allowed to choose the *law of a state* as the governing law for their contract but not *lex mercatoria*.[42] The latter was disfavored for a few reasons: first, it is not made by legislators through a democratic process,[43] which is concerned with sovereignty[44]; secondly, it may not be 'defined' or 'codified' or 'internationally recognized'[45]; thirdly, even if it is defined, codified and internationally recognized, it is often incomplete and usually has lacunas[46] 'since remedies, if they are to be effective, would have to [eventually] flow from the law of a country'.[47] However, with the development of *lex mercatoria* arising out of contemporary international business transactions, a school of scholars advocated that *lex mercatoria* should also be accepted to be applied by national courts in international litigation if it has been chosen by the parties, especially when compared with international commercial arbitration where *lex mercatoria* is broadly accepted.[48] They argued that to reject precise, codified and internationally-recognized *lex*

[37]See Article 145 (1) of GPCL and Article 126 (1) of CCL, both of which say, 'Foreign contractual parties can choose the law to resolve their contractual disputes unless otherwise stipulated by the law'; supra paras. 55–56.

[38]See Xu (1989, pp. 648, 649) and Chen (2008, pp. 115, 123–124).

[39]See Article 2 of the 2007 Interpretation; Chen, ibid, p. 124.

[40]See Article 3 of LAL; supra paras. 71–74.

[41]See Zhang (2006, pp. 289, 292).

[42]See Lando and Nielsen (2007, pp. 29, 31) and Zhang (2006, pp 522–523). This is still the situation under Rome I Regulation, see Articles 2 and 3 (1) of Rome I Regulation; Dicey et al. (2006, pp. 1567–1568).

[43]See Lando and Nielsen, ibid, p. 34.

[44]See Kruger Note, p. 14.

[45]See Lando and Nielsen (2007, p. 32).

[46]See Lando and Nielsen, ibid; Kruger Note, p. 14.

[47]See Cheshire et al. (2008, pp. 698–699).

[48]See Bonomi (2008, pp. 165, 170–171), Lando and Nielsen (2007, pp. 30–34) and Juenger (1997, pp. 204–205).

mercatoria is an unnecessary restriction on party autonomy in international litigation.[49] Furthermore, *lex mercatoria* has the advantage of being a 'neutral' system of law to the parties.[50] In addition, *lex mercatoria* could be made complete in itself.[51] Even if it is not, the mechanism of *dépeçage* in contractual choice of law[52] should still allow *lex mercatoria* to apply once chosen.[53]

139. In China, *lex mercatoria* was not mentioned in Article 5 of FECL as an alternative to the *law of a state*.[54] Neither is it in Article 145 of GPCL and Article 126 of CCL.[55] Given that Chinese civil and commercial law is not sophisticated yet, the general stance is that *lex mercatoria* could play a supplementary role if there is no relevant provision for a legal issue in Chinese law when Chinese law is the applicable law for the case.[56] In the relevant laws and Interpretations, there is no answer to the question whether *lex mercatoria* can directly be chosen as the applicable law. Neither could one find such a provision in LAL. Courts' practice, however, indicated that *lex mercatoria* could be applied if chosen by the parties.[57] It, therefore, might be possible that *lex mercatoria* could be accepted as one of the options for the parties' choice in the future in China.

140. Another issue that should be noted here is the position of international treaties in Chinese law. If China has ratified an international treaty and a case falls into the scope of that treaty, that treaty should enjoy priority over Chinese law, except where China has made a reservation,[58] and directly be applicable to the case e.g. the United Nations Convention on Contracts for the International Sale of Goods (hereinafter, 'CISG').[59] The question that concerns more here is not this but whether the parties can directly choose an international treaty which China may have not ratified yet as the applicable law for their contract. No answer exists in the current effective laws. It seems that there are quite a few scholars suggesting international treaties to be included in the scope.[60] To the present author, their

---

[49] See Juenger, ibid, 204; Bonomi, ibid.

[50] See Lando and Nielsen (2007, p. 33).

[51] See Nygh (1995, pp. 269, 309), Lando and Neilson, ibid, p. 33.

[52] See infra para. 145.

[53] See Bonomi (2008, pp. 165, 171).

[54] See Article 5 of FECL.

[55] See Article 145 of GPCL; Article 126 of CCL.

[56] See paragraph 3, Article 142 of GPCL; paragraph 3 of Article 5 in FECL. Also see Article 5 of Interpretation I on LAL.

[57] See a case as cited in Huang et al. (2009, pp. 415, 430) in which UCP 500 was chosen by the parties and applied by a Chinese court; Guo and Xu (2008, pp. 122, 127–128, 138).

[58] See Article 142 (2) of GPCL.

[59] As said in the Introduction of this book, this Convention came into force in China on 1 January 1988, see Chen (2008, pp. 115–116, 118–119); Article 4 of Interpretation I on LAL. For a case where a Chinese court has directly applied this convention, see Zhang (2006, pp. 289, 330–331).

[60] See Zhang, ibid, p. 330.

suggestion might be too bold and problematic because it would have the effects that private parties could ‘force’ China to accept a treaty that China might not want to ratify. In the latest Interpretation I on LAL, it is, however, clearly said:

> Where the parties invoke an international convention not ratified by China in their contract, People’s courts can determine the rights and obligations of the parties according to that convention, provided that the application of the convention will not violate the public interests of China and mandatory rules in Chinese laws and Chinese administrative regulations.[61]

The Means of Choice: Explicit or Implicit?

141. In reality, the real choice of the parties can be explicit or implicit.[62] To fully respect party autonomy, it is, therefore, necessary to recognize both explicit and implicit choices made by the parties,[63] which might be the reason why many legal systems have accepted both the parties’ explicit and implicit choices for the governing law regarding their contract.[64] Nevertheless, it is not always easy, sometimes even very difficult to infer if the parties have made a real implicit choice if they did not make an explicit one.[65]

142. While, in China, the FECL and GPCL did not put any limitation on the means of choice,[66] the 1987 Interpretation on FECL declared clearly that only explicit choice made by the parties was acceptable for the purpose of easier and uniform application of the law, given Chinese judges’ lack of experiences dealing with foreign cases.[67] LAL re-confirmed this stance.[68] Nevertheless, courts’ practice had run out of this limitation. In court proceedings, if one party invoked the substantive law of a state and the other party did not raise objection or both parties invoked the substantive law of the same state, normally *lex fori* (Chinese law), it had been decided that it should be inferred that the parties had implicitly chosen the substantive law of that state as the governing law for their contract.[69] This

---

[61]See Article 9 of Interpretation I on LAL.

[62]See Cheshire et al. (2008, pp. 701–702), Juenger (1997, p. 199) and Dicey et al. (2006, p. 1573).

[63]See Lando and Nielsen (2007, pp. 29, 34).

[64]See Kruger Note, p. 16; Juenger (1997, pp. 199–200) and Zhang (2006, p. 524).

[65]For the difficulties related to this issue, see Hill (2004, pp. 325, 327–332, 346–347), Dicey et al. (2006, pp. 1573–1577) and Cheshire et al. (2008, pp. 703–705); Kruger Note, p. 16.

[66]Neither did the CCL.

[67]See paragraph 2 of Part 2; supra para. 59.

[68]See supra para. 73.

[69]E.g. see *Changjiang Economic Combined Development (Group) GmbH Chongqing Company versus Orient Choice Limited* (2007) Yu High Court Civ Final No. 250; Guo and Xu (2008, pp. 130–131, 140). Japanese courts did the same thing as Chinese courts, see Okuda (2008, pp. 301, 303–305).

practice has been incorporated into the 2007 Interpretation and the Interpretation I on LAL[70] despite it has been insisted that the choice of the parties should be made in an explicit way.[71] Theoretically, there is a logical problem here: on the one hand, Article 3 of LAL and the 2007 Interpretation says only explicit choice is permissible; on the other hand, one kind of exemplary implicit choice has been accepted.[72] Furthermore, not to recognize implicit choice in other situations will certainly go against the principle of party autonomy in some cases and can be regarded as 'rigid'[73] despite it might be able to avoid the difficulties involved in implicit choice.[74] It is predictable that implicit choice may not be acceptable in the near future in China although some suggested that the rigidity regarding the means of choice should be relaxed.[75]

The Timing and Alternation of Choice

143. The issues of the timing of choice, whether the parties can alter their choice and if so, when at latest the alternation should be made are related to the extent to which party autonomy is allowed in terms of temporal dimension.[76] In China, these issues have not been touched in FECL, GPCL and CCL. However, Paragraph 2 of Part 2 of the 1987 Interpretation on FECL said: 'If the parties had chosen the applicable law for their contract at the time of conclusion of the contract or after their disputes arose, the chosen law shall be applied by the court hearing the case ...'[77] Subsequently, Paragraph 4 added that 'after the case is filed, the parties should still be allowed to choose the applicable law for their contract until the formal trial starts [if they did not do so according to Paragraph 2] ...'[78] Put them together, it could be said that the parties were allowed to make their choice before the formal court trial of their case.[79] Nevertheless, it often occurred that the parties could reach consensus on the applicable law for their contractual disputes after the formal court trial started, probably because only by then they began to realize the issue of choice of law that they had not realized before and would like to

[70]See Article 4 (2) of the 2007 Interpretation and Article 8 of Interpretation I on LAL.

[71]See Article 3 of the 2007 Interpretation and Article 3 of LAL.

[72]See Okuda (2008, pp. 301, 306), n 30.

[73]See Okuda, ibid, 306.

[74]See supra para. 141.

[75]See Huang (2005, p. 314). Cf. the situation under Rome I Regulation where implicit choice is recognized, see Article 3 (1) of Rome I Regulation.

[76]See Zhang (2006, pp. 317–318).

[77]See Paragraph 2 of Part 2 of the 1987 Interpretation on FECL.

[78]See Paragraph 4 of Part 2 of the 1987 Interpretation on FECL.

[79]See Xu (1989, pp. 648, 650).

determine it themselves rather than leave it with the judges.[80] Indeed, courts had accepted the choices of the parties made after the formal trials even before the promulgation of the 2007 Interpretation that authorized the expansion of the time limit on parties' choice up to the closing of the oral arguments in the first instance.[81] As to the alternation of choice, although the 1987 Interpretation on FECL did not say it was permissible, courts had also accepted it in practice.[82] The issues of timing of choice and alternation of choice were eventually put together in the 2007 Interpretation, Article 4 (1) of which says: 'Based on consensus, the parties should be allowed to make a choice of the applicable law for their contract or alter their choice until the closing of the oral arguments in the first instance'.[83] Once again, this stance was confirmed in Interpretation I on LAL.[84]

144. Undoubtedly, improvements have been made by the 2007 Interpretation and Interpretation I on LAL.[85] However, it was argued that the parties should be allowed to make their choice or alter their choice until the closing of the oral arguments in 'the instance determining the facts' whether it is a first or second instance, 'or else the principle of unity of the oral arguments would be offended'.[86] According to the Chinese Civil Procedure Law (hereinafter, 'CPL'), both factual and legal issues could be re-tried in the second instance.[87] The parties, therefore, should be allowed to make a choice or alter their choice in the second instance as what is permitted in the first instance according to the principle of 'unity of oral arguments'.[88] It is true that the parties could possibly change their mind on the issue of choice of law for their case during their arguments in the second instance.[89] Nevertheless, if the parties were permitted to make a choice or alter their choice in the second instance, the newly-chosen substantive law different from that applied to the case in the first instance would have to be applied to the case in the second instance so that the parties would lose an instance for their case in terms of substantive legal issues.[90]

---

[80]According to statistics, in China, around 70 % of choices made by the parties for the applicable law were done after the formal court trials started, see Guo and Xu (2008, p. 130).

[81]E.g. see *New World Trade Company (Hong Kong) versus Nanjing Baowang Lumbering Company Ltd.* (2006) Ning Civ 5 First Instance No. 61; *also* see Article 4 of the 2007 Interpretation.

[82]E.g. see *Shanghai Huazhong Lina Knitting Company Ltd. versus Veken (Hong Kong) Textile Ltd.* (2007) Hu High Court Civ 4 (Economic) Final No. 45.

[83]See Article 4 (1) of the 2007 Interpretation. Cf. Article 3 (2) of Rome I Regulation.

[84]See Article 8 of Interpretation I on LAL.

[85]See Huang et al. (2008, p. 436).

[86]See Okuda (2008, pp. 301, 305–306).

[87]See Article 168 of CPL.

[88]See Okuda (2008, pp. 301, 305–306).

[89]Ibid.

[90]In China, normally one case can have two instances, see supra para. 6.

Is *Dépeçage* Allowed?

145. In different jurisdictions, *dépeçage* is allowed more or less in the area of contractual conflicts.[91] In some legal systems, the parties can even choose different laws for different parts of their contract.[92] This kind of *dépeçage* has not been authorized in China in any law or Interpretation although it was proposed.[93] Given that China is a country of civil law tradition which prefers legal certainty and general social justice to flexibility and individualized fairness, a deep *dépeçage* as mentioned may not be suitable to Chinese judicial practice. [94] However, this does not mean that *dépeçage* is totally unacceptable to Chinese law. Article 143 of the GPCL and paragraphs 179–181 of the 1988 Interpretations on GPCL indicate that the legal capacity of contractual parties can be treated independently.[95] It is believed that the formality of contract should also be regulated in its own way.[96] It seems that *dépeçage* has been accepted to a limited extent in China for contractual conflicts.[97]

The Limitations on Choice

146. While party autonomy is broadly accepted, it is not absolute in the sense that various limitations may be put on it in different legal systems.[98] In China, the traditional devices like the doctrines of 'public policy' and 'evasion of law' could be exercised to deny the application of a foreign law chosen by the parties.[99] On the other side of the coin, mandatory rules in Chinese law must be applied over a foreign law even if the parties have designated that law as the applicable law for their contract.[100] However, throughout the relevant laws and Interpretations, no

[91]See supra paras. 88–89.

[92]E.g. this is allowed in the EU, see Article 3 (1) of Rome I Regulation.

[93]See Zhu (2007, pp. 283, 295).

[94]See Chen (2010, pp. 159–181).

[95]Cf. Article 13 of Rome I Regulation, see supra paras. 55, 59.

[96]See Article 10 of CCL; Zhang (2006, p. 316). Cf. Article 11 of Rome I Regulation.

[97]See Zhang, ibid, p. 322. For general discussion of this issue in Chinese conflicts of law, see supra paras. 88–89.

[98]See Kruger Note, pp. 8–14.

[99]Of course, they can also be generally exercised in other situations. See Article 11 of Interpretation I on LAL; Articles 6 and 7 of the 2007 Interpretation; Article 150 of GPCL; paragraph 194 of the 1988 Interpretation on GPCL.

[100]See Article 4 of LAL; Article 10 of Interpretation I on LAL; Article 6 of the 2007 Interpretation; paragraph 194 of the 1988 Interpretation on GPCL. Cf. Articles 3 (3) (4) and 9 of the Rome I Regulation.

provision requires any link or connection between the chosen law and the contract, which is confirmed in Article 7 of Interpretation I on LAL.[101] Contracts concerning 'weaker' parties such as consumers and employees used to have not been singled out in China, which meant these contracts had been treated in the same way as other contracts and no specific limitations on party autonomy were imposed for them.[102] The situation has changed for these special contracts since the legislation of LAL, in which these contracts are given special rules that are different from those for normal contracts.[103]

147. In contrast with other jurisdictions, a unique limitation on party autonomy exists in Chinese law for foreign investment contracts.[104] To protect national economic interests and also probably national sovereignty to some extent, it is believed that only Chinese law, rather than any other law including a foreign law chosen by the parties, should directly be applicable to a list of foreign investment contracts.[105] In other words, any choice of foreign law made by the parties for these contracts shall be null and void.[106] Initially, three kinds of contracts were enumerated in the FECL and later on, maintained in the CCL, namely Chinese-foreign equity joint venture contracts, Chinese-foreign contractual joint venture contracts and Chinese-foreign co-operation contracts on the exploration and exploitation of natural resources.[107] In the 2007 Interpretation, another five have been added to the list i.e. contracts on the transfer of shares in a Chinese-foreign equity joint venture, Chinese-foreign contractual joint venture or wholly foreign-funded enterprise; contracts on becoming a contractor acquiring the rights of management by a foreign natural person, foreign legal person or any other foreign organization of a Chinese-foreign equity joint venture or a Chinese-foreign contractual joint venture established within the territory of the People's Republic of China; contracts on the purchase by a foreign natural person, foreign legal person or any other foreign organization of share equity held by a non-foreign-funded enterprise shareholder within the territory of the People's Republic of China; contracts on the subscription by a foreign natural person, foreign legal person or any

[101]See Xiao (2005, p. 188). The same is true under Rome I Regulation, see Article 3. However, there has been a debate on this among Chinese scholars. Cf. Article 40 (2) of Macau Civil Code where a reasonable connection is required.

[102]The same was true in the Inter-American Convention on the Law Applicable to International Contracts, see Juenger (1997, p. 204). However, it was argued these contracts should be treated differently in China, see supra para. 76. Cf. Articles 6, 7 and 8 of Rome I Regulation.

[103]See infra paras. 192–195.

[104]See Huang et al. (2008, p. 438).

[105]See Xiao (2005, p. 189); Huang (2005, p. 317).

[106]See Xu (1989, pp. 648, 650–651).

[107]See Article 5 (2) of FECL; paragraph 3 of Part 2 of the 1987 Interpretation on FECL; Article 126 (2) of CCL; supra paras. 55, 59.

other foreign organization to the increased registered capital of a non-foreign-funded limited liability company or limited-by-shares company within the territory of the People's Republic of China; contracts on the purchase by a foreign natural person, foreign legal person or any other foreign organization of assets of a non-foreign-funded enterprise within the territory of the People's Republic of China.[108] In addition, there is an open-ended provision which says 'Other contracts [that should be] subject to the law of the People's Republic of China as prescribed by a law or administrative regulation of the People's Republic of China'.[109] The expansion of the list was doubted by some critics. It was argued that party autonomy should be respected as much as possible in a mature market-oriented economy[110]; it is not plausible any more to say that Chinese enterprises and businessmen are lack of international business experiences so that they need protections as provided in the FECL that was made shortly after the opening-up; the list, therefore, could be reduced or removed rather than expanded.[111] Furthermore, from a comparative perspective, one can see the list, and also of course the expansion of the list is not appropriate if one looks at other legal systems.[112] Moreover, the list could cause difficulties for Chinese law to achieve a harmonized position respecting some international treaties such as the 1965 Washington Convention on the Settlement of Investment Disputes between States and Nationals of Other States.[113] The parochial attitude of expanding the list to protect national interests, therefore, should be discarded.[114] There is much to commend in these arguments.

148. One point, however, has to be clarified here: Chinese law must directly be applicable *only* in these contracts and *only* if all the conditions related to these contracts prescribed in the laws are satisfied.[115] Other contracts and contracts that cannot satisfy all the conditions shall still be subject to the doctrine of party autonomy. For example, while a contract on a Chinese-foreign equity joint venture should be governed by Chinese law, once an enterprise based on such a contract is established, a contract between this enterprise and other enterprises should still be allowed to be governed by the law chosen by the parties.[116]

---

[108]See Article 8 (1)–(8) of the 2007 Interpretation, supra para. 59.

[109]See Article 8 (9) of the 2007 Interpretation. For all these contracts to be exclusively subject to Chinese law, they must be performed within the territory of China, see Article 8 of the 2007 Interpretation.

[110]See He (2006, p. 225).

[111]See He, ibid, 230–231.

[112]See He, ibid.

[113]See He, ibid.

[114]See Huang et al. (2008, pp. 438–439).

[115]See Huang (2005, pp. 317–318).

[116]See Huang, ibid.

10.1.2 The Applicable Law in the Absence of the Parties' Choice

10.1.2.1 The Statuary Rules

149. If the parties did not make a choice of law for their contract,[117] the 'most closely connected' test should be applied to determine the applicable law i.e. the contract shall be governed by the law of the place with which the contract is most closely connected, which is a principle well established in China by the FECL, the 1987 Interpretation on FECL, the GPCL, the CCL and the 2007 Interpretation.[118] This test, however, is quite abstract and how to apply it in practice could be a big problem.[119] It is generally believed that in China, only objective factors should be counted in applying the test.[120]

150. Unlike other legal instruments that has only given the test without more, the 2007 Interpretation, after stating the test in Article 5 (1), goes on to say in Article 5 (2): 'In determining the applicable law according to the most closely connected principle, the people's court shall take into account the factors of the nature of the contract in dispute and the obligation performed by one party that can best embody the essential characteristic [characteristic obligation] of the contract and other factors to find out the law of the place with which the contract is most closely connected'.[121] To further give judges guidance for practice on the one hand and restrict their discretionary power in applying the test on the other,[122] while the 1987 Interpretation on FECL prescribed fixed traditional-style choice of law rules for 13 kinds of contracts,[123] the 2007 Interpretation prescribes for 17, whose names and designated applicable laws are as follows:

[117]This may happen for a few reasons such as a consensus on the governing law cannot be reached between the parties or the contract is concluded without consulting lawyers first, see Cheshire et al. (2008, pp. 707–708).

[118]See Article 5 (1) of FECL; Paragraph 4, Part 2 of the 1987 Interpretation on FECL; Article 145 (2) of GPCL; Article 126 (1) of CCL; Article 5 of the 2007 Interpretation; supra paras. 55, 59.

[119]Although this test seems to have been broadly accepted for contractual conflicts, different jurisdictions are applying it differently, see Zhang (2006, pp. 322–323).

[120]See Chen (2008, pp. 115, 123). This understanding can also be proved by the courts' practice, see infra paras. 156–186. Cf. the situation under the Inter-American Convention where subjective factors could be taken into account in applying the test, see Juenger (1997, pp. 195, 205). For the situation under Rome I Regulation, see Dicey et al. (2006, pp. 1581–1582).

[121]See Article 5 (2) of the 2007 Interpretation. In other laws and interpretations, one cannot find this sentence or a similar sentence.

[122]See Zhang (2006, p. 325).

[123]For the names of the 13 kinds of contracts and the applicable laws that were designated for them, see paragraph 6, Part 2 of the 1987 Interpretation, supra para. 59; Xu (1989, pp. 651, 652).

(1) Contract on sales: the law of domicile of the seller upon the conclusion of the contract shall be the governing law; or the law of domicile of the buyer shall be the governing law, if the contract is negotiated and concluded at the place of domicile of the buyer or the contract expressly provides that the goods shall be delivered at the place of domicile of the buyer.
(2) Contract on processing with supplied materials, assembling with supplied parts and other processing works: the law of domicile of the processor shall be the governing law.
(3) Contract on supplying equipment for a plant: the law of the place of installation shall be the governing law.
(4) Contract on sales, lease or mortgage of real estate: the law of the place where the real estate is located shall be the governing law.
(5) Contract on lease of movables: the law of domicile of the leaser shall be the governing law.
(6) Contract on pledge of movables: the law of domicile of the pledgee shall be the governing law.
(7) Contract on loan: the law of domicile of the lender shall be the governing law.
(8) Insurance contract: the law of domicile of the insurer shall be the governing law.
(9) Financial leasing contract: the law of domicile of the lessee shall be the governing law.
(10) Contract on construction works: the law of the place of construction works shall be the governing law.
(11) Warehousing or safekeeping contract: the law of domicile of the warehouseman or keeper shall be the governing law.
(12) Contract on guarantee: the law of domicile of the guarantor shall be the governing law.
(13) Contract on commission: the law of domicile of the person commissioned shall be the governing law.
(14) Contracts on issuance, sales and assignment of bonds: the law of the place of issuance of bonds, the law of the place of sales of bonds and the law of the place of assignment of bonds shall be the governing law respectively.
(15) Contract on auction: the law of the place where the auction is held shall be the governing law.
(16) Contract on brokerage: the law of domicile of the broker shall be the governing law.
(17) Contract on intermediation: the law of domicile of the intermediary shall be the governing law.[124]

[124]See Article 5 (2) of the 2007 Interpretation. With the development of economy, the number of categories of contracts had increased since the 1987 Interpretation on FECL. There is no such a list in FECL, GPCL, CCL and LAL. Cf. Article 4 (1) of Rome I Regulation, where 8 kinds of contracts are listed and given traditional-style choice of law rules.

151. One can see that, echoing what has been said earlier, the concept of 'characteristic obligation' is heavily relied on to build up the fixed choice of law rules for the different kinds of contracts. For some contracts, the place of characteristic performer i.e. the place of the party effecting the characteristic obligation of the contract is employed as the connecting factor whereas for other contracts, the place of characteristic performance i.e. the place where the characteristic obligation of the contract is performed is utilized.[125] After enumerating the list, there is an escape clause immediately following, which says: 'If a contract said above is significantly more closely connected with a place other than the one designated in the rules, the law of that place shall be applied'.[126]

152. The whole structure of Article 5 of the 2007 Interpretation might simply be summarized as: a general clause stating the test that should be applied in the absence of parties' choice; two of the most important factors that should particularly be taken into account in applying the test; a series of fixed traditional-style choice of law rules that designate the applicable law for each kind of contracts respectively; and a general escape clause that allows judges to disregard those fixed rules.[127] However, one may wonder: what is exactly the relationship among the different paragraphs of Article 5 and how should these paragraphs coordinate and interact with one another in practice?

153. Unfortunately and also probably strangely, there has been little debate on these questions in China so far.[128] A holistic reading of Article 5 gives one the

[125]Generally speaking, while No. (1) (2) (5) (6) (7) (8) (9) (11) (12) (13) (16) (17) belong to the former, No. (3) (10) (14) (15) belong to the latter. No. 4 is a special rule for immovable properties. In the 1987 Interpretation on FECL, it was the same that both the place of characteristic performer and the place of characteristic performance was used, see supra para. 59. Cf. under the Rome I Regulation and its predecessor, the 1980 Rome Convention on the law applicable to contractual obligation (Rome Convention), it is mainly the place of characteristic performer that is used as the connecting factor, see Article 4 (1) (2) of Rome I Regulation and Article 4 of Rome Convention. In Swiss law where the concept of characteristic obligation was originated, it was the place of characteristic performance, rather than the place of characteristic performer, that was used as the connecting factor, see D'Oliveira (1977, pp. 303, 304–308). Interestingly, although the Rome Convention insisted on the place of characteristic performer, some English judges preferred the place of characteristic performance to the place of characteristic performer in practice as the most closely connected place with the contract where the two places were different, see Hill (2004, pp. 325, 341–343, 346). However, others argued in favor of the place of characteristic performer, see Lein (2008, pp. 177, 184).

[126]See Article 5 (3) of the 2007 Interpretation. This escape clause was also available in the 1987 Interpretation on FECL, see supra para. 59. There is no escape clause in FECL, GPCL, CCL and LAL accordingly, owing to the reason that there is no list in them.

[127]See Article 5 of the 2007 Interpretation. The structure for applying the test was quite similar in the 1987 Interpretation on FECL, see paragraphs 4 and 6, Part 2 of the 1987 Interpretation. Cf. the structure of Article 4 in Rome Convention which is also quite similar.

[128]There had also been little debate for the corresponding provisions in the 1987 Interpretation. But in the EU, there has been serious debate on the similar questions for Article 4 of Rome Convention, different approaches have been suggested, generally see Hill (2004, p. 325), Atrill (2004, p. 549) and Fentiman (2002, p. 50).

impression that those fixed choice of law rules in the middle should be subject to the general opening clause at the beginning and the general escape closing clause at the end. Those fixed rules, therefore, seems to essentially be presumptions only and probably be weak presumptions indeed. Their function is thus supplementary and directing and not commanding in nature. This understanding will undoubtedly lead to more flexibility and less certainty in applying Article 5. It might even be able to find support from one of the fixed rules. For the most common contract in practice i.e. contract of sales, while the first rule in the list points to the law of the place of characteristic performer in the first instance, it allows this law to be easily displaced if certain conditions are satisfied.[129] One may argue that this is a flexible choice of law rule for contract of sales in itself and it cannot be taken over to prove anything for the relationship among the paragraphs of Article 5. One, however, may have to agree that to some extent, this rule indicates that Chinese law prefer finding the most closely connected place which might have to be done in an uncertain and flexible way to just applying a simple rule in the name of the 'most closely connected' test but cannot find the most closely connected place. Going along this line, accordingly, the presumptions in the fixed rules should not be strong and Article 5 as a whole should be applied in a flexible way. Nevertheless, given that China is a country of civil law tradition, Chinese judges are normally not quite experienced in dealing with international cases and legal certainty has long been preferred, those fixed rules may have been given *just* for the purpose of commanding judges to apply them directly in most cases, whereby the goal of legal certainty and easy application of law could be achieved. Going along with this reasoning, then one may agree that the presumptions in the fixed rules should be read as being quite strong and the closing escape clause of Article 5 should be exercised only in an exceptional way.[130]

154. In the latest legislation of LAL, Article 41 says: '... in the absence of choice by the parties, the governing law shall be the law of the place where the person who is to effect the characteristic obligation for the contract has his habitual residence or the law of another place that has the closest connection with the contract'.[131] To this Article, one may put the following questions: must the law of the person who is to effect the characteristic obligation of a contract always apply if there is such a characteristic obligation in that contract?[132] Or can that law be displaced by the law of another place if that place is more closely connected with the contract according to this Article? In other words, does Article 41 mean that

---

[129]Cf. Article 4 (1) (a) of the Rome I Regulation where the law of the place of characteristic performer cannot be so easily displaced.

[130]Cf. the situation under the Rome I Regulation where legal certainty is preferred to flexibility and the fixed rules could only be disregarded exceptionally, see Article 4 (3) (4) of Rome I Regulation.

[131]See Article 41 of LAL.

[132]In some contracts, it might be difficult to identify or there might be no characteristic obligation, see infra para. 188.

the closest connection test will be applicable only in the situation where there is no characteristic obligation in a contract or that the closest connection test should still be the prevailing principle whether or not there is a characteristic obligation in a contract and this article only indicates the preference for the place of characteristic performer in the application of the closest connection test or even does not indicate the preference but just emphasize one of the most important factors as Article 5 (2) of the 2007 Interpretation does?[133] In the making of LAL, the second reading draft deleted the closest connection test and required the law of the characteristic performer or the place of characteristic performance should be directly applicable for the purpose of certainty.[134] Nevertheless, it was argued that the closest connection principle was necessary for contractual conflicts disputes and eventually added on.[135] The wording of Article 41 in the current version, to the present author, is quite ambiguous and how to apply it could be a difficult issue for the courts in practice.

155. Putting Article 41 of LAL and Article 5 of the 2007 Interpretation together, one probably still cannot tell exactly how to apply the closest connection test for contractual conflicts in Chinese PIL and resolve the problem regarding the relationships among the different paragraphs of Article 5 of the 2007 Interpretation. Moreover, even if Article 41 of LAL could be understood to give the preference for the law of characteristic performer, it could only give direction for the presumption rules based on characteristic performer in Article 5 (2) of the 2007 Interpretation to be read as strong but not for the presumption rules based on characteristic performance.[136]

10.1.2.2 The Practice in Courts

The Different Approaches Adopted to Find the Applicable Law Before the Implementation of the 2007 Interpretation: Courts' Practice in 2005–2007

156. Strictly speaking, in the period after the repeal of FECL and 1987 Interpretation on FECL and before the implementation of the 2007 Interpretation, the general 'most closely connected' test based on Article 145 (2) of GPCL and Article 126 (1) of CCL was the only choice of law rule that could be applicable for contractual conflicts disputes without the availability of the specific

[133]See supra paras. 150–152.

[134]See Article 43 of the draft of the second reading for LAL, this draft and the materials on discussing the draft are on file with the author.

[135]Ibid.

[136]See supra para. 150.

traditional-style presumptive choice of law rules for the respective different kinds of contracts. The practices in courts were various on the closest connection test in this period.

(1) Went on directly looking to the fixed choice of law rules contained in the 1987 Interpretation on FECL

157. As said, with the entry into force of CCL in 1999, the FECL and the 1987 Interpretation on FECL should not be applicable anymore and so should the fixed presumptive rules prescribed in the latter. The practice in some courts, however, demonstrated otherwise.

158. In the case of *Changzhou Lida Instruments Company Ltd. versus USA Nilkota Inc.*,[137] the claimant, Changzhou Lida through its agent, Donghua Foreign Trade Company, sold electronic tools to the defendant, USA Nikota. The sale contract was signed by the claimant's agent and the defendant with the defendant being aware of the agency relationship. While the claimant performed its obligations of delivering the goods, the defendant failed to make the payment. The claimant then sued the defendant in the Intermediate People's Court of Changzhou, Jiangsu Province.[138] After confirming the validity of the sale contract between the claimant and the defendant, the judges stated that the applicable law for the sale contract should be the law of the seller's business place in accordance with the principle of closest connection. The seller i.e. Changzhou Lida's business place in this case was in China. Therefore, the judges decided that China had the closest connection with the contract and Chinese law, accordingly, should be the governing law for the case.[139] In another case of *Changzhou Kaiyi Traveling Things Company Ltd. versus Lifang Company Ltd. (Taiwan)* where a processing contract was in dispute,[140] the judges said: '[A]ccording to the closest connection principle, the law of the processor's business place should be the applicable law for contracts on processing of raw materials'.[141] The processor in this case was Changzhou Kaiyi Company, a Chinese company whose business place was in Changzhou, China so that China was thought to be most closely connected with the contract and Chinese law was thus applied as the governing law.[142]

159. Although in both cases, the judges did not explicitly say that they were referring to the fixed choice of law rules given in the 1987 Interpretation on FECL in making the decision on the applicable law for the cases, one could see that essentially it was those fixed choice of law rules that dominated their minds when they were applying the most closely connected test even if those fixed rules were

[137](2005) Chang Civ 3 First Instance No. 27.

[138]Ibid.

[139]Ibid.

[140](2006) Chang Civ 3 First Instance No. 29.

[141]Ibid.

[142]Ibid.

said to have been repealed. While in the case of *Changzhou Kaiyi*, the cited sentence clearly indicated that the judges were resorting to Article 6 (4) of Part II of the 1987 Interpretation on FECL, in the case of *Changzhou Lida*, it could be seen that the judges were resorting to Article 6 (1) of Part II of the 1987 Interpretation on FECL.[143]

(2) The place of performance/characteristic performance of the contract as the determinative factor

160. Another significant trend that could be discerned from the courts' practice was that some Chinese judges always took the place of performance of the contract for the one that had the closest connection with the contract.

161. In the case of *Tianfuxing Industry GmbH (Hong Kong) versus Shangqiu Haiqiao Trade Company Ltd.*,[144] the claimant, Tianfuxing Industry GmbH, a Hong Kong company, concluded a contract with the defendant, *Shangqiu Haiqiao Trade Company Ltd.*, a company in Henan Province, the mainland China. According to their contract, the defendant should produce beef sparerib soup cans for the claimant and deliver the goods via FOB to the port of Qingdao or Lianyungang for shipment. However, for some reasons, the defendant was unable to deliver the goods although it had produced some beef sparerib soup cans for the claimant. Later on, it was sued by the claimant for breach of contract. As regards the applicable law for this case, the judges said:

> The place of performance designated in the contract concluded between Tianfuxing Company and Haiqiao Company was in Henan Province, the mainland China, and the performance of the contract did take place [partly] in the mainland China. Therefore, the law of the mainland China should be the governing law for the dispute, and the rights and obligations between the two parties should be adjudicated by the law of the mainland China.[145]

162. In this case, the place of performance of the contract thus was said and considered by the judges as the determinative factor in applying the closest connection test. However, in contrast with a simple sale contract where delivery of the goods is normally the characteristic obligation of the contract, this case concerned a contract that had two important obligations i.e. producing and delivering the goods. The performance of both obligations should have taken place in the mainland China and the performance of one of the obligations did partly take place in China i.e. producing the goods. One might be able to see from the above citation that in this case when the judges said the place of performance of the contract, they were only thinking of the place of producing rather than delivering the goods or both. However, this case did indicate that the judges intended to apply the law of the place of performance of the contract as the governing law.

---

[143] See Article 6 (1) (4) of Part II of the 1987 Interpretation on FECL.

[144] (2006) Zheng Civ 3 First Instance No. 214.

[145] Ibid.

163. In the case of *Lv Rong versus Zhong Guang Company Limited (Hong Kong)*,[146] the claimant, Lv Rong from Sichuan Province concluded a construction contract with the defendant, *Zhong Guang Company Limited*, a company from Hong Kong. The construction project was carried out in Guangzhou. Disputes arose when the payment was not made by the Hong Kong company. Regarding the applicable law for this case, the judges said:

> The place of performance for the disputed contract in this case is Guangzhou. Therefore, in the absence of the parties' choice of the applicable law, the law of the mainland China should be the governing law in accordance with the closest connection principle.[147]

164. Although the wording in the judgment of this case referred to the place of performance of the contract, it is natural for one to relate it with the place of characteristic performance. When the judges said 'the place of performance for the disputed contract in this case is Guangzhou', to the present author, they were actually pointing to the place of the characteristic performance of the construction contract. The said place of performance of the contract was just the place of the characteristic performance in this case.

165. As a matter of fact, in quite a lot of other cases, the place of performance of the contract was said and utilized by Chinese judges as the determining factor for applying the closest connection test and when it was so, the place of performance of the contract usually meant the place of the characteristic performance of the contract.[148] According to the current author's observation, it is fair to say that in many cases, judges in China have been and are still using the phrases of 'the

[146](2005) Sui Intermediate Court Civ 3 First Instance No. 490.

[147]Ibid.

[148]E.g. also see *Shandong Boshui Pump Company Ltd. versus Guan Qiaoling (Macao)*, (2005) Sui Intermediate Court Civ 3 First Instance No. 65; *Suzhou Taifeng Glass Adornment Company Ltd. versus Phoneix Imports Co. Ltd.*, (2006) Su Intermediate Court Civ 3 First Instance No. 0012; *Yuetian Science and Trade Stock Company (Japan) versus Shanghai Qi'an Industry Company Ltd.*, (2006) Hu High Court Civ 4 (Economic) Final No. 46; *Wuxi Dahua Clothing Company Ltd. versus South Korea Xiyu Aite Stock Company*, (2007) Xi Civ 3 First Instance No. 005; *Enterprise P. Boucher Ltee (Canada) versus Henan Yuanfeng Leather Goods Company Ltd.*, (2007) Xin Civ 3 First Instance No. 30; *Suzhou Liansheng Chemistry Company Ltd. versus Changzhou Changlin Textile Printing and Dyeing Company Ltd. and Zhou Baicheng (Taiwan)*, (2007) Su Intermediate Court Civ 3 First Instance No. 0097; *Suzhou Liansheng Chemistry Company Ltd. versus Changzhou Changlin Textile Printing and Dyeing Company Ltd. and Zhou Baicheng (Taiwan)*, (2007) Su Intermediate Court Civ 3 First Instance No. 0097; *China Tabacco Henan Imports and Exports Company Ltd. versus Hong Kong Yingqi Tabacco Company*, (2005) Zheng Civ 3 First Instance No. 194; *Want Want Holdings Ltd. (Singapore) versus Zhuhai Jinguang Oils and Fats Industry Company Ltd.*, (2006) Hu High Court Civ 4 (Economic) Final No. 64.

place of performance of the contract' and 'the place of the characteristic performance of the contract' interchangeably and the two concepts mean the same thing to them.

(3) The domicile of one party alone or together with other factors as being determinative

166. In the case of *Anzhi Electronic Materials Hong Kong Company Ltd. versus Xuzhou Jingda LCD Screen Company Ltd.,*[149] the claimant, Anzhi Company was located in Hong Kong while the defendant, Jingda Company was a company in Xuzhou, Jiangsu Province. The claimant long-term supplied AZ optical-resistant materials to the defendant. Their dispute revolved around the delivery of goods and the payment for one transaction. In determining the applicable law, the judges simply said:

> [I]n this case, the domicile of the defendant is in Xuzhou City, Jiangsu Province. Therefore, the mainland China should be most closely connected with this case, and the governing law of this case is the law of the mainland China.[150]

167. Another similar decision was made in the case of *Axtra HK Limited versus Shanghai Youcai Electronic Science and Technology Company Ltd.*[151]

168. It was, however, not often that the domicile of one party alone could be regarded as being determinative in applying the closest connection test. More often was that the domicile of one party could come together with other factor(s) to determine the most closely connected place. For instance, in the case of *Shouan Industrial Fire Protection GmbH versus Zhen Huang Lin Law Office (HK) and Huifu Financing Company Ltd.,* the domicile of the claimant and the place of the conclusion of the contract were put together as being decisive for the closest connection principle.[152]

(4) The place of conclusion of the contract highlighted as one important factor together with other factors as being possibly determinative

169. In the case of *Suzhou Liansheng Chemistry Company Ltd. versus Changzhou Changlin Textile Printing and Dyeing Company Ltd. and Zhou Baicheng (Taiwan),*[153] the claimant Suzhou Liansheng concluded a sale contract with the first defendant Changlin Textile Printing and Dyeing for whom the second defendant, Zhou Baicheng provided guarantee. The claimant and the first defendant were both from Jiangsu Province and the sale contract was concluded and carried out in

---

[149](2007) Xu Civ 3 First Instance No. 2.

[150]Ibid.

[151](2007) Hu High Court Civ 4 (Economic) Final No. 10.

[152](2006) Sui High Court Civ Final No. 191; also see *Wuxi Dahua Clothing Company Ltd. versus South Korea Xiyu Aite Stock Company*, (2007) Xi Civ 3 First Instance No. 005.

[153](2007) Su Intermediate Court Civ 3 First Instance No. 0097.

Jiangsu Province, too.[154] The second defendant was from Taiwan and it had to bear joint liabilities according to the guarantee agreement attached to the main contract of sale.[155] The claimant sued the two defendants in order to claim the payment for the contract. As far as the governing law for the dispute between the claimant and the second defendant was concerned, the judges said:

> We consider that since the defendant *Zhou Baicheng* is from Taiwan, the jurisdiction and the applicable law for this dispute should be determined by referring to the rules for the civil cases involving foreign interests. … Since the parties did not make a choice of the applicable law for the contract, according to Article 126 of the Chinese Contract Law, the law of the place having the closest connection with the contract should be applied. The places of conclusion and performance of this contract [the sale contract] were both in Jiangsu Province. Therefore, the law of the mainland China which is most closely connected with the contract should be the governing law of the case.[156]

170. To the present author, the judges in this case might have mixed up the sale contract with the subsidiary guarantee contract. According to the above citation, it seemed that in deciding the case, the judges had put the second defendant into the shoes of the first one as if the second defendant had signed and were a party of the sale contract because of the joint liabilities. It, however, did demonstrate that the place of conclusion of the contract could be a meaningful factor in applying the closest connection test to them. Indeed, as shown above, in the case of *Shouan Industrial Fire Protection GmbH*, the fact that the place of conclusion of the contract and the place of the domicile of the claimant were the same had been enough to establish that place as being most closely connected with the contract. The factor of the place of conclusion of the contract was also highlighted in some other cases.[157]

(5) The place of conclusion, performance and the subject matter of the contract together as being determinative

171. In the case of *Enterprise P. Boucher Ltee (Canada) versus Henan Yuanfeng Leather Goods Company Ltd.*,[158] the claimant was a Canadian company and the defendant was a Chinese company from Henan Province. The claimant and the defendant concluded an oral agreement, according to which the claimant should supply 10 containers wet blue to the defendant. The claimant claimed that it delivered the goods to China according to the sale contract and received a letter of confirmation from the defendant but the defendant failed to pay. However, the defendant asserted that the agreement between them should be a processing

[154]Ibid.

[155]Ibid.

[156]Ibid.

[157]See supra para. 168; *Want Want Holdings Ltd. (Singapore) versus Zhuhai Jinguang Oils and Fats Industry Company Ltd.*, (2006) Hu High Court Civ 4 (Economic) Final No. 64; *Enterprise P. Boucher Ltee (Canada) versus Henan Yuanfeng Leather Goods Company Ltd.*, (2007) Xin Civ 3 First Instance No. 30.

[158](2007) Xin Civ 3 First Instance No. 30.

contract rather than a sale contract and it, therefore, had no obligation to make the payment for the wet blue; contrarily, the claimant should pay the defendant for the processing work the defendant had done. Respecting the governing law for this dispute, the judges said:

> We consider that, since the parties didn't choose the applicable law for the dispute, according to the provision of Article 126 (1) in the Chinese Contract Law which says '[w] here parties to the foreign related contract failed to select the applicable law, the contract shall be governed by the law of the country having the closest connection with the contract', the applicable law for this dispute should be determined by applying the closest connection principle. The place of conclusion, the place of performance, and the place of the subject matter of the contract are all in the PRC. Therefore, we decide to apply the law of PRC which is most closely connected with the contract.[159]

172. In this case, to the judges, the place of conclusion, the place of performance and the place of the subject matter of the contract were in the same place so that this place was the most closely connected with the contract.

(6) The place of the main facts with legal meaningfulness as the determinative factor

173. In the case of *Huayi Beijing Xinglin Medical Treatment Technique Company Ltd. versus Roche Diagnostics (Hong Kong) Ltd.*,[160] the factor of 'the main facts with legal meaningfulness' had appeared to become the determinative one for applying the closest connection test. The claimant, a Beijing company, concluded an agreement with the defendant, a Hong Kong company. By that agreement, the claimant could buy medical products from the defendant and became the general agent for the sale of the defendant's products in Northern China. The agreement listed the detailed territorial scope for the market that included the provinces of Heilongjiang, Jilin, Liaoning, Shandong, Xinjiang, Hebei, Neimenggu and Gansu and the municipality of Tianjin. The agreement was signed and sealed by the claimant and the defendant in November 1997 and May 1999 respectively. Subsequently, the defendant delivered the products to Beijing according to the orders placed by the claimant. The claimant sold the products in Northern China, not only in the listed areas but also in the municipality of Beijing. A subsidiary company of the defendant was established in Shanghai in 2000 and the claimant had started to send the orders to the Shanghai subsidiary company instead of the defendant since June 2001. The claimant continued to purchase the products from the Shanghai subsidiary company and sold them in Northern China, including Beijing until one day in October 2003, the Shanghai subsidiary company refused to supply the products any more, the reason for which was that the defendant offered an exclusive dealership in Beijing to another Beijing company in October 2003. The claimant then launched the litigation to protect its rights of sale in Beijing and claim the economic losses sustained. There was no choice of law

---

[159]Ibid.

[160](2005) Hu High Court Civ Final No. 1038.

clause in the contract and the parties did not make a choice during the court proceedings.[161] The judges in the first instance said:

> Given that the disputes arose out of the process of promotion and sale activities of the ROCHE diagnostic instruments manufactured in Germany and other relevant products, and the activities were performed in Beijing (China) where the main facts with legal meaningfulness took place, the court has the power to apply the law of the country which has the closest connection with the contract and relevant legal facts to govern the case i.e. Chinese law.[162]

174. The determination of the governing law for this case was upheld by the judges in the second instance.[163] The factor of the so-called 'main facts with legal meaningfulness' was stressed in this case. According to the decision of the judges, Beijing was the place of the main facts with legal meaningfulness because the legally meaningful facts that took place in Beijing included the signing of the agreement by the claimant, the arrival of the delivered products and the sales activities.[164] The factor of the main facts with legal meaningfulness was also relied on as being determinative in the case of *Liang Guoneng versus Huang Ximei (Hong Kong)*.[165] However, it was not clear which fact was legally meaningful and why and how many such facts together could make a place being the one of the main facts with legal meaningfulness.

The Courts' Practice After the Implementation of the 2007 Interpretation

175. The 2007 Interpretation was given in accordance with Article 145 of GPCL and Article 126 of CCL for the purpose of making the abstract closest connection test more workable in practice.[166] However, after the 2007 Interpretation came into effect, while some courts have followed it, other courts have not but continued to apply Article 145 of GPCL or/and Article 126 of CCL only to find the applicable law by the most closely connected test.

(1) The practice in the courts that have followed the 2007 Interpretation

176. In the case of *Panographs Publishing PTY Ltd. versus Guangzhou Changcheng Ceramic Company Ltd.*,[167] the claimant, an Australian company concluded a processing contract with the defendant, a Chinese company according to which, the defendant should produce 70,000 cups for the claimant that could meet the local leading standard in California, the US. The claimant paid 36,480 USD to the defendant as the

---

[161] Ibid.

[162] Ibid.

[163] See *Huayi Beijing Xinglin Medical Treatment Technique Company Ltd. versus Roche Diagnostics (Hong Kong) Ltd.* (2005) Hu High Court Civ Final No. 1038.

[164] Ibid.

[165] (2005) Sui Intermediate Court Civ 3 First Instance No. 229.

[166] See supra para. 129.

[167] (2007) Sui Intermediate Court Civ 4 First Instance No. 106.

deposit for performing the contract. Later on, it was, however, found out that the cups produced by the defendant could not meet the required standard. The claimant, therefore, refused to accept the cups and in the meantime, it had to find another supplier for the cups and deliver the goods to its client by air transportation due to the time limitation. Thereafter, the claimant sued the defendant to claim the deposit back and the damages sustained.[168] As for the governing law, the judges said:

> Since this is a contractual dispute and the parties have not chosen the applicable law to deal with it, according to Article 126 (1) of the Chinese Contract Law, the law of the country which is most closely connected with the contract should be applied. The domicile of the processor which is the defendant in this case is in China. According to Article 5, paragraph 2 (2) of 'The Rules of the Supreme People's Court on Related Issues Concerning the Application of Law in Hearing Foreign-Related Contractual Dispute Cases in Civil and Commercial Matters' which says '[a]s for contracts on processing with supplied materials, assembling with supplied parts and other processing work, the law of domicile of the processor shall be the applicable law', it thus can be confirmed that China has the closest connection with this case. The Chinese law should be the applicable law for this dispute.[169]

177. This is a typical case in which judges directly applied a specific choice of law rule prescribed in Article 5 (2) of the 2007 Interpretation to find the applicable law after the 2007 Interpretation entered into force.

178. The case of *Guoya Textile Company Ltd. versus Zhuoyang Textile Company Ltd.* is another typical case of this kind, in which the claimant, a Jiangsu company and the defendant, a Hong Kong company concluded a contract on sale.[170] In determining the applicable law for the dispute arising out of the sale contract, the court said:

> The parties i.e. the seller and buyer did not make any explicit choice of the applicable law for their sale contract relationships. According to Article 5, paragraph 2 (1) of 'The Rules of the Supreme People's Court on Related Issues Concerning the Application of Law in Hearing Foreign-Related Contractual Dispute Cases in Civil and Commercial Matters', for disputes of contract of sale, if the parties have not made a choice of the applicable law by mutual consent, in accordance with the principle of closest connection, it can be sure that the law of the seller's domicile is the applicable law of the case. In this case, the domicile of the seller, Guoya Company is in the mainland of China, so we should apply the law of the mainland China in accordance with the principle of closest connection.[171]

179. Changzhou Huayuan Leidisi Company Ltd. versus Noy Ambiente S.P.A., Noy Vallesina Engineering S.R.L. and Green Holding S.P.A.[172] is a third case in which judges applied a specific traditional-style choice of law rule listed in Article 5 (2) of the 2007 Interpretation directly. In this case, the claimant was a Chinese company and the three defendants were Italian companies. The claimant and the first defendant, *Noy Ambiente S.P.A.* concluded a sale contract in the city of Changzhou, Jiangsu Province in 2000. According to the contract, the first defendant should deliver two sets of equipments that could meet the standards required by the

[168]Ibid.

[169]Ibid.

[170](2006) Chang Civ 3 First Instance No. 47.

[171]Ibid.

[172](2008) Chang Civ 3 First Instance No. 30.

claimant to Shanghai and Beijing respectively; the first defendant should also assume the obligations of maintenance and replacement of the equipments during the period of installation and probation including the expense arising out of the relevant activities. The first defendant failed to supply the equipments in time, which caused economic loss to the claimant. Moreover, the first defendant's products could not meet the standard demanded by the claimant. In addition, the claimant paid the expense of maintenance for the defendant. The claimant launched litigation to claim for the maintenance costs and the damages for the contract. Since the second defendant and the third defendant were companies that were separated from the first defendant after the contract came into effect, they were required to undertake joint liabilities according to Chinese law and called to participate in the proceedings.[173] As to the governing law for this case, the judges said:

> This case is a dispute arising from an international sale contract. Since the defendants *Noy Ambiente S.P.A.*, *Noy Vallesina Engineering S.R.L.* and *Green Holding S.P.A.* are registered in Italy, this case is a foreign-related civil and commercial dispute. According to Article 5 of 'The Rules of the Supreme People's Court on Related Issues Concerning the Application of Law in Hearing Foreign-Related Contractual Dispute Cases in Civil and Commercial Matters', as for the sale contract, when the parties did not make a choice of the governing law, the law of the domicile of the seller should normally be the applicable law according to the principle of closest connection; in a case where the contract is negotiated and concluded at the domicile of the buyer, or the contract clearly stipulates that the seller shall fulfill the obligation of delivery at the domicile of the buyer, the law of domicile of the buyer shall be the applicable law. In this case, the claimant, *Huayuan Leidisi* and the defendant *Noy Ambiente S.P.A.* did not make an explicit choice of the governing law for the contract. The place of conclusion of the contract was in Changzhou City, Jiangsu Province, China. Therefore, according to the principle of closest connection, the law of PRC should be the applicable law of this case.[174]

180. This case is, however, not as straightforward as the two cases cited earlier. On the one hand, in making the decision on the applicable law, the judges only mentioned the place of conclusion of the contract and did not investigate the issue of the place of negotiating the contract although according to the second half of Article 5 (2) (1), one possibility for the law of the domicile of the buyer to be applicable is only when the contract was both negotiated and concluded in the place of the domicile of the defendant[175]; on the other hand, this case was more complicated than a simple international sale contract because it concerned the installation, maintenance and possible replacement of the sold products (equipments). To the present author, the judges sorely and awkwardly fitted the case into the rule. Although the result for the applicable law was right because China evidently had the closest connection with the contract in this case, the short analysis without taking into account the factors such as the installation, maintenance and possible replacement of the sold products was clearly incomplete and unsatisfactory.

181. In all the three cases cited above, the judges had invoked the specific fixed choice of law rule listed in Article 5 of the 2007 Interpretation directly. While the

---

[173]Ibid.

[174]Ibid.

[175]See Article 5 (2) (1) of the 2007 Interpretation.

case of *Panographs Publishing PTY Ltd.* resorted to Article 5 (2) (2) and found the law of the domicile of the characteristic performer (the processor) was applicable,[176] the case of *Guoya Textile Company Ltd.* was about a typical international contract on sale for which the first half of Article 5 (2) (1) was applied.[177] Although the case of *Changzhou Huayuan Leidisi Company Ltd.* was also about an international sale contract, it was the second half of Article 5 (2) (1) that the case was fitted into.[178]

182. From the judgments of these three cases, one could see that the judges realized that where the parties did not make a choice of law for their contract, the most closely connected test should be applied; they, then, looked to Article 5 (2) of the 2007 Interpretation to find a specific choice of law rule into which they could fit their case no matter whether they could do so comfortably or not; after that, according to the connecting factor in the concerned specific choice of law rule, they found the most closely connected place and the corresponding applicable law but without further questioning whether or not that place was really most closely connected with the contract in dispute. To them, once a specific choice of law rule was applied, the closest connection principle had been followed; the specific choice of law rules in Article 5 (2) of the 2007 Interpretation were equivalent to the closest connection principle, which could be evidenced by the wording such as '... it thus can be confirmed ...'[179] and '... it can be sure ...'[180] This process seemed to have become the standard procedure for finding the applicable law in many courts that had applied the 2007 Interpretation.[181] So far, the author has not

[176]See supra paras. 176–177.

[177]See supra para. 178.

[178]See supra paras. 179–180.

[179]See supra para. 176.

[180]See supra para. 178.

[181]See *Wujin Jinling Lamps and Lanterns Manufactory versus Technolamp(Hong Kong) Limited* (2007) Chang Civ 3 First Instance No. 78; *Changzhou Dahua Imports and Exports Group Company Ltd. versus Supreme Dragon Electronics LLC (United Arab Emirates) and Ors*, (2006) Chang Civ 3 First Instance No. 11; *Shanghai Saifeng International Trade Company Ltd. versus Industrial and Commercial Bank of China (Branch of Changzhou)*, (2006) Chang Civ 3 First Instance No. 26; *Shao Xiaolu versus Yang Qihui and Rankam Group Limited (Hong Kong)* (2007) Chang Civ 3 First Instance No. 24; *Guangzhou Fangcun Rural Credit Union versus Lin Weiji (Hong Kong) and Wu Bizuan* (2007) Sui Intermediate Court Civ 4 First Instance No. 12; *Rui Hua Investment Holding Limited (Mauritius) versus Chongqing Huaxin Thermal Spring Entertainment Company Ltd.* (2007) Yu 5th Intermediate Court Civ First Instance No. 408; *Shanghai Yisheng Textile Trade Company Ltd. versus Nanhua Textile Group Company Ltd. (Hong Kong)* (2007) Tong Intermediate Court Civ 3 First Instance No. 0253; *Changzhou Shifang International Trade Company Ltd. versus New Step Garments Company Limited* (2008) Chang Civ 3 First Instance No. 48; *Rui Hua Investment Holding Limited (Mauritius) versus Chongqing Yujiu Construction Projects Company Ltd.* (2008) Yu 5th Intermediate Court Civ First Instance No. 17; *Yosun Hong Kong Corporation Limited versus Chongqing Hexing Jiangyuan Science and Technology Development Company Ltd.* (2008) Yu 1st Intermediate Court Civ First Instance No. 193; *Rui Hua Investment Holding Limited (Mauritius) versus Chongqing Mechanism Instruments Imports and Exports Company Ltd. and Chongqing Longshui Lake Tour and Holiday Company Ltd.* (2008) Yu 5th Intermediate Court Civ First Instance No. 133; *Li Gang (Australia) versus Jiujiang Xinhua Clothing Factory*, (2008) Gan Civ 4 Final No. 11.

found any case where Article 5 (3) was applied to rebut a presumptive fixed choice of law rule in Article 5 (2).

(2) The practice in the courts that have not followed the 2007 Interpretation

183. As a matter of fact, after the 2007 Interpretation entered into force, it had not been followed in practice by quite a few of courts. In these courts, the judges still only invoked Article 145 (2) of the GPCL or/and Article 126 (1) of the CCL to apply the closest connection test to find the governing law in the absence of the parties' choice. That is to say, the judges had still employed the various approaches adopted before the 2007 Interpretation without referring to the specific choice of law rules listed in Article 5 (2) of the 2007 Interpretation.[182]

---

[182]See supra paras. 158–174. E.g., see *IMT ASIA PTE LTD. (Singapore) versus Nanjing Duma Science and Technology Trade Company Ltd.*, (2007) Ning Civ 5 First Instance No. 54; *Taicang Shunfeng Knitting Company versus Sihong Group Corporation Ltd. (Hong Kong) and Ors* (2007) Su Intermediate Court Civ 3 First Instance No. 0030; *Taidexing Accurate Electronic (Kunshan) Company Ltd. versus Hong Kong Guomei Investment Company Ltd.*, (2007) Su Intermediate Court Civ 3 First Instance No. 0052; *Qunyi Industry GmbH (Taiwan) versus Yaxin Industry GmbH and Ors*, (2007) Su Intermediate Court Civ 3 First Instance No. 0094; *Suzhou Liansheng Chemistry Company Ltd. versus Changzhou Changlin Textile Printing and Dyeing Company Ltd. and Zhou Baicheng (Taiwan)* (2007) Su Intermediate Court Civ 3 First Instance No. 0097; *Bank of China Branch of Suzhou Chengzhong versus Ji Yajun and Xie Zifang*, (2007) Su Intermediate Court Civ 3 First Instance No. 0167; *DAC China SOS (Barbados) SRL versus Zhenjiang Feichi Automobile Group Corporation Ltd.*, (2007) Zhen Civ 3 First Instance No. 54; *DAC China SOS (Barbados) SRL versus Zhenjiang Jingkou Restaurant* (2007) Zhen Civ 3 First Instance No. 55; *DAC China SOS (Barbados) SRL versus Zhenjiang Minxin General Merchandize Trade Company Ltd.*, (2007) Zhen Civ 3 First Instance No. 56; *Enterprise P. Boucher Ltee (Canada) versus Henan Yuanfeng Leather Goods Company Ltd.* (2007) Xin Civ 3 First Instance No. 30; *Axtra HK Limited versus Shanghai Youcai Electronic Science and Technology Company Ltd.*, (2007) Hu High Court Civ 4 (Economic) Final No. 10; *DAC China SOS (Barbados) SRL versus Meita Special Fireproof Board (Jiangsu) Company Ltd.* (2008) Zhen Civ 3 First Instance No. 48; *DAC China SOS (Barbados) SRL versus Zhenjiang Material Industry and Trade Company* (2008) Zhen Civ 3 First Instance No. 88; *Hangzhou Qichang Textile Company Ltd. versus YOU KI WOON* (2008) Su Intermediate Court Civ 3 First Instance No. 0002; *Huafang Textile GmbH versus Cui Haiji* (2008) Su Intermediate Court Civ 3 First Instance No. 0008; *Chuangshiji Fastener Company Ltd. versus KIM JONG CHIL* (2008) Su Intermediate Court Civ 3 First Instance No. 0010; *Deng Jiankang versus Guo Chongguang (Taiwan)* (2008) Su Intermediate Court Civ 3 First Instance No. 0022; *Ningbo Nanrong Mechanical Company Ltd. versus Yipin Company*, (2008) Su Intermediate Court Civ 3 First Instance No. 0067; *Wuxi Longxin Textile Company Ltd. versus Donghua Textile Company Ltd. (Hong Kong)* (2008) Xi Civ 3 First Instance No. 50; *Trisome-Cosmos International Limited (British Virgin Islands) versus Jiangyin Longfei Clothing Company Ltd. and Jiangyin Xinshengye Textile and Clothing Company Ltd.* (2008) Xi Civ 3 First Instance No. 73; *Nanjing Langguang Electronic GmbH versus Lampus Photoelectron Co., Ltd.* (2008) Ning Civ 5 First Instance No. 23; *Jiangsu International Entrust Company Ltd. versus Delu Investment Development Company Ltd.* (2008) Ning Civ 5 First Instance No. 36; *SPG CO., LTD. (South Korea) versus Feidashi Sunning Air-Conditioner (Nanjing) Company Ltd.*, (2008) Ning Civ 5 First Instance No. 55; *Jinju Development Clutch Gold Company Ltd. (Taiwan) versus Hongjie Circuit (Changshu) Company Ltd.* (2009) Su Intermediate Civ 3 First Instance No. 0014; *Ellsworth Adhesives Asia Limited versus Jiatong Technology (Suzhou) Company Ltd.* (2009) Su Intermediate Civ 3 First Instance No. 0021.

Lex Fori Favoritism Under the Cover of the Closest Connection Test in Chinese Courts' Practice

184. Both before and after the implementation of the 2007 Interpretation, another noticeable phenomenon in the practice was some Chinese judges' strong inclination to apply *lex fori* i.e. Chinese law as the governing law.

185. The most notorious might be the pattern of 'one-step decision' in finding the applicable law in which an Article of the law was invoked, then, the decision was made without any reasons or analysis being given. This pattern of judgments is typically like the following:

> According to Article 145 of the GPCL/Article 126 of the CCL/Article 41 of the LAL/Article 5 of the 2007 Interpretation, the mainland China is most closely connected with the contract, therefore, the law of mainland China should be applicable.[183]

186. In other courts, there might be some given reasons why Chinese law should be the applicable law but very often the explanation upon the reasons took a very little part of the judgment. The process of measuring the connections usually could not be clearly seen. Why some factors should be counted but others should not was unknown. By reading the judgments, one would have the impression that the reason why some factors were mentioned but others not was just because those mentioned factors could enhance the connections between China and the contract in the case so that the application of Chinese law could be made more persuasive or say, have more excuses.[184]

Analysis

187. In the absence of the parties' choice, while GPCL and CCL have prescribed the closest connection test for determining the applicable law, the 2007 Interpretation tries to concretize and give practical contents to this abstract principle. The investigation of the Chinese courts' practice demonstrates that the application of the 'most closely connected' principle by Chinese courts both before and

---

[183]E.g., see *Guangzhou Fangcun Rural Credit Union versus Lin Weiji (Hong Kong) and Wu Bizuan*, (2007) Sui Intermediate Court Civ 4 First Instance No. 12; *Rui Hua Investment Holding Limited (Mauritius) versus Chongqing Huaxin Thermal Spring Entertainment Company Ltd.*, (2007) Yu 5 Intermediate Court Civ First Instance No. 408; *Rui Hua Investment Holding Limited (Mauritius) versus Chongqing Mechanism Instruments Imports and Exports Company Ltd. and Chongqing Longshui Lake Tour and Holiday Company Ltd.*, (2008) Yu 5th Intermediate Court Civ First Instance No. 133; and *Huafang Textile GmbH versus Cui Haiji*, (2008) Su Intermediate Court Civ 3 First Instance No. 0008.

[184]E.g. see *Anzhi Electronic Materials Hong Kong Company Ltd. versus Xuzhou Jingda LCD Screen Company Ltd.* (2007) Xu Civ 3 First Instance No. 2; *Changzhou Huayuan Leidisi Company Ltd. versus Noy Ambiente S.P.A., Noy Vallesina Engineering S.R.L. and Green Holding S.P.A.* (2008) Chang Civ 3 First Instance No. 30.

after the 2007 Interpretation was quite 'divergent and unsuccessful' as agreed by some other commentators.[185] Whereas some Chinese courts did like the fixed traditional-style choice of law rules so that they had still referred to the fixed rules when they were even not legally available and have closely followed the 2007 Interpretation,[186] other Chinese courts have continuously applied the flexible closest connection principle by taking into account various factors in different cases even after the implementation of the 2007 Interpretation.[187]

188. To those courts that like specific choice of law rules, the implementation of the 2007 Interpretation, which had refreshed those rules in the 1987 Interpretation on FECL and added some more other rules, meant a real and urgent help for their practice. In deciding cases, although they realized that the general closest connection principle should be the prevailing test, they treated the presumptive rules almost the same as the principle. They always tried to find a specific choice of law rule in the 2007 Interpretation they can fit their case in whether or not they could really find a suitable one in the list. Once they found a specific choice of law rule, they then apply it without further questioning the real connections between the place designated by that rule and the contract. As said, the author did not find any case where the escape clause had been invoked. To these courts, it seems that there is no need of Article 5 (3) in the 2007 Interpretation and the presumption rules can be said to be extremely strong, or say, almost equal to the closest connection test. This attitude goes along with that of some legislators who wanted to delete the test and make the law of the place of characteristic performer or characteristic performance directly applicable in the legislation of LAL. There might be no problem with this stance for simple cases which could easily fit into the rules. However, the presumptive choice of law rules are hung on the concept of characteristic obligation. If in a case, there is no characteristic obligation or the case is concerned with a complicated contract for which it is difficult to identify which obligation is the characteristic one, sorely squeezing the contract into a rule might not be a good idea.[188] It might also be possible that a case could not be squeezed into any of the 17 kinds of contracts even if one tries hard. In this situation, the abstract test could work better, which might explain why in making the LAL, some argued that the closest connection test was necessary and eventually added on.

189. At the other end of the spectrum, however, there were some courts that did not look to or even slightly refer to the specific presumption choice of law rules in making their decisions both before and after the implementation of the 2007

[185]See Guo and Xu (2008, pp. 145–147, 149) and Huang et al. (2009, p. 439).

[186]See supra paras. 157–159, 176–182.

[187]See supra para. 183.

[188]See Cheshire et al. (2008, pp. 712–714) and Hill (2004, pp. 334–336). The concept of characteristic obligation (performance) was rejected by the Inter-American Convention in applying the test, see Juenger (1997, pp. 205–206).

Interpretation.[189] While before that, their practice was legal because the 1987 Interpretation on FECL was formally repealed, it is not so after that because the SPC's Interpretation should be legally binding to all lower courts.[190] In these courts, after the implementation of the 2007 interpretation, they have continued to adopt the various approaches that had been exercised before.[191] In finding the applicable law, the different factors could come to play to be determinative to various extents.[192] The reason for them to do so might be that they did not know the promulgation of the 2007 Interpretation or did not study or were unwilling to study how to apply it or just wanted to keep their old habit. If this was the reason, the mistake could be corrected or at least be reduced with the time passing. However, given the current communication technology and the court training system in China, this reason might be untrue or at least partly wrong. The practice in these courts might be able to indicate that they would like to apply the more flexible test and want to read the presumption rules as rather weak. Although they did not follow the 2007 Interpretation, in applying the closest connection test established by Article 145 of GPCL, Article 126 of CCL and Article 41 of LAL, one or both of which they usually invoked in the judgments, very often, they referred to the place of performance/characteristic performance of the contract.[193] As a result, it might be that in many cases the applicable law found by these courts and those following the 2007 Interpretation could be the same especially when the place of the characteristic performer was just the place of characteristic performance. Therefore, the actual situation with these courts might not be as bad and uncertain as first imagined. In addition, by applying the flexible test, they could have leeway and reach a better result in a complicated case.[194]

190. Whether the courts mainly applied the fixed choice of law rules or the flexible closest connection test only, one common problem revealed was that Chinese judges have strong *lex fori* favoritism as their counterparts do in many other jurisdictions.[195] It has even been difficult for the author to find a case where a foreign law was applied. Many judges, by different means, tried to apply Chinese law as possible as they could. According to another two empirical researches, Chinese law was applied as the governing law in as many as 94 % foreign-related cases tried in Chinese courts in 2007, 97 % in 2008. [196] As far as contract was concerned, one could only see UCP or CISG or a foreign law was occasionally applied as the governing law by a Chinese court if not Chinese law.[197] However, it

[189]See supra para. 187.

[190]See supra paras. 7–10.

[191]See supra para. 187.

[192]See supra paras. 157–174.

[193]See supra paras. 160–165.

[194]See supra para. 182.

[195]See Symeonides (2000, pp. 6–8).

[196]See Huang et al. (2009, pp. 425–439, 2008, pp. 441–452).

[197]Ibid.

is also true that Chinese judges could treat cases having foreign element(s) as foreign-related rather than domestic cases and some have observed that Chinese judges are becoming more and more liberal in applying foreign law.[198]

191. According to the law, the determination of the applicable law in the absence of the parties' choice should normally be a three-step process.[199] Courts' practice, however, showed an 'all or nothing' approach as regards the specific choice of law rules in the 2007 Interpretation. To some Chinese courts, the rules are the same as the closest connection principle and mean all while in other courts, the rules have been totally ignored and mean nothing. This situation can be improved by the SPC who can issue a 'Notice' or a similar document to resolve the problems.[200] Given that China is a country of civil law tradition, judges are not experienced in dealing with international cases and legal certainty has long been preferred, a mere open-ended abstract principle is not desirable. It is suggested that in the Notice or a similar document to be given by the SPC, the following should be included and emphasized: first, the 2007 Interpretation must be followed; secondly, those specific choice of law rules are neutral and bilateral and should not be manipulated just for the purpose of making Chinese law applicable; thirdly, the rules must be read as very strong but not absolute and Article 5 (3) could be applicable exceptionally; fourthly, if a contract cannot properly be fitted into any specific choice of law rule, the general closest connection principle should be applied.

10.1.3 Special Contracts

192. As mentioned already, the policy of protecting the weaker parties including consumers and employees has been adopted by LAL.[201] Choice of law rules for consumer and employee contracts, independent from those for other contracts, are now given in Articles 42 and 43 of LAL respectively.

10.1.3.1 Rules for Consumer Contracts

193. As far as consumer contracts are concerned, the applicable law should normally be the consumer's law i.e. the law of the place where the consumer has his

[198]See Guo and Xu (2008, pp. 137–138).

[199]See supra paras. 149–155.

[200]As said above, it is normal in China that the SPC can issue a Notice to call the attention of the lower courts to follow a legal instrument or provide more detailed guidance for their practice, generally see supra paras. 7–11.

[201]See supra paras. 75–76.

habitual residence.[202] However, this protection is not absolute in that if the supplier did not engage in any business activity related to the case in the place of the consumer's habitual residence, the law of the place where the product or service is supplied should be the governing law.[203] This is a kind of balance leaning towards the supplier lest the consumers be excessively protected by unduly sacrificing the supplier's interests. In addition, the consumer can also have the freedom to opt into the law where the service or product is supplied if he wishes.[204] If he does do so, however, Article 42 does not mention whether the mandatory rules protecting the consumer's interests in the consumer's law i.e. the law of his habitual residence must still be applied or not.[205]

10.1.3.2 Rules for Employment Contracts

194. As to employment contracts, the applicable law should normally be the law of the place where the employee carries out his work.[206] Although Article 43 does not explicitly say that place should be where the employee *habitually,* rather than *temporarily*, carries out his work, this Article, to the present author, could only be rightly understood in this way according to the context of the Article.[207] The law of the employer's main business place can be applicable only if it is difficult to identify the employee's working place. In the case of an employee being dispatched, the law of the place from where the employee is dispatched may be applicable.[208] No party autonomy, however, is allowed for employment contracts, in which area party autonomy could have been more utilized, compared with that in consumer contracts, especially when the employees are professionals such as chief executive officers (CEOs) working for large enterprises.[209]

195. It is, therefore, now the case that consumer contracts and employee contracts will be subject to the relevant Articles in LAL rather than the 2007 Interpretation. However, there is no special arrangement for insurance contracts in LAL yet and insurance contracts will still be governed by the latter as one of the 17 kinds of contracts listed.[210]

---

[202]See Article 42 of LAL. Cf. Article 6 (1) of Rome I Regulation which says similarly.

[203]See Article 42 of LAL. Cf. Article 6 (1) (3) of Rome I Regulation.

[204]See Article 42 of LAL. Cf. Article 6 (2) of Rome I regulation.

[205]Cf. Article 6 (2) of Rome I Regulation.

[206]See Article 43 of LAL. Cf. Article 8 of Rome I Regulation.

[207]Ibid.

[208]Ibid.

[209]Cf. Article 8 (1) of Rome I Regulation.

[210]See Point 8, Paragraph 2 of Article 5 of the 2007 Interpretation. Cf. Article 7 of Rome I Regulation.

10.2 Tort

196. In LAL, there are also general choice of law rules for general torts and special choice of law rules for some special torts, which will be examined one by one in the following text.

10.2.1 Rules for General Torts

197. In LAL, the general choice of law rules for general torts can be found in Article 44, which says:

> Liabilities arising out of tort shall be governed by the law of the place of tort; however, if the parties have their habitual residences in the same place, the law of their common habitual residence shall apply; where the tort has occurred, if the parties have chosen the governing law for their tort dispute, the law chosen shall apply.[211]

198. Compared with Article 146 of GPCL that contains the old Chinese tort conflict rules and had been repealed when LAL came into force,[212] this new Article has abandoned the requirement of 'double actionability'.[213] In addition, it also deleted the 'common nationality' rule when introducing the 'common habitual residence' rule to replace the 'common domicile' rule.[214] These changes are sound because the abandonment of 'double actionability' requirement for tort conflicts is the modern trend[215]; while the connection by nationality could be tenuous, the concept of domicile might be more difficult to be determined than habitual residence.[216]

199. These general rules are supposedly applicable to all torts except those special torts for which some specific choice of law rules have been prescribed.[217] One can see that actually there are three independent but inter-connected general choice of law rules in Article 44. The hierarchy of the applicability of the three rules can simply be summarized as follows: first, if the question of choice of law regarding a tort comes to surface after that tort has occurred, the parties can make a choice of the applicable law for the concerned tort; secondly, without the choice of the

[211]See Article 44 of LAL.

[212]See Article 51 of LAL.

[213]Cf. paragraph 3 of Article 146 of GPCL, supra para. 56.

[214]See Article 44 of LAL; paragraph 2 of Article 146 of GPCL.

[215]In Regulation (EC) No. 864/2007 of the European Parliament and of the Council of 11 July 2007 on the law applicable to non-contractual obligations (hereinafter, 'Rome II Regulation'), one cannot find this requirement, either.

[216]See Cheshire et al. (2008, p. 154 et seq).

[217]See infra paras. 204–212.

parties, whether the dispute arises before or after the occurrence of the tort, if only the parties have their habitual residence in the same place, the law of that place shall apply; thirdly, failing the parties' choice and the common habitual residence exception, the basic choice of law rule for tort applies i.e. the law of the tortious place is the applicable one.[218] As mentioned, compared with the old rules in GPCL improvements have been made but there are problems with these new rules.[219]

200. With regard to the doctrine of party autonomy, in recent years for the purpose of legal certainty this doctrine in the field of private international law has gradually been extended from contract to other areas including tort and it has been accepted for choice of law respecting tort disputes in quite a few jurisdictions.[220] While it is good to see that LAL has been geared up to the modern trend, permitting the parties to choose the governing law for their post-tort disputes,[221] one might wonder to what extent the freedom of the parties should be allowed in this area. By nature, contract law is supplementary to the parties' will/contract. It is, thus, seemingly natural for the parties to be allowed to choose any law they like to govern/supplement their contract/will so that the expectations of the parties can be met by the application of the chosen law.[222] In contrast, tort law is more 'local and mandatory'; the parties' freedom, thus, should accordingly be restricted more at conflicts level.[223] Whereas it is fine for the parties to choose any law, without much constraint, to govern their contract,[224] it might be wiser to confine the parties' choice to the laws of those jurisdictions who do have legitimate interests to claim for the concerned tort e.g. the law of one of the parties, the law of the tortious place and the law of the forum.[225] Even if the parties are allowed to have a 'wild' choice, the mandatory rules for the concerned tort in those interested jurisdictions might probably have to be taken into account by some way and to some extent.[226] In LAL, however, one can find neither any direct limitations on the parties' choice nor any provision commanding Chinese courts to show respect to mandatory rules of a foreign jurisdiction, no matter how strong the connection between the disputed tort and that foreign jurisdiction might be, although there is a provision providing for the application of local Chinese mandatory rules.[227]

---

[218]See Article 44 of LAL.

[219]See supra para. 56.

[220]See Cheshire et al. (2008, p. 837 et seq).

[221]Cf. in Rome II Regulation, however, freely-negotiated choice of law made by the parties pre-tort is also allowed, see Article 14 of Rome II Regulation.

[222]See supra para. 134.

[223]See Han (2005, p. 205 et seq).

[224]E.g. see Article 3 of Rome I Regulation.

[225]See Cheshire et al. (2008, p. 766).

[226]Cf. Under Rome II Regulation, although the parties' choice is not confined to the alternatives as suggested, there are quite a few limitations imposed on it, see Cheshire et al., ibid, p. 839 et seq.

[227]See Article 4 of LAL; supra para. 77.

201. According to Article 44 of LAL, if only the parties have common habitual residence, the law of the place where the parties both have their habitual residence shall supersede the law of the tortious place.[228] This exception to the basic rule may bring about reasonable results in many loss-allocation conflicts cases but it cannot necessarily be justified in some others especially in those conduct-regulating conflicts ones.[229] A typical explanatory example is that both parties from the same place have left their common habitual residence by chance and one has committed tort to the other in a foreign place. In this scenario, the law of their common habitual residence is suitable to govern their dispute if the dispute is mainly about damages arising out of the tort i.e. a question of loss-allocation between them because they live under the same economic environment provided by the market of the same place and the amount of damages awarded can be reasonably determined only according to their common local standard (law). Nevertheless, if the dispute is mainly about whether a tort has been committed i.e. a question of conduct-regulating, the law of the place where the act in question has been carried out is suitable, rather than that of their common habitual residence.[230] Moreover, for this exception rule to apply, the concept of habitual residence has to be defined. As said, although In LAL, there is no definition for this key concept, it has now been defined in Interpretation I on LAL.[231] In addition, when the law of the parties' common habitual residence is applied, one probably would also have to, to some extent, take into consideration the mandatory rules in the law of the place of tort being committed or the law of the place of damage being sustained. These rules may be required to be applied by the strong national interests of those concerned states either in regulating conducts or in allocating loss.[232] LAL, however, does not give Chinese judges any discretion to do so.

202. As to the basic rule, an immediate question with the application of this rule is: shall the tortious place refer to the place where the tortious act is committed or the place where the damage arising out of tortious act is sustained? While Article 44 of LAL does not give answer to this question itself, Paragraph 187 of the 1988 Interpretation on GPCL says both these places should be regarded as tortious places and where they are different from each other, the court hearing the case could choose between them at its discretion, normally the one whose law is more unfavorable to the tortfeasor.[233] It is the author's belief that this approach will continue to be adopted in practice.[234] The next question then is: how to

[228]See supra para. 197.

[229]For the concepts of loss-allocation conflicts and conduct-regulating conflicts, see Symeonides (2008a, pp. 1741, 1760 et seq); Symeonides (2008b, pp. 173, 188 et seq).

[230]See Cheshire et al. (2008, p. 804 et seq).

[231]See supra para. 98.

[232]See Symeonides (2008a, pp. 1741, 1747, 1752 et seq).

[233]See paragraph 187 of the 1988 Interpretation on GPCL, supra para. 59.

[234]Cf. the place of damage has been chosen as the criterion for the basic rule in Article 4 (1) of Rome II Regulation.

identify the tortious place in a real case? The place of where the tortious act is committed or where the damage arising out of the tortious act is sustained may be obvious in easy cases such as traffic accident cases and personal physical injury cases. In those difficult cases, it is, however, very hard to know exactly where the damage is sustained or where the tortious act is committed e.g. in a case where the perishable foods have gradually rotted when they were transported in a refrigerated truck across a few jurisdictions because of the breakdown of the refrigeration at some unknown point.[235] One further question might be asked: what if the tortious act is committed or the damage is sustained in more than one place? It seems that the laws of the different places where the tortious act is partly committed or where the damage is partly sustained will have to be applied on a distributive basis.[236] To proceed along this way, however, is obviously undesirable because there would possibly be inconsistent judgments arising out of the application of the different substantive laws to the different parts of the same case. While the parties might be able to choose the applicable law to make the resolution of their dispute simpler on this occasion,[237] a general escape clause based on the closest connection test would be helpful, in particular when the doctrine of party autonomy is unworkable.[238]

203. In LAL, although the closest connection test has been established as a fundamental principle,[239] there is, unfortunately, no general escape clause based on the test that can work as a safety-valve to avoid the possible arbitrary results that can occur due to the rigid application of the above tort conflicts rules.[240] If there were, the application of the basic rule and the exception rule, to the present author, would be better off, especially in those complicated tort cases.

10.2.2 Rules for Special Torts

204. If it is a case concerned with a special tort for which some specific choice of law rules have been prescribed, those specific choice of law rules shall prevail over the general rules. In LAL, specific choice of law rules have now been given to three kinds of special torts cases, namely product liability cases, cases of infringement of personality rights and cases of infringement of IP rights.

[235]See Cheshire et al. (2008, p. 797).

[236]Ibid.

[237]See supra para. 199.

[238]See Cheshire et al. (2008, p. 797).

[239]See Article 2 of LAL; supra paras. 69–70.

[240]Cf. Article 4(3) of the Rome II Regulation.

10.2.2.1 Rules for Product Liability Cases

205. Recent years have seen fast growing number of product liability cases in Chinese courts.[241] In international arena, product liability cases have long been viewed as special tort disputes that need be dealt with by specific tort conflicts rules.[242] To meet the practical demand and give Chinese judges a consistent approach resolving problems arising out of product liability cases, specific choice of law rules are now prescribed in Article 45 of LAL, which says:

> Product liability shall be governed by the law of the place where the person sustaining the damage has his habitual residence; however, if the person sustaining the damage chooses the law of the tortfeasor's principal business place or the place of the damage being sustained or the tortfeasor did not engage in any business activity related to the case in the place where the person sustaining the damage has his habitual residence, the law of the tortfeasor's principal business place or the place of the damage being sustained shall apply.[243]

206. There is, thus, no common habitual residence rule for product liability cases, which is regretful to the current author.[244] It is the law of the place where the victim has his habitual residence that normally shall apply, regardless of where the damage is sustained or the product causing the damage is acquired.[245] This rule, at conflicts level, obviously favours the weaker party i.e. the victim, whose law is normally the applicable law for the case. This approach seems reasonable because the victim supposedly needs to continue his life in the place where he has his habitual residence with the awarded damages, the amount of which could be reasonably determined only according to his local standard (law). Further protection can be discerned from the immediately following part of Article 45 i.e. the victim can unilaterally choose the law of the tortfeasor's principal business place or the place of damage being sustained as the applicable law if he finds one of those laws could be more favourable to him in a particular case.[246]

207. Although it seems that the protection of the victim does not stop where the tortfeasor could only claim he could not have reasonably foreseen his product would enter into the market of the victim's place of habitual residence,[247] the protection for the victim does stop where the tortfeasor could prove he actually did

[241]See Zhu (2007, pp. 283, 304 et seq).

[242]See the Hague Convention of 2 October 1973 on the Law Applicable to Product Liability (hereinafter, 'Hague Product Liability Convention').

[243]See Article 45 of LAL. Cf. Article 5 of Rome II Regulation.

[244]Cf. Article 5 (1) of Rome II Regulation.

[245]Ibid.

[246]Ibid.

[247]Cf. Article 5 (1) of Rome II Regulation; Article 7 of the Hague Product Liability Convention.

not engage in any business activity related to the case in that place.[248] In the latter situation, the applicable law will be the law of the tortfeasor's principal business place or the place of the damage being sustained.[249] This is designed, on the other side, to protect the interests of the producer so that he would not surprisingly be subject to the law of a place whose territory he never set foot in.[250] The immediate one difficulty with the application of this rule is how one can judge if the tortfeasor has engaged in any business activity related to the case in the place of the victim's habitual residence or not. Selling the product in the place of the victim's habitual residence that later actually caused the damage is surely a clear business activity related to the case engaged in that place. How about only advertising for the whole category of products or even a similar product?[251] Another difficulty is: which law shall exactly be applied in a particular case, the law of the tortfeasor's principal business place or the law of the place of damage being sustained? A more sensible and better choice between the laws could be made if there were a general clause which could direct the judges to apply the closest connection test.[252]

208. In addition, product liability is often related to the rules of safety. When the applicable law in the case is a law other than that of the place where the tortious act is committed, probably due account would have to be taken of the local safety standard in that place to strike a proper balance between the interests of the parties.[253] One, however, cannot see any provision accepting this idea in LAL.

10.2.2.2 Rule for Infringement of Personality Rights

209. Cross-border infringement of personality rights has become much more frequent with the rapid development of modern technologies, especially the internet. This reality calls for harmonizing solutions to such kind of cases urgently across the globe.[254] Substantive laws in this aspect, however, are quite different from country to country.[255] Due to the divergences of substantive laws regarding personality rights, it is possible that an act is perfectly legal and protected according to the law in one country—for example, under the rules guaranteeing freedom of speech and the press which are even a constitutional concern in many countries—but

[248]See Article 45 of LAL.

[249]Ibid. Cf. Article 5 (1) of Rome II Regulation.

[250]Cf. Article 5 (1) of Rome II Regulation.

[251]See Cheshire et al. (2008, p. 807).

[252]Cf. Article 5 (2) of Rome II Regulation.

[253]See Article 17 of Rome II Regulation; Cheshire et al. (2008, p. 855).

[254]See Warshaw (2006, p. 269 et seq).

[255]See Cheshire et al. (2008, p. 784 et seq).

could be a violation of personality rights i.e. a form of defamation in another.[256] The sharp divergences of the laws and the importance of the concerned rights make harmonization in this area rather difficult.[257]

210. To provide a solution for Chinese judges encountering with this sort of cases, a new specific choice of law rule for infringement of personality rights is now available in Article 46 of LAL, which states:

> The law of the victim's habitual residence shall be applicable to violation of his personality rights by internet or any other means including the rights of name, image, reputation and privacy.[258]

211. This rule is compatible with the rule in Article 15 of LAL which says that the contents of personality rights shall also be determined according to the law of the rights holder's habitual residence.[259] One can see that both rules, at conflicts level, favour the victim.[260] Difficulties, however, can be predicted for the application of these rules in practice. Suppose a victim has his habitual residence in a country whose substantive law on protection of personality rights e.g. reputation is much laxer than that in China and he launches litigation in a Chinese court, the Chinese court would probably have to refuse the application of the law of his habitual residence designated by these rules if the Chinese court thinks its local standard on protection of reputation is so important that to do otherwise would offend local public policy as recognized in Article 5 of LAL.[261] On the other hand, suppose a victim has his habitual residence in a country whose substantive law on protection of personality rights—once again, take reputation as an example—is much stricter than that in China but he launches litigation in a Chinese court for whatever reasons, the Chinese court would probably also have to refuse the application of the law of his habitual residence designated by the above rules by the doctrine of public policy if the Chinese court thinks its local standard on freedom of speech is too dear to be reconciled.[262]

10.2.2.3 Rules for Infringement of IP Rights

212. As can be seen, this has already been done in the above text where choice of law rules for IP rights are examined.

---

[256]Generally see Garnett and Richardson (2009, p. 471 et seq); Cheshire et al., ibid.

[257]This can be evidenced by the legislative history of the Rome II Regulation, see Cheshire et al., ibid, p. 770 et seq.

[258]See Article 46 of LAL.

[259]See Article 15 of LAL.

[260]Cf. the choice of law rules for defamation cases in English law, see Cheshire et al. (2008, p. 869 et seq).

[261]See Article 5 of LAL, supra para. 77.

[262]Ibid.

213. There are no arrangements yet in LAL for specific choice of law rules respecting other special torts such as unfair competition, environmental damage, industrial action and traffic accidents.[263]

214. A systematic examination of conflict rules for cross-border torts in LAL demonstrates that the Chinese legislation has largely followed the European model i.e. a few general rules are prescribed for general torts plus a series of specific choice of law rules for each special tort although the number of special torts to which specific choice of law rules have been given in the Chinese legislation is not as many as that in its European counterpart.[264] In China, besides those general tort conflict rules, specific choice of law rules are now available for product liability cases, cases on infringement of personality rights and IP rights. As anticipated, in constructing those rules, the modern trend in the world has generally been followed, which can be evidenced by the acceptance of party autonomy.[265] Regretfully, the popular doctrine of the closest connection, however, has not yet been introduced in LAL to relax the rigidity of those tort conflict rules although it has been established as a fundamental principle for the whole law. In addition, there is generally a lack in LAL of reasonable care that needs to be taken of the laws of those jurisdictions interested in the concerned torts although they are not the governing law.

10.3 Unjust Enrichment and Negotiorum Gestio

215. It is hard to imagine when there is no systematic substantive rules for unjust enrichment and *negotiorum gestio* in a country, there could be systematic conflict rules for them in that country. As a matter of fact, before LAL, there were no conflict rules at all for these non-contractual obligations in Chinese law.[266] LAL, as the first-ever comprehensive Chinese conflicts code, has now prescribed a set of conflict rules for them.

216. Nevertheless, unlike what has been done in the European Union where these two non-contractual obligations shall primarily be subject to the governing law for the foundational legal relationship, which they are closely connected with or have arisen out of,[267] LAL resorts to the principle of party autonomy in the first instance.[268] If the primary rule does not work, although both LAL and Rome II

[263]Cf. Articles 6, 7 and 9 of the Rome II Regulation.

[264]*Generally* see Rome II Regulation.

[265]See He (2009, pp. 210, 234).

[266]See Huo (2011, pp. 1065, 1091).

[267]See Articles 10 (1) and 11 (1) of Rome II Regulation.

[268]See Article 47 of LAL, which says: 'Unjust enrichment and *negotiorum gestio* shall be governed by the law chosen by the parties; failing which, by the law of the common habitual residence of the parties; failing which, by the law of the place where unjust enrichment or *negotiorum gestio* occurred'.

Regulation defer to the law of the place of common habitual residence of the parties, failing which further to the law of the place of the unjust enrichment or *negotiorum gestio* has occurred, there is, in LAL, no escape clause based on the closest connection doctrine that does have a role in Rome II Regulation for these two non-contractual obligations.[269]

---

[269]Cf. Articles 10 (2) (3) (4) & 11 (2) (3) (4) of Rome II Regulation.

Part III
International Civil Procedure (ICP)

217. In this part, as done before, the legal sources of ICP in China will be systematically reviewed first. Thereafter, rules on international jurisdiction, service of documents, taking of evidence, and recognition and enforcement of foreign judgments will be examined chapter by chapter. At the end, rules of international commercial arbitration in China will also be briefly explored. As said, although court cases are not a formal legal source in China, they can be persuasive in practice and indicate the future trend of development, for which the Chinese doctrine of *forum non conveniens* is a good illustration. While this doctrine was not statutorily recognized in China, courts' practice accepted it, which led the SPC to have eventually incorporated it into its latest interpretation on CPL. Therefore, this doctrine will be examined by discussing court cases in Chap. 12 where fine-tuning of international jurisdiction in China is examined. Some court cases will also be studied to demonstrate the Chinese practice regarding recognition and enforcement of foreign judgments in Chap. 15 and foreign arbitral awards in Chap. 16.

Chapter 11
Legal Sources of ICP in China

11.1 Domestic Legislations

218. As far as international civil proceedings are concerned, like in many other jurisdictions, the principle of *lex fori* is firmly laid down in China i.e. all civil proceedings that take place within the territory of China shall be conducted according to Chinese law.[1] The main and primary source where one can find Chinese international civil procedure rules is Chinese Civil Procedure Law (CPL). This law, which establishes the general framework and prescribes detailed rules for international civil proceedings in China, has gone through two amendments since it was first tentatively enacted in 1982 and thereafter formally adopted in 1991 by the National People's Congress.[2]

219. Amendments and changes as have been made, throughout the whole course of the legislative development, Chinese CPL has kept the 'dual-track' structure i.e. foreign-related civil proceedings and pure domestic civil proceedings generally shall be subject to their respective own systems and rules.[3] Under this structure, foreign-related civil proceedings shall firstly refer to those special rules specifically designed for them in Title IV of CPL, which includes rules on general principles of international civil procedure,[4] international jurisdictional

[1]See Article 4 of Chinese Civil Procedure Law (CPL). Also see Ehrenzweig (1960, pp 637–688).

[2]The drafting group of Chinese CPL was founded in 1979, soon after Mr. Xiaoping Deng came back into power and advocated his famous opening-up policy and the first Chinese CPL did not come into being until 1982 with the title of 'Civil Procedure Law of the People's Republic of China (Provisional)'. The 'provisional' CPL had been implemented for almost ten years until 1991 when the 'formal' Chinese CPL was adopted. For changes made to Chinese CPL in 1991, see Ye (2004, pp. 15–17); also see Wei Jiang, 'The Drafting and Amendments of Civil Procedure Law', on file with the author. The First Amendment to CPL was made in 2007. For the background of and changes brought about by the First Amendment, generally see Zhang (2011, pp. 25–27), The Second Amendment was adopted recently on August 31, 2012 and has come into force since January 1, 2013. For changes made, see the Decision of NPC on Adoption of the Amendment to the Civil Procedure Law of the People's Republic of China passed on August 31, 2012. This decision and a full text of Amendment II are on file with the author. Also see Tu and Li (2013, pp. 633–658).

[3]For more detailed discussion with regard to the 'dual-track' structure, see Tu and Li (2013, pp. 633–658).

[4]See Articles 259–264, Chapter 23 of CPL.

G. Tu, *Private International Law in China*, DOI 10.1007/978-981-287-993-6_11

rules,[5] rules on service of documents abroad and relevant terms,[6] international arbitration rules,[7] and rules on international judicial assistance.[8] If there is no applicable special provision prescribed in Title IV for a matter of foreign-related civil proceedings, rules for domestic civil proceedings given in other parts of CPL can be borrowed and resorted to.[9] Therefore, the general picture for international civil proceedings in China is that those special foreign-related civil procedural rules should be given priority and domestic procedural rules can supplement them to make them complete where necessary. One, however, should not have the misunderstanding that most parts of a foreign-related civil litigation can be completed according to those special rules only and the truth is the opposite that even a foreign-related civil litigation still has to, on many occasions, rely on those domestic procedural rules although those special applicable rules in Title IV of CPL should be applied first if there are such rules or there is any conflict. The reason is simply that compared with the whole CPL, Title IV is rather short and limited and given what has been said in Article 259 of CPL, many domestic procedural rules have to be borrowed and applied in practice even if it is a foreign-related case.[10] Therefore, in the following text where the specific topics of international civil procedure are examined, the relevant domestic rules existing in a Title other than Title IV but internationally applicable will also be taken into discussion where it is suitable to do so.

220. Apart from the general law i.e. Chinese CPL, some special international civil procedural rules for maritime litigation can be found in the Special Procedure Law for Maritime Litigation of the People's Republic of China (hereinafter, MPL) which was adopted by the Standing Committee of NPC on 25 December 1999 and has come into force since 1 July 2000. MPL comprehensively covers procedural issues of international maritime litigation in China and provides provisions for jurisdiction,[11]

---

[5]See Articles 265–266, Chapter 24 of CPL.

[6]See Articles 267–270, Chapter 25 of CPL.

[7]See Articles 271–275, Chapter 26 of CPL.

[8]See Articles 276–283, Chapter 27 of CPL.

[9]See Article 259 of CPL, which says: 'Provisions in this Title [Special Provisions on Foreign-Related Civil Procedures] shall apply to foreign-related civil actions within the territory of the People's Republic of China. Where this Title is silent, other relevant provisions of this Law shall apply'.

[10]See Article 259 of CPL.

[11]International jurisdiction rules are prescribed in Chapter II of MPL, which contains Articles 6–9.

Article 6 of MPL says:

> Maritime territorial jurisdiction shall be conducted in accordance with the relevant provisions of the Civil Procedure Law of the People's Republic of China. However, the maritime territorial jurisdiction below shall be conducted in accordance with the following provisions:
>
> (1) A lawsuit brought on maritime tortious act may be, in addition to the provisions of Articles 19 to 31 of the Civil Procedure Law of the People's Republic of China, under jurisdiction of the maritime court of the place of its port of registry;
>
> (2) A lawsuit brought on maritime transportation contract may be, in addition to the provisions of Articles 82 of the Civil Procedure Law of the People's Republic of China, under jurisdiction of the maritime court of the place of its port of re-transportation;

protective measures[12] and service of documents.[13] However, MPL is only a special law to CPL and the former has to be supplemented by the latter in many cases

---

Footnote 11 (continued)

(3) A lawsuit brought on maritime charter parties may be under jurisdiction of the maritime court of the place of its port of ship delivery, port of ship return, port of ship registry, port where the defendant has its domicile;
(4) A lawsuit brought on a maritime protection and indemnity contract may be under jurisdiction of the maritime court of the place where the object of the action is located, the place where the accident occurred or the place where the defendant has his domicile;
(5) A lawsuit brought on a maritime contract of employment of crew may be under jurisdiction of the maritime court of the place where the plaintiff has his domicile, the place where the contract is signed, the place of the port where the crew is abroad or the port where the crew leaves the ship or the place where the defendant has his domicile;
(6) A lawsuit brought on a maritime guaranty may be under jurisdiction of the maritime court of the place where the property mortgaged is located or the place where the defendant has his domicile; a lawsuit brought on a ship mortgage may also be under jurisdiction of the maritime court in the place of registry port;
(7) a lawsuit brought on ownership, procession, and use, maritime liens of a ship, may be under jurisdiction of the maritime court of the place where the ship is located, the place of ship registry or the place where the defendant has his domicile;

Article 7 says:

The following maritime litigation shall be under the exclusive jurisdiction of the maritime courts specified in this Article:

(1) A lawsuit brought on a dispute over harbor operations shall be under the jurisdiction of the maritime court of the place where the harbor is located;
(2) A lawsuit brought on a dispute over pollution damage for a ship's discharge, omission or dumping of oil or other harmful substances, or maritime production, operations, ship scrapping, repairing operations shall be under the jurisdiction of the maritime court of the place where oil pollution occurred, where injury result occurred or where preventive measures were taken;
(3) A lawsuit brought on a dispute over a performance of a maritime exploration and development contract within the territory of the People's Republic of China and the sea areas under its jurisdiction shall be under the jurisdiction of the maritime court of the place where the contract is performed;

Article 8 says:

'Where the parties to a maritime dispute are foreign nationals, stateless persons, foreign enterprises or organizations and the parties, through written agreement, choose the maritime court of the People's Republic of China to exercise jurisdiction, even if the place which has practical connections with the dispute is not within the territory of the People's Republic of China, the maritime court of the People's Republic of China shall also have jurisdiction over the dispute';

Article 9 says:

'An application for determining a maritime property as ownerless shall be filed by the parties with the maritime court of the place where the property is located; an application for declaring a person as dead due to a maritime accident shall be filed with the maritime court of the place where the competent organ responsible for handling with the accident or the maritime court that accepts the relevant maritime cases'.

[12]See Chapters 3, 4, 5, 6 and Articles 13, 14, 52, 53, 63, 64 of MPL.

[13]Rules regarding service of documents are stipulated in Chapter VII, containing Articles 80–81.

Article 80 says:

In serving a maritime litigation document, the relevant provisions of the Civil Procedure Law of the People's Republic of China are applicable, and the following methods may also be adopted:

although the special rules in the former for maritime matters shall prevail if there are any such rules.[14]

221. In the following text, it is thus the international procedure rules in CPL that will mainly be examined and the rules in MPL will not be mentioned unless necessary.

11.2 Interpretations of the SPC

222. As mentioned in the previous text of this book, Judicial Interpretation released by the Supreme People's Court (SPC) is also one of the most important sources of international civil procedure law in China.[15] Corresponding to the legislations mentioned just now, the SPC has issued a series of Judicial Interpretations in different forms, which cover general issues or some specific aspects of international civil procedure.[16] Among the various Interpretations, the most important one used to be the 'Opinions of the Supreme People's Court on Some Issues Concerning the Application of the Civil Procedure Law of the People's Republic of China' (hereinafter, 1992 Interpretation on CPL) publicized on 14 July 1992, which has recently been replaced and updated by the 'Interpretation of the Supreme People's Court on the Application of the Civil Procedure Law of the People's Republic of China' (hereinafter, 2015 Interpretation on CPL) publicized on 4 February 2015. Following its predecessor, the latter comprehensively construes the Articles in CPL including those Articles concerning foreign-related civil proceedings such as those of jurisdiction,[17] recognition and enforcement of foreign

Footnote 13 (continued)

> (1) to serve on an agent ad litem commissioned by the person on whom the litigation document is to be served; (2) to serve on a representative office or branch office established in the People's Republic of China by the person on whom the service is to be made or on his business agent; (3) to serve by employing other appropriate methods by which the receipt can be confirmed. A legal document relating to the arrest of a ship may also be served on the captain of the ship involved;

Article 81 says:

> If the person who has the obligation of receiving a legal document refuses to sign and receive the legal document, the person serving the document shall record on the receipt the situations. After the person serving the document and the witness have affixed their signatures or seals to the receipt, the legal document shall be left at his domicile and the service shall be deemed completed.

[14]See Article 2 of MPL, which says:

> Whoever engages in maritime litigation within the territory of the People's Republic of China shall apply the Civil Procedure Law of the People's Republic of China and this Law. Where otherwise provided for by this Law, such provisions shall prevail.

[15]See supra para. 20.

[16]See supra paras. 7–10.

[17]See Articles 1–34, 531–533 of the 2015 Interpretation on CPL.

judgments and international commercial arbitration.[18] In addition, based on CPL, the SPC has also issued an Interpretation specifically addressing jurisdictional issues regarding foreign-related civil and commercial litigation on 25 February 2002, namely 'Provisions of the Supreme People's Court on Some Issues Concerning the Jurisdiction of Civil and Commercial Cases Involving Foreign Elements' (hereinafter, 2002 Interpretation on International Jurisdiction)[19]; and Interpretations regarding international service of documents and taking of evidence, namely 'Several Provisions of the Supreme People's Court on the Service of Judicial Documents of Foreign-related Civil or Commercial Cases' adopted on 17 July 2006 (hereinafter, 2006 Interpretation on Service of Documents)[20] and 'Provisions of the Supreme People's Court on the Service of Judicial Documents and Taking of Evidence in Civil and Commercial Matters under International Conventions and Bilateral Treaties on Judicial Assistance' adopted on 7 April 2013.[21] There is also a Judicial Interpretation that follows the MPL i.e. 'Interpretation of the Supreme People's Court on the Application of the Special Maritime Procedure Law of the People's Republic of China' adopted on 6 January 2003.[22]

[18]See Articles 543–548 of the 2015 Interpretation on CPL.

[19]See infra paras. 227–229.

[20]See infra paras. 303–310.

[21]Apart from the inter-regional Arrangements mentioned in the General Introduction of this book, the SPC, based on CPL, has also unilaterally issued some Interpretations respecting inter-regional service of documents and taking of evidence, see 'Several Provisions of the Supreme People's Court on the Issues concerning the Service of Judicial Documents of Hong Kong- and Macao-related Civil and Commercial Cases' adopted on 9 March 2009; 'Notice of the Supreme People's Court on Further Regulating Investigation and Evidence Collection involving Hong Kong, Macao or Taiwan by People's Courts' adopted on 7 August 2011. In addition, based on CPL, the SPC has also unilaterally issued some Interpretations specifically for cases related to Taiwan, see 'Several Provisions of the Supreme People's Court on the Service of Litigation Documents in Taiwan-related Civil Matters' adopted on 17 April 2008; 'Provisions of the Supreme People's Court on the People's Courts' Handling of Cases of Mutual Judicial Assistance in Terms of Serving Legal Documents, Investigation and Evidence Collection between Both Sides of the Taiwan Strait' adopted on 14 June 2011; 'The Provisions of the Supreme People's Court on the People's Court's Recognition of the Judgments on Civil Cases Made by Courts of Taiwan Province' adopted on 22 May 1998; and 'Supplementary Provisions of the Supreme People's Court on the People's Courts' Recognition of Civil Judgments of the Relevant Courts of the Taiwan Region' adopted on 24 April 2009. The latter two have been recently replaced by the 'The Regulation of the Supreme People's Court on Recognition and Enforcement of Judgments in Civil Cases Made by the Courts of Taiwan Region' publicized on 1 July 2015.

[22]This Interpretation comprehensively construes the Articles in MPL including those for international civil procedure, see paragraphs 4, 5, 9, 10, 11, 13, 14, 53, 54 and 55.

11.3 International Conventions and Treaties

223. Once again, as said in the General Introduction of this book, international conventions and treaties which China has acceded to/ratified are also an important legal source for ICP in China.[23] Indeed, conventions and treaties China has acceded to/ratified are directly applicable and enjoy priority over domestic legislations and Judicial Interpretations.[24] In the area of international civil procedure, the most influential multi-lateral conventions and treaties China has participated in are 'Hague Convention on the Service Abroad of Judicial and Extrajudicial Documents in Civil or Commercial Matters' (hereinafter, Hague Service Convention); 'Hague Convention on the Taking of Evidence Abroad in Civil and Commercial Matters' (hereinafter, Hague Evidence Convention); and 'Convention on the Recognition and Enforcement of Foreign Arbitral Awards' (hereinafter, New York Convention).[25] Furthermore, China has concluded bilateral treaties respecting judicial assistance in civil and commercial matters with over 30 countries so far.[26] The majority of these bilateral treaties contain clauses concerning exchange of judicial information, abolishing the requirement of legalization, service of documents, taking of evidence, mutual recognition and enforcement of judgments in civil and commercial matters and arbitral awards.[27]

224. Based on these legal sources plus some court cases, the specific topics of international civil procedure in China will be discussed in the following text of this part.

[23]See supra para. 20.

[24]See Article 260 of CPL, which says: 'Where there is any discrepancy between an international treaty ratified or acceded to by the People's Republic of China and this Law, the provisions of the international treaty shall prevail, except clauses to which the People's Republic of China has declared reservations'.

[25]See supra para. 46.

[26]See supra para. 47.

[27]As already mentioned, in order to promote inter-regional judicial cooperation within China, several bilateral Arrangements concerning judicial assistance have been concluded between Mainland China and HK/Macau, see supra para. 39.

Chapter 12
International Jurisdiction and Its Fine-Tuning in China

12.1 Jurisdiction by Forum Level

225. As mentioned, generally there are courts at four different levels in China.[1] As far as subject matter jurisdiction is concerned, the court at county (district) level shall have general jurisdiction except those cases that shall be taken by higher courts as otherwise stipulated by Chinese law.[2] Therefore, in principle, civil cases of first instance are normally under the jurisdiction of the county (district) courts in China.[3] There are, however, three situations where an intermediate court (court at intermediate city or prefecture level) can exercise jurisdiction as the court of first instance, for which Article 18 of Chinese CPL says:

The intermediate people's courts shall have jurisdiction over the following civil cases as a court of first instance:

(1) Major foreign-related cases;
(2) Cases which have a major impact within their respective territories;
(3) Cases which are under the jurisdiction of the intermediate people's courts as determined by the Supreme People's Court.[4]

226. A 'major foreign-related case' is interpreted by the SPC as a case in which the disputed value is large or factual elements are complicated or there are a few parties living outside the territory of China. Implicitly, a minor or simple foreign-related case is still subject to the jurisdiction of a county/district court as the court of first instance.[5] So far, the SPC has determined two categories of cases as those

[1]See supra para. 6.

[2]See Article 17 of Chinese CPL, which says: 'The basic people's courts [courts at county (district) level] shall have jurisdiction over civil cases as the court of first instance, except as otherwise provided for in this Law'.

[3]Ibid.

[4]See Article 18 of Chinese CPL.

[5]See Article 1 of the 2015 Interpretation on CPL.

G. Tu, *Private International Law in China*, DOI 10.1007/978-981-287-993-6_12

that shall be subject to the jurisdiction of an intermediate court as the court of first instance i.e. maritime cases and cases related to patent disputes.[6] The exact standard for the cases that could be said to have a major impact within their respective territories mentioned in Article 18 used to be made respectively by different high courts at provincial level according to the actual situation within their territories with due attention paid to the elements of disputed value, the factual complexity and the influential effects.[7] One thing is, for sure, that for a case to be qualified as one that has a major impact and be heard by an intermediate court as the first-instance court, it must have a far-reaching effect in the territory of the concerned intermediate court and be unsuitable to be heard by any court at county (district) level within that territory. Going along this line, a high court at provincial level and the SPC can also hear a case as the court of first instance if the case has a major impact within its territory (the country).[8] In addition, as the highest court on the Chinese soil, the SPC can decide to hear any case which it thinks it is suitable to hear as the court of first instance.[9]

12.2 Centralized International Jurisdiction Over Foreign-Related Civil and Commercial Cases

227. According to what has been said just now, it seems that a court, wherever it sits, should have the chance of exercising jurisdiction over foreign-related cases if the requirements demanded by the law can be met.[10] However, due to the possible importance and complexity of some categories of foreign-related cases, based on CPL, the SPC issued an Interpretation in 2002, further stipulating that those cases shall be heard only in the courts specified therein.[11] Those categories of foreign-related cases singled out by the SPC in the Interpretation are:

(1) cases on disputes over contracts or torts involving foreign elements;
(2) cases on disputes over Letters of Credit;
(3) cases on revocation, recognition and enforcement of international arbitral award;

[6]See Article 2 of the 2015 Interpretation on CPL.

[7]See paragraph 3 of the 1992 Interpretation on CPL, which has now been deleted in the 2015 Interpretation on CPL.

[8]See Articles 19 & 20 (1) of CPL.

[9]See Article 20 (2) of CPL.

[10]See supra para. 225.

[11]It is the 2002 Interpretation on International Jurisdiction mentioned above, see supra para. 222.

(4) cases on the validity of international arbitration clauses in civil and commercial matters;
(5) cases on recognition and enforcement of foreign civil and commercial judgments.[12]

228. The courts that have been specified as competent to exercise international jurisdiction over those cases are enumerated in Article 1 of the Interpretation, which says:

The following courts shall exercise jurisdiction, as the court of first instance, over civil and commercial cases involving foreign elements:

(1) the people's court of an economic and technological development zone established under the approval of the State Council;
(2) the intermediate people's court located in the city which is the capital of a province or autonomous region or a municipality;
(3) the intermediate people's court of a special economic zone or a city separately listed according to the State Plan;
(4) any other intermediate people's court designated by the Supreme People's Court;
(5) the high people's court…[13]

229. One, therefore, should bear it in mind that all Chinese courts may have the chance of hearing a case of cross-border matters such as family or succession but not all courts in China can necessarily exercise international jurisdiction over foreign-related civil and commercial cases, for which it is normally the case that only those courts located in a well-developed area or important city have been given the power to try.[14]

---

[12]See Article 3 of the 2002 Interpretation on International Jurisdiction. However, it is said in the same Interpretation that if a case is on a border-trade dispute, real estate dispute or IP dispute that have occurred in a border province neighboring a foreign country, it shall not be covered by Article 3, see Article 4 of the 2002 Interpretation on International Jurisdiction.

[13]See Article 1 of the 2002 Interpretation on International Jurisdiction. For reference of a detailed list of the courts that are covered by Article 1 (1), see Annex of the Judgment Arrangement between Mainland China and Hong Kong: List of Basic People's Courts of the Mainland Authorized to Exercise Jurisdiction of the First Instance in Civil and Commercial Cases Involving Foreign, Hong Kong, Macao and Taiwan Parties as of 25 July 2014; supra para. 39.

[14]Jurisdiction over civil and commercial cases related to Hong Kong, Macau and Taiwan will be handled in the same way, see Article 5 of the 2002 Interpretation on International Jurisdiction.

12.3 International Jurisdiction Grounds

12.3.1 International Jurisdiction Grounds Specifically Prescribed in Title IV of CPL

230. There used to be four international jurisdiction grounds specifically prescribed in Title IV of Chinese CPL i.e. jurisdiction by connections, party autonomy, submission and exclusive jurisdiction.[15] After Amendment II which was made in 2012,[16] there are now only two international jurisdiction grounds that have been kept in Title IV i.e. jurisdiction by connections and exclusive jurisdiction.[17] However, one should not have the misunderstanding that party autonomy and submission as international jurisdiction grounds for Chinese courts have been deleted altogether from Chinese CPL. The truth is that these two grounds have now been combined with the corresponding domestic ones that are also internationally applicable.[18]

12.3.1.1 Jurisdiction by Connections

231. In Title IV of Chinese CPL, Article 265 says:

> Where an action is instituted against a defendant that has no domicile within the territory of the People's Republic of China for a contract dispute or any other property right or interest dispute, if the contract is signed or performed within the territory of the People's Republic of China, or the subject matter of action is located within the territory of the People's Republic of China, or the defendant has any arrestable property within the territory of the People's Republic of China, or the defendant has any representative office within the territory of the People's Republic of China, the people's court at the place where the contract is signed or performed, where the subject matter of action is located, where the arrestable property is located, where the tort occurs or where the domicile of the representative office is located may have jurisdiction over the action.[19]

232. In the Chinese academia, jurisdiction based on this Article is called 'jurisdiction by connections'.[20] One can see that on the one hand, the scope of this Article is really broad because it can apply if only it is a case of 'a contract dispute or any other property right or interest dispute'; on the other hand, according to this Article, a broad range of courts that may only have tenuous connection with the case can exercise jurisdiction over the case, for example the court where a contract

[15]See supra paras. 218–219; Articles 241–244 of Chinese CPL as amended in 2007.

[16]See supra paras. 218–219.

[17]See Articles 265–266 of Chinese CPL.

[18]See infra paras. 254–256.

[19]See Article 265 of Chinese CPL.

[20]See Liu (1994, pp. 465–467).

was signed or where the defendant has arrestable property having nothing to do with the contract can have jurisdiction over the case.[21] Therefore, this international jurisdiction ground could be exercised quite excessively or exorbitantly in practice.[22] Indeed, it can even be branded as 'Chinese exorbitant jurisdiction'.[23]

12.3.1.2 Exclusive Jurisdiction

233. In Title IV of Chinese CPL, Article 266 says: 'Actions instituted for disputes arising out of performance within the territory of People's Republic of China of contracts for Chinese-foreign equity joint ventures, Chinese-foreign contractual joint ventures or Chinese-foreign cooperative exploration and exploitation of natural resources shall be under the exclusive jurisdiction of the people's courts of the People's Republic of China'.[24] As a developing country, to attract foreign capital and investors has been a policy for long in China. Due to the importance of the three categories of contracts mentioned in the Article and strong national interests possibly involved therein, China does not want disputes related to them to be heard outside its territory. It is also reasonable for China to claim exclusive jurisdiction over these cases because disputes related to these contracts do normally have the strongest connection with China. However, China does not prohibit these cases from being arbitrated even by an arbitration tribunal outside China.[25]

12.3.2 Domestic Jurisdiction Grounds that are Internationally Available

234. As said, owing to Article 259 of Chinese CPL, rules for domestic litigation can be internationally applicable including those jurisdiction rules.[26] The jurisdiction grounds that are supposedly and seemingly made only for domestic cases but actually also for international cases are explored in the following text. Before doing so, one point, however, must be clarified first that these '*domestic but internationally available*' jurisdiction grounds are even more commonly and frequently relied on by Chinese courts in practice for exercising international jurisdiction over foreign-related cases than those specifically prescribed in Title IV of CPL.[27]

[21]E.g. see infra para. 264.

[22]Ibid.

[23]See Tu (2012, pp. 341, 343–344).

[24]See Article 266 of Chinese CPL.

[25]See Article 531 of the 2015 Interpretation on CPL.

[26]See supra para. 219.

[27]Ibid.

12.3.2.1 General Jurisdiction

235. Based on the ancient Rome doctrine of *actor sequitur forum rei*, like in many other civil law countries, general jurisdiction is grounded on the domicile of the defendant in Chinese law, regardless of whether the defendant is a natural person or a legal person.[28] A defendant shall/can be sued in his/its home forum for any cause of action.[29] To a natural person, domicile is the place he has registered with the police as his home; to a legal person, domicile is the place of its central administration or its registration place.[30] In the case where a natural person has not resided in his domicile for long, the place of his habitual residence shall prevail over and be regarded as his domicile.[31] For the purpose of jurisdiction, the concept of habitual residence is further defined as the place where a natural person has continuously resided for more than a year.[32] In addition, this general jurisdiction ground has been extended against any other defendant in a case concerning multiple-defendants.[33]

236. In contrast with Article 21, Article 22 allows general jurisdiction to be exercised by the court of the place where a plaintiff is domiciled or has his habitual residence against a defendant who is either under the police custody or imprisoned.[34]

12.3.2.2 Special Jurisdiction

Special Jurisdiction for Cases Concerning Personal Relationship (Status)

237. If the case is about personal relationship (status) between the defendant and the plaintiff where the defendant is not in the territory of China or the defendant's address is unknown or the defendant has been declared as having disappeared by a

[28]See Article 21 of Chinese CPL, which says: 'A civil action instituted against a citizen shall be under the jurisdiction of the people's court at the place of domicile of the defendant; or if the defendant's place of domicile is different from his or her place of habitual residence, the civil action shall be under the jurisdiction of the people's court at the place of habitual residence of the defendant; A civil action instituted against a legal person or any other organization shall be under the jurisdiction of the people's court at the place of domicile of the defendant; in a case of multiple-defendants where the defendants are domiciled or have habitual residences in more than one place, any court of the domicile/habitual residence of one defendant can exercise jurisdiction against all the defendants involved in the case'. Also see Tu (2009, p. 72).

[29]See Tu, ibid.

[30]See Article 3 of 2015 Interpretation on CPL. In the case of a partnership, it is the place of registration if it has no place of administration, see Article 5 of 2015 Interpretation on CPL.

[31]See Article 21 of Chinese CPL.

[32]See Article 4 of 2015 Interpretation on CPL.

[33]See Article 21 of Chinese CPL.

[34]See Article 22 (3) (4) of Chinese CPL.

court, the court for the place where the plaintiff is domiciled or has his habitual residence can have jurisdiction.[35]

238. In matters relating to maintenance, the court of the place where the maintenance creditor is domiciled can have jurisdiction over the case.[36]

239. If it is a dispute for guardianship, the court for the place where the ward is domiciled can have jurisdiction.[37]

240. In a case of divorce, if one of the couple has left his/her domicile for more than a year and the other sues for divorce, the court for the place where the other has his/her domicile can have jurisdiction; if both has left their domiciles for more than a year, the court where the defendant has his habitual residence shall have jurisdiction, failing which the court where the defendant has his residence[38]; if one of a Chinese couple living abroad wants to sue in a Chinese court, whether they have been married in China or abroad, the court for the place where anyone of them had the last domicile or residence or their marriage was concluded can have jurisdiction; where a divorced Chinese couple residing abroad have dispute over property located within China, the court where the main disputed property is located shall have jurisdiction.[39]

Special Jurisdiction for Contractual Matters

General Contracts

241. According to Article 23 of CPL, a dispute regarding contractual matters can be sued in the court for the place where the contract has been performed, apart from the place where the defendant is domiciled.[40] However, if the contract has not been performed and none of the contractual parties is domiciled in the agreed place of performance of the contract, it is only the court for the place where the defendant is domiciled can have jurisdiction.[41]

242. As said above, in Chinese law, the concept of the place of performance of the contract is interchangeable with the concept of the place of performance of characteristic obligation of the contract.[42] Therefore, this special jurisdiction rule essentially refers to the court for the place where the characteristic obligation of

---

[35]See Article 22 (1) (2) of Chinese CPL.

[36]See Article 9 of 2015 Interpretation on CPL.

[37]See Article 10 of 2015 Interpretation on CPL.

[38]See Article 12 of 2015 Interpretation on CPL.

[39]See Articles 13–17 of 2015 Interpretation on CPL.

[40]See Article 23 of Chinese CPL.

[41]See Article 18 of 2015 Interpretation on CPL; supra para. 235.

[42]See supra para. 165.

the contract has been performed.[43] Generally, for the purpose of this jurisdiction rule, the actual place of performance however shall be subordinate to the agreed place of performance in the contract.[44] This contrasts with the previous situation where the former normally shall prevail over the latter, which indicates that China is more willing to accept party autonomy for special jurisdiction regarding contractual matters than before.[45]

Special Contracts

243. Unlike in the EU where insurance contracts, consumer contracts and individual employment contracts are differentiated from general contracts, Chinese law has only prescribed particular special jurisdiction for insurance contracts and transportation contracts.[46]

244. For insurance contracts, the court for the place where the insured subject matter is located can have jurisdiction, apart from the court where the defendant is domiciled.[47] If the insured subject matter is a transportation vehicle or goods in transit, the court for the place where the vehicle is registered or the place of destination or where the harmful event has occurred can have jurisdiction.[48]

245. For transportation contracts, the court for the starting place or the place of destination can have jurisdiction, apart from the court of the defendant's domicile.[49]

Special Jurisdiction for Disputes Arising Out of Negotiable Instruments

246. For disputes arising out of negotiable instruments, the court for the place where the payment shall be made can have jurisdiction, apart from the court of the defendant's domicile.[50] In the previous Interpretation, the place of payment was defined as "the one designated in the concerned negotiable instrument. If the place

[43]This understanding can be evidenced by the special jurisdiction rules prescribed for a few specific kinds of contracts, see Articles 19–20 of 2015 Interpretation on CPL.

[44]See Articles 19–20 of 2015 Interpretation on CPL. Also see Article 18 of the 2015 Interpretation on CPL.

[45]See paragraphs 19–21 of 1992 Interpretation on CPL.

[46]See Sects. 3, 4, 5 of Council Regulation (EC) No 44/2001 of 22 December 2000 on jurisdiction and the recognition and enforcement of judgments in civil and commercial matters (hereinafter, Brussels I Regulation).

[47]See Article 24 of Chinese CPL; supra para. 235.

[48]See Article 21 of 2015 Interpretation on CPL.

[49]See Article 27 of Chinese CPL; supra para. 235.

[50]See Article 25 of Chinese CPL; supra para. 235.

of payment is not clearly indicated, it shall be the place of domicile or the principal business place of the payer".[51] This definition has been deleted by the latest 2015 Interpretation on CPL.

Special Jurisdiction for Internal Affairs of a Corporation

247. Internal affairs of a corporation, generally speaking, refer to those affairs of internal management and governance, such as its incorporation, dissolution, legal capacity, internal structure, and determination of shareholders and their roles in management and portions of profits.[52] Before Amendment II made in 2012, it was mainly the general principle of *actor sequitor forum rei* in CPL that could apply to the issue of jurisdiction over internal affairs of a corporation.[53] Under this principle, very possibly the competent court for the dispute over internal affairs was not the court for the place of domicile of the concerned corporation when the defendant in the dispute was not the corporation itself but for instance, one of its shareholders or directors.[54] In such a case, the access of necessary evidence such as registration information kept in the local Industry and Commercial Administrative Bureau where the concerned corporation was incorporated could be rather inconvenient and costly. The frailty can now be cured to some extent by Article 26, a new Article inserted into the group of special jurisdiction rules in CPL, which states:

> Disputes arising out of the establishment of a corporation, confirmation of shareholder's membership, profit distribution, dissolution and other similar matters can be subject to jurisdiction of the court where the corporation is domiciled.[55]

248. With the adoption of Amendment II, the court for the place where the corporation is domiciled can, therefore, exercise special jurisdiction over internal affairs of that corporation even if the corporation itself is not the defendant in the case, apart from the general jurisdiction it may exercise against the corporation when the corporation itself is the defendant in the case.[56]

---

[51]See paragraph 26 of 1992 Interpretation on CPL.

[52]See Kaplan (1968, pp. 433, 438); the United States Restatement (Second) of Conflicts of Laws, § 302–310.

[53]See Article 22 of CPL as amended in 2007; supra para. 235.

[54]Ibid.

[55]See Article 26 of CPL; Article 22 of 2015 Interpretation on CPL. There used to be no such a provision in the group of special jurisdiction rules, see Articles 22–33 of CPL as amended in 2007.

[56]See Article 21; supra para. 235.

Special Jurisdiction for Tort

General Torts

249. For a dispute of tort, the court for the tortious place can have jurisdiction, apart from the court for the place where the defendant is domiciled.[57] The tortious place includes not only the place where the tortious act is committed but also the place where the damage is sustained. For the purpose of internet-related torts, the place of tortious act can refer to the place where the concerned electronic instrument such as the computer is located while the place of damage can refer to the place of the victim's domicile.[58]

Special Torts

250. If a tort occurs during the course of transportation, the court for the place where the harmful event has happened or the place of the earliest arrival can have jurisdiction, apart from the court of the defendant's domicile.[59]

251. A tort arising out of product liability or provision of service can be sued in the court for the place where the product was manufactured or where the product was sold or where the service was provided or where the tort has occurred, apart from the court for the place of the defendant's domicile.[60]

252. A maritime tort can also be sued in a court other than the court for the place where the defendant is domiciled.[61]

12.3.2.3 Exclusive Jurisdiction

253. Further to the exclusive jurisdiction mentioned above,[62] there are also some domestic exclusive jurisdictional rules that are internationally applicable.[63] Article 33 of CPL says:

The following cases shall be subject to exclusive jurisdiction of the courts specified in this Article:

(1) Where a dispute is about an immovable property, the court for the place where the immovable property is located shall have jurisdiction;
(2) Where a dispute is arising out of harbour operation, the court for the place where the harbour is located shall have jurisdiction;

---

57 See Article 28 of CPL; supra para. 235.

58 See Articles 24–25 of 2015 Interpretation on CPL. Also see supra para. 202.

59 See Article 29 of Chinese CPL; supra para. 235.

60 See Article 26 of 2015 Interpretation on CPL; supra para. 235.

61 See Articles 30-32 of Chinese CPL; supra para. 235.

62 See supra para. 233.

63 See Article 33 of Chinese CPL.

(3) Where a dispute is about succession, the court for the place of the deceased's domicile upon death or where the main property to be inherited shall have jurisdiction.

In the latest 2015 Interpretation on CPL, Article 33 (1) has been extended to cover disputes arising out of contracts respecting agricultural land lease, contracts respecting housing lease (tenancy), contracts respecting constructing immovables and contracts respecting sale of policy-related housing.[64]

12.3.2.4 Prorogation of Jurisdiction

254. As mentioned above, two jurisdiction grounds respectively based on choice of court agreement made by the parties and submission by the defendant that used to be specifically prescribed for international civil proceedings have now been deleted from Title IV of CPL by Amendment II.[65] This, however, does not mean that these two grounds of jurisdiction will not be viable any more for international civil proceedings. The fact is that now, Article 34 allowing choice of forum and Article 127 confirming the validity of defendant's submission shall apply universally to both domestic and foreign-related actions.[66]

255. Article 34 of CPL still insists on the principle of 'actual connection' and that the choice of court agreement must be made in written form.[67] Though it has been indicated in a series of Chinese legislations that the 'written form' shall refer to documents concluded in writing and those made by other means of communication which is capable of tangibly representing its content as well, this expanded definition was not formally incorporated into CPL.[68] It is, however, the current author's belief that it would be the expanded definition that would be adopted in Chinese judicial practice.[69] According to Article 34, parties to a dispute over a contract or any other right or interest in a property may, without violating rules

[64]Ibid; Article 28 of 2015 Interpretation on CPL.

[65]See supra para. 230.

[66]See Articles 34 & 127 of CPL; supra para. 230.

[67]The principle of 'actual connection' means that the parties are only allowed to choose a forum which must have substantial connection with the case. These two requirements were demanded previously, see Articles 25, 242 of CPL as amended in 2007; Article 34 of CPL.

[68]See Article 11 of Chinese Contract Law, stipulating that 'The term "written form" refers to a form which is capable of tangibly representing its content, such as written instruments, letters and electronically transmitted documents (including telegrams, telexes, facsimiles, electronic data interchange and email), etc.'; Article 4 of Law of Electronic Signature of the People's Republic of China adopted on August 28, 2004, saying: 'Any data message that can show the contents it specifies in material form, and may be picked up for reference and use at any time, shall be regarded as complying with the written form as prescribed by laws and regulations'.

[69]Also see Tu (2007, pp. 347, 347–356).

concerning jurisdiction by forum level and exclusive jurisdiction, choose the court for the place where the defendant is domiciled, or where the contract is performed or signed, or where the plaintiff is domiciled, or where the subject matter is located or any other place that has actual connection with the dispute as the court having jurisdiction over their dispute by a written agreement.[70] Compared with the previously applicable rule, to parties of domestic disputes, the scope of cases for which they are allowed to choose a forum to resolve their dispute is now extended from the only contractual disputes to contractual disputes plus others where property interests are involved.[71] Moreover, the parties can also choose a court of a place which is actually connected to the dispute other than those explicitly enumerated[72]; To parties of foreign-related actions, the change is that quite a few exact places where the courts supposedly allowed to be chosen are located have been added as the illustration of the places that are actually connected to the disputes.[73] It is, therefore, predictable that in future, the parties need not prove that their chosen forum is actually connected to the dispute, provided that that forum is located in one of the above-listed places.[74]

256. Previously, jurisdiction based on submission by the defendant was only expressly accepted for foreign-related actions[75] and there was doubt whether this jurisdictional ground was available for domestic proceedings. To clarify the situation, this jurisdictional ground is now re-arranged in Article 127 which has extended its applicability to both foreign-related and domestic actions.[76] Compared with the former version, a safeguard clause, however, has been added to ensure that provisions in CPL regarding jurisdiction by forum level and exclusive jurisdiction will not be violated.[77]

---

[70]See Article 34 of CPL.

[71]Ibid. Cf. Article 25 of CPL as amended in 2007 which says: 'Parties to a contract may, without violating rules concerning jurisdiction by forum level and exclusive jurisdiction, choose the court for the place where the defendant is domiciled, or where the contract is performed or signed, or where the plaintiff is domiciled, or where the subject matter is located as the court having jurisdiction over the dispute by a written agreement'.

[72]Ibid.

[73]See Article 34 of CPL. Cf. Article 242 of CPL as amended in 2007, which says: 'Parties to a foreign-related dispute over a contract or any other right or interest in a property may choose a court for the place that is actually connected to the dispute as the court having jurisdiction over the dispute by a written agreement. Rules concerning jurisdiction by forum level and exclusive jurisdiction shall not be violated if a people's court of the People's Republic of China is chosen as the court having jurisdiction'.

[74]See Article 34 of CPL. Also see Articles 29–34, 531 of 2015 Interpretation on CPL.

[75]See Article 243 of CPL as amended in 2007, which says: 'If the defendant in civil litigation involving foreign elements raises no objection to the jurisdiction of a people's court and files his defense with the court, he shall be deemed to have accepted that that people's court has jurisdiction over the case'.

[76]See Article 127 of CPL.

[77]See Article 127 of CPL. Cf. Article 243 of CPL as amended in 2007.

257. From the above discussion, it can be seen that except some additional grounds of exclusive jurisdiction, choice of forum by the parties and jurisdiction based on plaintiff's domicile in few unusual circumstances, the ancient doctrine of *actor sequitur forum rei* in Roman law is firmly accepted as the basis for general jurisdiction. Furthermore, this doctrine is included again and re-emphasized in most of special jurisdictional rules which are basically based on territorial connections between the case and the forum. These special jurisdiction rules are secondary to the general one although they cover a wide range of different areas. The Chinese jurisdictional law, thus, has closely followed the civil law tradition in which the same set of jurisdictional rules as those domestic ones, with some adjustments being possibly made for international cases, can usually also be applicable to international cases on the presumption that domestic courts and foreign courts are 'wholly comparable and interchangeable elements of a universal organization for the administration of justice'.[78] In constructing jurisdictional law, the starting point is the defendant's domicile and some special rules are utilized to complement this basic rule to meet practical needs plus exclusive jurisdiction, submission and party autonomy. Also as in many other civil law countries where judicial discretion is generally not preferred for jurisdictional matters, one cannot find any rule in Chinese law that can generally authorize a Chinese court to discretionarily transfer a case over which it has jurisdiction to another court, whether in a domestic or international context. It is this jurisdictional background that sets the tone for the Chinese version of *forum non conveniens*.

12.4 Fine-Tuning International Jurisdiction in China: Forum Non Conveniens in Chinese Judicial Practice

258. Forum non conveniens is a popular doctrine in common law countries.[79] It is a useful tool for fine-tuning the exercise of international civil jurisdiction,[80] by which judges can enjoy a kind of general discretionary power to decline cases when there is a clearly more appropriate forum for trial abroad or the local forum is clearly inappropriate although jurisdiction can be established in the local forum.[81] This doctrine is, however, generally unacceptable to civil law countries and declining jurisdiction is even constitutionally prohibited in some of those countries.[82] Nevertheless, substitutes for this doctrine, though usually limited in

[78]See Struycken (1978, pp. 356–357).

[79]See Fawcett (2005, pp. 1, 10).

[80]See von Mehren (2002, pp. 9, 306).

[81]See Fawcett (2005, pp. 2, 10). In the US, judges, however, can decline a case without having established local jurisdiction, generally see Tu (2007, pp. 529–537).

[82]See Fawcett (2005, pp. 21–27).

terms of the exercisable discretionary power, do often exist in civil law countries, especially in the area of family law.[83] Historically, China is a country of civil law tradition and this doctrine had not been accepted in Chinese law.[84] It, however, has increasingly attracted the attention of Chinese lawyers since 1990s and was de facto applied by the Supreme People's Court and some lower Chinese courts in practice although there was no statutory authorization. Having examined international jurisdiction rules applicable in Chinese courts, this section intends to explore how the exercise of international jurisdiction is fine-tuned in China.

259. As said already, although the doctrine of *forum non conveniens* was not statutorily authorized in China, the SPC and some lower Chinese courts had accepted it in practice. In this section, a few available publicized cases regarding the application of this doctrine will be examined to show how this doctrine has evolved in China. The judicial practice of Chinese courts can basically be divided into two periods: before and after the SPC's 2005 Notice[85] which had systematized and provided some useful guidance for the doctrine.

12.4.1 Cases Before the SPC's 2005 Notice

12.4.1.1 Two Seminal Cases

260. It is generally agreed that the first Chinese case concerning this doctrine is *Bank of East Asia (Hong Kong) v. Dong Peng Trade & Development Corporation.*[86] In this case, both the appellant, Bank of East Asia (BEA) and the respondent, Dong Peng Trade & Development Corporation (Dong Peng Corp.) were registered, located and run in Hong Kong with the appellant having a representative organ in Shenzhen, Guangdong Province, the mainland China.[87] Dong Peng Corp. applied in Hong Kong for a Letter of Credit (LC) to be issued by BEA for which the beneficiary was an American company. When Dong Peng Corp. found a fraud of the beneficiary, it demanded that BEA should not make the payment but BEA rejected Dong Peng Corp.'s request and paid.[88] As a result, relying on Article 243 [now Article 265] of CPL that allows a legal person to be sued in the place where it has a representative organ,[89] Dong Peng Corp. sued BEA in the intermediate court of Shenzhen in 1993 but the Shenzhen court's jurisdiction was

[83]Ibid.

[84]See Wang (2006, pp. 72, 78).

[85]See infra para. 273.

[86]See (1995) No. 3 of the Second Economic and Supervision Division of Guangdong High Court; Shi and Teng (2003, pp. 60, 61), Xi (2002, pp. 81, 85).

[87]Ibid.

[88]Ibid.

[89]See supra para. 231. At that time, it was Article 243 of the 1991 version of CPL.

challenged by BEA, arguing that the doctrine of *forum non conveniens* should be applied and this case should be tried in Hong Kong.[90] BEA's challenge to jurisdiction was rejected by the Shenzhen court and further by the Guangdong High Court when BEA appealed to the latter. BEA, however, did not give up easily and successfully requested the Guangdong High Court to launch the supervision procedure for re-trial on the jurisdictional matter in 1995. During the proceedings of re-trial, Guangdong High Court asked the opinion of the SPC before making its decision. With the consent of the SPC in its reply, the Guangdong High Court ruled that the case shall be dismissed by the mainland court, saying:

> In this case, the parties have explicitly agreed that Hong Kong court shall have non-exclusive jurisdiction. And both of the parties are companies from Hong Kong, the dispute has nothing to do with the mainland China. Hong Kong court shall, according to the agreement of the parties, have jurisdiction and try the case for the purpose of the convenience of litigation.[91]

261. It was in the same year that the SPC itself directly decided a case related to the application of the doctrine. In the case of *Yongqiao Corporation Ltd. (Yongqiao) & Zhongqiao Guohuo Investment Corporation Ltd. (Zhongqiao) v. Jiahua International Corporation Ltd. (Jiahua) & Ruixiang Corporation Ltd (Ruixiang)*, all the four parties were registered and located in Hong Kong.[92] Jiahua, Ruixiang and Yongqiao were shareholders of Zhongqiao. While Yongqiao had a representative organ in Guangdong province, Zhongqiao was investing in real estate in Guangdong. Based on Article 243 [now Article 265] of CPL that allows a legal person to be sued in the place where it has a representative organ or arrestable property,[93] Jiahua and Ruixiang filed a case against Yongqiao and Zhongqiao with Guangdong High Court, complaining that their interests as minority shareholders of Zhongqiao had been damaged because Yongqiao was the major shareholder of Zhongqiao and had taken advantage of that position to manipulate the operation of Zhongqiao. Although Yongqiao and Zhongqiao challenged jurisdiction, Guangdong High Court insisted that it had jurisdiction over the case because Yongqiao had a representative organ in Guangdong and Zhongqiao had arrestable property within its territory.[94] Yongqiao and Zhongqiao, then, took the case to the SPC who overruled the decision of the Guangdong High Court and said:

> The two respondents [Jiahua and Ruixiang] and the appellant, Yongqiao are all Hong Kong companies and Zhongqiao which was invested by the three is also a company registered in Hong Kong. As to the dispute within a Hong Kong-based company among the different shareholders, the court for the place where the company is registered shall have

[90]See (1995) No. 3 of the Second Economic and Supervision Division of Guangdong High Court.

[91]Ibid.

[92]See (1995) No. 138 Economic Final of the SPC.

[93]See supra para. 231.

[94]See (1995) No. 138 Economic Final of the SPC.

exclusive jurisdiction. Guangdong High Court is not a court of that place and it shall not exercise jurisdiction just because a representative organ or arrestable property of the defendant is located in Guangdong.[95]

262. The situation in this case might be a bit different from that in the case of *Bank of East Asia (Hong Kong)* because 'exclusive jurisdiction of a foreign court' was concerned here.[96] The exclusive jurisdiction ground mentioned in the SPC's ruling, however, was neither agreed by Chinese law domestically nor internationally.[97] It is hard to see why and how the possible exclusive jurisdiction of a 'foreign' court that could not be approved by local courts could have impact on local courts in declining their own jurisdiction.

263. Despite the fact that the Guangdong High Court and the SPC did not explicitly say they declined jurisdiction in the above two cases by the doctrine of *forum non conveniens*, it is submitted that in making the decision, the two Chinese courts had the doctrine in their minds.[98]

12.4.1.2 Some More Cases

264. In 1999, another two cases which had quite similar factual-pattern were litigated in Guangdong High Court and further appealed to the SPC for the application of the doctrine i.e. *Sumitomo Bank v. Xinhua Real Estate Ltd.*[99] and *Round-flow Company Ltd. v. Sun Chung Estate Company Ltd.*[100] Both of the two cases were concerned with a loan contract between two Hong Kong-based companies in which there were a non-exclusive jurisdiction clause conferring jurisdiction upon Hong Kong Court and a choice of law clause favoring Hong Kong Law. Moreover, in both of the two cases, there was a guarantor from the mainland China which was Guangdong Development Bank in the case of *Sumitomo Bank* and Jiangmen Branch of Guangdong Development Bank in the case of *Round-flow Company Ltd.* The only difference was that in the case of *Sumitomo Bank*, the mainland guarantor, Guangdong Development Bank issued a Standby Letter of Credit to the lender, the Sumitomo Bank for the borrower, Xinhua Real Estate Ltd. In both of the two cases, when there was a dispute arising out of the loan contract and the borrower sued the lender in the mainland China, the Guangdong High Court took up the case by the jurisdictional ground of 'defendant's arrestable

---

[95]Ibid.

[96]See supra para. 260.

[97]See supra paras. 233, 253. China has not agreed with an exclusive jurisdiction ground like that in any bilateral or multilateral treaty it has ratified. Cf. Article 22 (2) of Brussels I Regulation.

[98]See Shi and Teng (2003, pp. 60, 62).

[99]See (1999) No. 194 Economic Final of SPC.

[100]See (1999) No. 317 Economic Final of SPC.

property within the territory'[101] on the reasoning that the lender could be regarded as having arrestable property within the mainland China because the lender could realize their potential property rights and obtain their potential property in the mainland China from the mainland guarantor.[102] Furthermore, in both of the two cases, the lender challenged the jurisdiction of Guangdong High Court and appealed to the SPC, which overruled the decision of the Guangdong High Court.[103] In the case of *Sumitomo Bank*, when overturning the Guangdong High Court's verdict, the SPC said:

> Due to the reason that both of the parties are registered companies in Hong Kong, the disputed loan contract was signed and performed in Hong Kong and the parties have chosen Hong Kong law as the governing law for the contract, Hong Kong court is more appropriate to take jurisdiction and Guangdong High Court is an inappropriate court.[104]

265. This paragraph was echoed and largely repeated in the case of *Round-flow Company Ltd.* although the wording was slightly different.[105] However, the SPC did not say whether the Guangdong High Court was right on treating a legal person as having arrestable property in China if only it could possibly realize its potential property rights through a guarantor in China as shown in the two above cases. In other words, the SPC did not elaborate on whether the Guangdong High Court should have jurisdiction over the two cases at all in the first place. It seems that the SPC had implicitly agreed with the Guangdong High Court upon that point but overruled its decision just because it was not appropriate to try the case.[106]

266. The SPC took an interesting turn in the case of *Hong Kong Branch of Guohua Commercial Bank (Guohua) v. Shantou Hongye Corp. Ltd. (Hongye) & Shantou Special Economic Zone Xinye Development Corp. Ltd. (Xinye).*[107] In this case, both Hongye and Xinye signed an irrevocable guarantee contract with Guohua to provide guarantee for Grand Empire Holdings Ltd. (Grand Empire) which had a loan contract with Guohua, promising that they would jointly bear responsibilities for the loan. During the course of insolvency proceedings against Grand Empire in Hong Kong that was initiated by HSBC (Hong Kong) because of the Grand Empire's default, Guohua sued the two mainland guarantors in Guangdong High Court, asking them to pay back the money on loan and the incurred interests according to the guarantee contracts.[108] Probably having the two

[101] See Article 265 of CPL, supra para. 231.

[102] See (1999) No. 194 Economic Final of SPC; (1999) No. 317 Economic Final of SPC.

[103] Ibid.

[104] See (1999) No. 194 Economic Final of SPC.

[105] See (1999) No. 317 Economic Final of SPC.

[106] See Shi and Teng (2003, pp. 60, 62).

[107] See (2000) No. 177 Economic Final of the SPC.

[108] Ibid.

cases decided by the SPC in 1999 in its mind, the Guangdong High Court declined jurisdiction, saying:

> According to Article 20 of the guarantee contract between Guohua and Hongye and that between Guohua and Xinye which says 'Hong Kong law shall govern this guarantee contract and Hong Kong court shall have non-exclusive jurisdiction over any dispute arising out of this guarantee contract', this case shall be governed by Hong Kong law. Due to the reason that the main contract (loan contract) to which the guarantee contracts are subordinate was signed and performed in Hong Kong …… and Hongye, Xinye and Guahua all agreed with the non-exclusive jurisdiction of Hong Kong court. Therefore, Hong Kong court is more appropriate to exercise jurisdiction over the disputes regarding the guarantee contract between Guohua and Hongye and that between Guohua and Xinye in accordance with the parties' agreement and for the purpose of the convenience of litigation.[109]

267. Guohua, however, appealed to the SPC, arguing that this case should be tried in the Guangdong High Court because the Guangdong High Court was more appropriate to hear the case in terms of enforcement of the eventual judgment against the two mainland defendants. The SPC allowed the appeal and said:

> [According to the agreements of the parties], the governing law chosen by the parties is Hong Kong law and Hong Kong shall have non-exclusive jurisdiction over the case. It is clear that the jurisdiction of Hong Kong court is non-exclusive and cannot exclude jurisdiction of other courts. Therefore, if a party files the case with another court that has jurisdiction, that court can exercise jurisdiction according to law. Guangdong High Court is the court for the place where the two defendants are domiciled and should have jurisdiction over the case [according to Article 22 [now Article 21] of CPL] …… Hongye and Xinye are two mainland companies with properties located in the mainland, if the mainland court exercises jurisdiction, the trial proceedings and the judgment enforcement of the case will be more convenient.[110]

268. The SPC's decision in this case was followed by a lower court's case. In *Guo & Ye Partnership Legal Firm of Hong Kong (Guo & Ye) v. Huayang Color Printing Ltd. of Xiamen (Huayang)*, the defendant, Huayang engaged the plaintiff, Guo & Ye for legal service, whereby the defendant could be listed in the Hong Kong Exchange.[111] Afterwards Huayang failed to be listed and did not pay the legal service fees, as a result of which Guo & Ye sued Huayang in Hong Kong court on 29 June 2003 and again in the Intermediate Court of Xiamen, Fujian Province, China on 7 July 2003.[112] Although the defendant admitted jurisdiction of the Xiamen Intermediate Court, it argued that Xiamen Intermediate Court was the court of *forum non conveniens* and should decline jurisdiction because many crucial facts of the case had to be ascertained in Hong Kong, the case had big influence and attracted a lot of media attention in Hong Kong and the parties had chosen Hong Kong law as the governing law. In addition, the plaintiff had filed the

[109]Ibid.

[110]See (2000) No. 177 Economic Final of the SPC.

[111]See the Gazette of the SPC (2004), p. 397.

[112]Ibid.

same case with Hong Kong court already. Therefore, to the defendant, Xiamen Intermediate Court should refer the case to Hong Kong court which was the court of *forum conveniens*, or else there would be parallel proceedings.[113] On the other side, the plaintiff, Guo & Ye insisted that the case be kept in the Xiamen Intermediate Court because Xiamen Intermediate Court was the one for the place where the defendant was registered and domiciled and accordingly, it had legitimate jurisdiction over the case. To the plaintiff, the court of the defendant's domicile was the most convenient forum; if the case was to be tried in Hong Kong, the judgment would not be able to be executed because the defendant had no property in Hong Kong.[114] After hearing the arguments of the two parties, the Intermediate Court of Xiamen decided on 13 August 2003:

> This case is concerned with the issues of parallel proceedings and *forum non conveniens* that exist in international civil litigation …… it does not matter whether there is a *lis pendens* in Hong Kong and that cannot become a barrier for Chinese court to take up a case …… According to Article 24 [now Article 21] of CPL, Xiamen Intermediate Court shall have jurisdiction because the defendant is domiciled in Xiamen. Of course, Hong Kong court also has jurisdiction over this case because the concerned contract was performed in Hong Kong, the parties have chosen Hong Kong law as the governing law and Hong Kong court as the court having non-exclusive jurisdiction over the case …… If this case is heard in Hong Kong and there is a judgment rendered against Huayang, the parties will still have to re-litigate in the mainland because Huayang has no property in Hong Kong for execution [and Hong Kong's judgment cannot be executed in the mainland, either]. To avoid double proceedings and protect the interests of the parties timely and efficiently, Xiamen Intermediate Court is the most appropriate forum for this case and it cannot decline jurisdiction by the reason of *forum non conveniens*.[115]

269. One can see that as in the case of *Hong Kong Branch of Guohua Commercial Bank*, the defendant's domicile and the enforceability of the possible judgment became two determinative factors for Xiamen Intermediate Court to keep the case in its hands.[116] Moreover, this case might also be able to reflect some Chinese courts' attitude towards a foreign *lis pendens*.

270. Another interesting lower court case that should be noted here is *Pu Shanggen & Others v. Tian Linzhen & Yantai Hanya Lighting Corp. Ltd. (Hanya)* in which the eight plaintiffs and one of the defendants, Tian Linzhen were all from South Korea and the other defendant, Hanya was a company invested by Tian Linzhen, registered and domiciled in Yantai, Shandong Province, China.[117] The dispute between the plaintiffs and the defendants was originated from South Korea where the eight plaintiffs invested in a company which was run by the defendant, Tian Linzhen and unfortunately went bankrupt. The eight plaintiffs came to China and find Tian Linzhen, pressing him to repay the money invested back in South

[113]Ibid.

[114]Ibid.

[115]Ibid.

[116]See supra para. 267.

[117]See (2005) No. 23 Qing Fourth Civil Division of Qingdao Intermediate Court.

Korea, who unwillingly wrote a 'loan note' and a 'guarantee letter' in the name of the two defendants promising to pay back the money. Afterwards the defendants could not live up to their promise within the time, as a result of which the plaintiffs sued in the Intermediate Court of Qingdao, who took jurisdiction by saying:

> The defendant, Hanya is domiciled in Yantai, Shangdong Provinve ... this court has jurisdiction because it is the court for the place where the defendant is domiciled [and this court also has jurisdiction against Tian linzhen according to Article 22 [now Article 21] of CPL which says: 'If there is more than one defendant in a case and the defendants are domiciled in different territories, the court for the place where any defendant is domiciled can have jurisdiction against all defendants'].[118]

271. Although the two defendants argued that there was a *lis pendens* in South Korea and this case should be dismissed in China [by the doctrine of *forum non conveniens*], the Qingdao Intermediate Court said:

> Even if Korean court is hearing the same case, the jurisdiction of this court shall not be influenced unless the defendants can prove that Korean court has exclusive jurisdiction over the case. As to parallel proceedings between Chinese court and Korean court, there is no available solution provided in the bi-lateral treaty on judicial assistance between the two countries and neither in any other treaty on 'parallel proceedings' nor according to any kind of 'reciprocity'. Therefore, this court cannot agree with the defendant and shall continue to try and make a verdict on the case.[119]

272. In contrast with the case of *Guo & Ye*, the Qingdao Intermediate Court refused to decline the case solely because one of the defendants was domiciled in China.[120] Its attitude towards possible foreign exclusive jurisdiction mirrored that of the SPC reflected in the case examined earlier.[121] Moreover, the judgment of the Qingdao Intermediate Court once again demonstrated the firm stance of Chinese courts towards a foreign *lis pendens*.[122]

12.4.2 Systematization and Public Announcement of the Doctrine in the SPC's 2005 Notice

273. After about one decade's Chinese courts' practice of the doctrine, the SPC systematized and publicly announced the doctrine on 26 December 2005 in its 'Notice on the Dissemination of the Minutes of the Second Country-wide Trial-work

[118]Ibid.

[119]See (2005) No. 23 Qing Fourth Civil Division of Qingdao Intermediate Court.

[120]Cf. the situation in the cases of *Guo & Ye* and *Hong Kong Branch of Guohua Commercial Bank*, see supra paras. 266–268.

[121]See supra paras. 261–262.

[122]See supra paras. 267–268.

Conference for Foreign-related Commercial and Maritime Cases' (SPC's 2005 Notice or 2005 Notice).[123] Paragraph 11 of the SPC's 2005 Notice said:

> In dealing with a foreign-related commercial case, if a Chinese court finds it is not convenient to exercise jurisdiction, that court can dismiss the case by the doctrine of *forum non conveniens*. To apply the doctrine, the following conditions must be met:
>
> (1) the defendant requests the application of the doctrine or challenges the jurisdiction of Chinese court and the court filed with the case thinks the doctrine could possibly be applicable;
> (2) the Chinese court filed with the case has jurisdiction over the case;
> (3) the parties do not have an agreement conferring jurisdiction on Chinese court;
> (4) the case does not fall into exclusive jurisdiction of Chinese courts;
> (5) the case is not concerned with the interests of Chinese nationals, corporates or other organizations;
> (6) the main legal facts of the dispute do not happen within the Chinese territory and Chinese law is not the governing law for the case, and if the case is tried in China, there will be great difficulties in ascertaining the facts of the case and applying the governing law;
> (7) there is a foreign court that has jurisdiction over the case and is more convenient to try the case.[124]

274. Before going further, it is necessary to know the legal status of the SPC's 2005 Notice. According to the Preamble, this Notice and also Paragraph 11 on the doctrine in it must be implemented by lower courts, they therefore seemed legally binding.[125] It, however, has to be noted that the Notice was just a notice on disseminating the minutes of an important conference and according to the SPC itself, it did not belong to any kind of 'Interpretations of the SPC' which are legally binding in China.[126] Nevertheless, the Notice could not be disregarded by lower courts. The real situation was between the two ends and the Notice was 'persuasive, authoritative and guidance-providing'.[127]

275. Once the legal effect of the Notice and the relevant paragraph on the doctrine in it was known, one need explore whether there was anything new that had been provided by the Notice for the doctrine. As can be seen in the above cited paragraph, Points (1), (2) and (7) were common pre-requirements for the application of the doctrine.[128] Points (3), (4) commanded that Chinese courts could not

---

[123] See supra para. 259. Before this Notice, in 2004, the Fourth Division Court of the SPC actually publicized a document that said something about the doctrine, most contents of which were incorporated into the SPC's 2005 Notice, see 'Answers to the Practical Questions Arising out of Hearing Foreign-related Commercial and Maritime Cases'.

[124] See paragraph 11 of the SPC's 2005 Notice.

[125] See the Preamble of the SPC's 2005 Notice.

[126] See Articles 5 & 6 of Provisions of the Supreme People's Court on the Judicial Interpretation Work; supra paras. 7–10.

[127] See supra para. 9.

[128] These pre-requirements are also applicable to the British version of *forum non conveniens*, see Fawcett (2005, pp. 1, 11–16).

apply the doctrine to decline a case when they had exclusive jurisdiction over the case according to Chinese law or they had jurisdiction because of the parties' choice. While Point (5) emphasized the disconnection between the case and China, Point (6) touched the real convenience of hearing a case i.e. the convenience of ascertaining the facts of the case and application of the governing law. If one looks back at all the above examined cases in which the doctrine had been applied, it seems that all of them could have satisfied the seven conditions. However, although paragraph 11 of the SPC's 2005 Notice had publically acknowledged the doctrine and could provide some helpful guidance for the future, it could not cover all the details for the application of the doctrine, some of which had come to surface in the examined cases and some of which would possibly arise in the future cases. It is submitted that the right way to understand the Chinese version of the doctrine was to study the Paragraph and courts' cases especially those of the SPC together.

12.4.3 Cases After the SPC's 2005 Notice

12.4.3.1 One More Case in the SPC

276. In 2006, one more case on the doctrine reached the SPC. *Shenzhen Energy Investment Group (Shenzhen Energy Group) v. Zhu Lanting* is a case in which Zhu Lanting, a Hong Kong citizen sold the shares of a Hong Kong company in his hands to Shenzhen Energy International Investment Co. Ltd, Hong Kong (Shenzhen Energy Hong Kong) which was a subsidiary of Shenzhen Energy Group and registered in Hong Kong.[129] In their contract, Shenzhen Energy Hong Kong and Zhu Lanting agreed that the transaction should be governed by Hong Kong law and subject to the jurisdiction of Hong Kong court.[130] In 2005, Zhu Lanting, however, sued the parent company, Shenzhen Energy Group in Guangdong High Court to invalidate the transaction. The Guangdong High Court classified the case as a contractual dispute with one party i.e. Shenzhen Energy Group being a mainland company and thus took jurisdiction over the case because the defendant, Shenzhen Energy Group was domiciled in Guangdong. Shenzhen Energy Group challenged the jurisdiction of Guangdong High Court and appealed to the SPC, arguing that the case should be referred to Hong Kong court [by the doctrine of *forum non conveniens*] because both parties of the contract [Shenzhen Energy Hong Kong and Zhu Lanting] were from Hong Kong, the subject of the contract was the transfer of the shares of a Hong Kong company and the parties had agreed with jurisdiction of Hong Kong law and Hong Kong court. Although the SPC found that the transaction was actually made between Zhu Lanting and

[129]See (2006) No. 3 Civil Final of the Fourth Division of the SPC.

[130]Ibid.

Shenzhen Energy Group but through its subsidiary, Shenzhen Energy Hong Kong, whereby Shenzhen Energy Group could therefore be a qualified defendant, the SPC denied the contractual relationship between Zhu Lanting and Shenzhen Energy Group and upheld the jurisdiction of Guangdong High Court because the defendant, Shenzhen Energy Group was domiciled in Guangdong.[131] Regardless of the classification, this case, however, might have indicated that it would be difficult for a Chinese court to decline jurisdiction when its jurisdiction is based on the defendant's domicile within China even if the case does not have many other connections with China.[132]

12.4.3.2 Some Lower Court Cases

277. Since the SPC's 2005 Notice was distributed, lower courts have referred to it in making their decisions on the application of the doctrine of *forum non conveniens*. However, courts in different territories have decided cases differently even when the cases have the same or quite similar factual pattern.

278. Chae Jae Yeon v. Puguang Fiber Corp. Ltd. (Puguang Corp.) is a case in which the appellant, Chae Jae Yeon was a national of South Korea but invested a company in Qiandao, Shandong Province and the respondent, Puguang Corp. was a company registered and located in South Korea.[133] Back in their home country, South Korea, there was a dispute on a sales contract between Puguang Corp. and H. K International Ltd. which was actually run by Chae Jae Yeon. Due to the default of H. K International Ltd., Chae Jae Yeon was asked to pay instead and forced to have written a note in South Korea promising to honor the payment. Chae Jae Yeon, however, did not keep his promise, as a result of which Puguang Corp. sued him in the Qingdao Intermediate Court which took jurisdiction over the case because it thought Chae Jae Yeon invested a company in Qingdao and thus could be regarded as having arrestable property in China.[134] Chae Jae Yeon applied for the application of *forum non conveniens*, arguing that this case should be heard in South Korea because both of the parties were South Korean, main facts of the case had happened there and the governing law should be South Korean law.[135] His arguments, however, were not accepted by the Qingdao Intermediate Court which, after citing the whole Paragraph 11 of the SPC's 2005 Notice, said:

> The application of *forum non conveniens* is to make the hearing of a case more convenient … it should not be a tool for [the defendant] Chae Jae Yeon to evade the jurisdiction of a court that should have jurisdiction. In this case, Chae Jae Yeon habitually lives in

[131]Ibid.

[132]See supra para. 269.

[133]See (2009) No. 15 Lu Civil Fourth Division Final of Shandong High Court.

[134]See ibid; supra para. 231.

[135]See (2009) No. 15 Lu Civil Fourth Division Final of Shandong High Court.

> China and has invested a company in China. Therefore, if the case is heard in China, there is no great difficulty in 'ascertaining the facts of the case and applying the governing law'. Accordingly, there is no need to apply the doctrine of *forum non conveniens* at all in this case.[136]

279. Thereafter, Chae Jae Yeon appealed to the Shandong High Court which, after systematically re-examining the case, said:

> To take jurisdiction on the ground of Chae Jae Yeon [the defendant] having arrestable property in China is not improper in this case and the arguments on the applicability of *forum non conveniens* ...... cannot be supported.[137]

280. Conversely, in a few similar cases, the Jiangsu High Court has drawn a different conclusion. In the case of *Aiken Chemical Industry Corporation (Aiken Corp.) v. Yuyan Paint Corporation (Yuyan Corp.) & Neiao Special Steel Corporation (Neiao Corp.)*, all parties were South Korean companies.[138] They had a long-term business relationship in which Aiken Corp. supplied chemical materials to Yuyan Corp., the latter turned them into paints for the use of Neiao Corp. who would then write Yuyan Corp. a cheque that would be endorsed by Yuyan Corp. for the payment of Aiken Corp. In August 2007, Aiken Corp., however, was refused by the bank in South Korea to have the six cheques honored that had been written by Neiao Corp. and endorsed by Yuyan Corp. Due to this, Aiken Corp. launched litigation in the Suzhou Intermediate Court against Yuyan Corp. and Neiao Corp., both of which had investment in Suzhou, Jiangsu Province.[139] The Suzhou Intermediate Court took up the case because it thought 'According to Article 243 [now 265] of CPL, the court for the place where the arrestable property is located should have jurisdiction'.[140] It, however, declined jurisdiction after the challenging of Yuyan Corp. and Neiao Corp. by the doctrine of *forum non conveniens* and said:

> Although there is no explicit provision on *forum non conveniens* in Chinese law, Chinese judicial practice did not repel it. In this case, Suzhou Intermediate court does not have exclusive jurisdiction according to Chinese law and the parties did not have an agreement conferring jurisdiction on Chinese court ......; there is great difficulty in ascertaining the facts of the case and applying the governing law if the case is heard here ......; South Korean court has jurisdiction over this case and is more convenient to try the case ......; and no interests of Chinese nationals, corporations or other organizations are concerned and Chinese interests will not be damaged if the case is heard in South Korea. Therefore, according to the doctrine of *forum non conveniens*, this case shall be declined.[141]

[136]Ibid.

[137]See (2009) No. 15 Lu Civil Fourth Division Final of Shandong High Court.

[138]See (2010) No. 26 Su Commercial Foreign Final of the Jiangsu High Court.

[139]Ibid.

[140]See supra para. 231.

[141]See (2010) No. 26 Su Commercial Foreign Final of the Jiangsu High Court.

281. Unhappy with the verdict of the first instance court, Aiken Corp. appealed to the Jiangsu High Court. After citing the whole Paragraph 11 of the SPC's 2005 Notice, the Jiangsu High Court echoed the reasoning of the Suzhou Intermediate Court and concluded:

> In this case, although [the two defendants] Yuyan Corp. and Neiao Corp. have arrestable property in Suzhou, according to which the Suzhou Intermediate Court should have jurisdiction over the case, the doctrine of *forum non conveniens* can be applied to decline the case.[142]

282. In another two cases that had the same factual pattern as this case, the Suzhou Intermediate Court and Jiangsu High Court made the same decisions and sent away the cases by the doctrine of *forum non conveniens*.[143]

283. The different approaches adopted in the Shandong High Court and Jiangsu High Court demonstrated that further details had to be spelled out by the SPC for the uniform application of the doctrine although general guidelines had been provided by the SPC's 2005 Notice. While the case of *Chae Jae Yeon* had indicated that some Chinese courts would not give up their own international jurisdiction easily, Jiangsu High Court was one of those who could be more liberal in applying the doctrine of *forum non conveniens*. Given the far disconnection between a case and China, it might be better for a Chinese court not to hear the case as the Jiangsu High Court had confirmed.

12.4.4 Analysis and Synthesis

12.4.4.1 The Nature of the Chinese Version

284. As shown above, the Chinese international jurisdiction regime closely follows the model of civil law tradition. Unlike the situation in many common law countries where the jurisdiction system is usually open and consists of broad, general, even 'crude' principles,[144] the Chinese regime is, generally speaking, a coherent and closed system in which a series of refined and predetermined jurisdiction rules are laid down which are supposedly able to cover all the situations in real life and always point to the courts of *forum conveniens* for real cases.[145] The broad discretion that common law judges need to modify and fine-tune those wide, general or crude jurisdiction rules is, therefore, regarded as being unnecessary in a civil law

---

[142]See (2010) No. 26 Su Commercial Foreign Final of the Jiangsu High Court.

[143]See *Seoul Industry Corporation v. Yuyan Paint Corporation & Neiao Special Steel Corporation* (2010) No. 27 Su Commercial Foreign Final of the Jiangsu High Court; *Dahao Chemical Industry Corporation v. Yuyan Paint Corporation & Neiao Special Steel Corporation* (2010) No. 53 Su Commercial Foreign Final of the Jiangsu High Court.

[144]See Fawcett (2005, pp. 1, 19–21). For the typical example of the traditional jurisdiction system in England, see Cheshire et al. (2008, pp. 353–424).

[145]See Tu (2009, pp. 114–118).

country such as China.[146] This may explain why there is no statutory conferment of a general discretionary power upon Chinese judges for jurisdictional matters.[147] The rejection of a general discretion for jurisdictional matters also conforms to the composition of judiciary in China. In contrast with common law judges, Chinese judges are selected 'graduates' rather than experienced lawyers.[148] They are merely like civil servants who are constrained by the rules given by the legislature and have to strictly and faithfully follow those pre-designed rules.[149] They have not and cannot be entrusted with much discretion for the purpose of legal certainty.[150] A doctrine of *forum non conveniens* like the British or American version which gives judges broad discretionary power, thus, cannot and should not be adopted in China.[151]

285. The reality, however, has another side that on the one hand not every jurisdiction rule in the Chinese system is properly-and well-designed such as some of the rules in Article 265 of CPL[152]; on the other hand, a so-called generally-well-crafted jurisdiction rule even like that based on the domicile of the defendant could produce a very distasteful result in a particular case.[153] An absolute rejection of discretion is, therefore, not realistic and desirable. As a matter of fact, the Chinese judicial practice had called for the introduction of some discretion to dealing with international jurisdictional matters. In response to the needs of judicial practice, the SPC sensibly accepted and publicized the Chinese doctrine of *forum non conveniens*. The above text demonstrates how the Chinese doctrine has been applied by Chinese courts to relax the excessive rigidity of Chinese jurisdiction rules and decline undue Chinese court's jurisdiction in the circumstances.

286. Nevertheless, unlike the British doctrine the application of which is to compare the different alternative *fora* and search for the natural forum for each individual case in the name of serving 'the interests of all the parties and the ends of justice',[154] the employment of the Chinese doctrine is to send away those cases far disconnected with China and spare Chinese judicial resources with the simultaneous intention of protecting private interests of the parties. The stringent Chinese attitude towards declining jurisdiction by the doctrine was confirmed by paragraph 11 of the SPC's 2005 Notice.[155] Indeed, the cases examined in the above text indi-

---

[146] Ibid.

[147] See supra paras. 257–258.

[148] See supra paras. 16–18; Tetley (2000, pp. 677, 705).

[149] See Kerameus (1987, pp. 493, 494).

[150] See Fawcett (2005, pp. 1, 23).

[151] For the British version, see Beaumont (2005, p. 207); for the American version, see Del Duca and Zaphiriou (2005, p. 401).

[152] See supra para. 231.

[153] E.g., see supra para. 268. Also See Beaumont (1998, pp. 75, 76).

[154] See *Spiliada Maritime Corp. v. Cansulex Ltd.* [1987] AC 460, 476; Briggs (1987, p. 1).

[155] See supra para. 273.

cate that this doctrine has been applied in China only in the situation where an exorbitant jurisdiction arising out of Article 265 of CPL was concerned and when the case had very little connection with China.[156]

287. It, therefore, can be concluded that the Chinese version of *forum non conveniens* is a doctrine that gives quite limited discretion to Chinese judges and Chinese judges can decline a case by the doctrine only when the local forum is clearly inappropriate (inconvenient).[157] One could even say, strictly speaking, the Chinese version is not a real doctrine of *forum non conveniens* [like the British one] but only a *forum non conveniens* substitute although Chinese lawyers have habitually used the same term.[158]

12.4.4.2 The Application of the Chinese Version

288. Having made clear the nature of the Chinese version, it is necessary to further reflect upon the application of the Chinese doctrine. Apart from the common prerequisites that the seized Chinese court must have jurisdiction over the case, the defendant must have put forward the motion and there must be an alternative forum,[159] it is said that once a case is declined by the doctrine in China, it has been dismissed rather than stayed (suspended).[160] Furthermore, the practice of attaching conditions on declining jurisdiction by the doctrine has not been developed in China so far.[161] None the less, some factors have been identified for the application of the doctrine which will be examined in more detail now.

Exclusive Jurisdiction

289. The reason why a country claims exclusive jurisdiction over some cases is often that the country wants to preserve its own jurisdiction in those cases so that it can ensure 'special' interests of its own or its citizens to be protected.[162] The area where exclusive jurisdiction can be reasonably claimed is usually

[156]E.g. see supra para. 260.

[157]Cf. the situations in other civil law countries, see Fawcett (2005, pp. 1, 24–27).

[158]Ibid.

[159]See supra para. 273.

[160]This can be seen from the beginning sentence of paragraph 11 of the SPC's 2005 Notice in which the word 'dismiss' is used, see supra para. 273. Scholars have the same opinion, see Xi (2002, pp. 81, 92). Cf. the situation in the UK, see Beaumont (2005, pp. 207, 209–212).

[161]See Xi, ibid. Cf. the situation in the US, see *In re Union Carbide Corp Gas Plant Disaster at Bhopal, India in Dec, 1984*, 634 F Supp 842 (SDNY 1986); 809 F2d 195 (2d Cir 1987); Bies (2000, p. 489).

[162]See Xi (2002, pp. 81, 88–89).

sovereignty-sensitive or concerning strong national interests.[163] In China, it is thought that giving up exclusive jurisdiction means going against the public interests and unduly giving up judicial sovereignty.[164] Thus, when a Chinese court has exclusive jurisdiction over a case, it is not allowed to apply the doctrine to decline its jurisdiction whatever other elements the case may have, according to Point (4) of paragraph 11 of the SPC's 2005 Notice.[165] Accordingly, when the jurisdictional ground is based on Articles 33 and 266 of CPL, it is not possible for a Chinese court to apply the doctrine and dismiss the case.[166] Indeed, one has not found and cannot find such a case in Chinese judicial practice.

290. Nevertheless, how about the situation where a Chinese court has jurisdiction over a case which is not exclusive according to Chinese law but a foreign court can claim exclusive jurisdiction over the same case according to its own law or even Chinese law? Will a Chinese court decline the case by the doctrine under this situation? Paragraph 11 of the SPC's 2005 Notice does not give us an answer for the questions. However, the cases of *Yongqiao & Zhongqiao* and *Pu Shanggen & Others* seemed to have indicated that Chinese courts can show respect and are willing to refer the case to the concerned foreign court in such a situation.[167] In addition, if there is a case in which both a Chinese court and a foreign court can claim exclusive jurisdiction according to its own law respectively, it is predictable that the Chinese court will not apply the doctrine to dismiss the case although no case is reported for this yet.

Choice of Court Agreement

291. According to Point (3) of paragraph 11 of the SPC's 2005 Notice, if there is an agreement between the parties conferring jurisdiction upon a Chinese court, that Chinese court cannot apply the doctrine to decline its jurisdiction.[168] A Chinese court, therefore, cannot apply the doctrine when it has jurisdiction owing to Article 34 of CPL.[169]

292. There are, however, two kinds of choice of court agreements in international business transactions i.e. exclusive and non-exclusive.[170] Article 34 of CPL and paragraph 11 of the SPC's 2005 Notice do not make a distinction between

[163]Ibid; Article 22 of the Brussels I Regulation.

[164]See Xi (2002, pp. 81, 89).

[165]See supra para. 273.

[166]See supra paras. 233, 253.

[167]See supra paras. 261–262, 270–271.

[168]See supra para. 273.

[169]See supra para. 255.

[170]See Fawcett (2001, pp. 234, 234–235) and Peel (1998, pp. 182, 182–183).

them. It is safe to say that a Chinese court will definitely not apply the doctrine to decline a case if the parties have made an exclusive choice of that Chinese court. Deducing along the line of Article 34 of CPL and paragraph 11 of the SPC's 2005 Notice, it might also be safe to say that a Chinese court will not apply the doctrine to decline a case, either when the parties have made a non-exclusive choice of that Chinese court although there has been no case endorsing this stance so far.[171]

293. Turning to the opposite direction, Chinese judicial practice has indicated that a Chinese court will apply the doctrine to decline its own jurisdiction if the parties have made an exclusive choice of court agreement pointing to a foreign court.[172] The case of *Hong Kong Branch of Guohua Commercial Bank*, however, has demonstrated that a Chinese court can still take jurisdiction and keep the case in its hands even if there is a non-exclusive choice of court agreement designating a foreign court.[173]

Parallel Proceedings

294. It is widely agreed that to avoid the risk of conflicting judgments, the more liberal the rules on recognition and enforcement of foreign judgments in a country are, the more urgent the need to effectively resolve the problem of parallel proceedings in that country is or vice versa.[174] China has rigorous rules on recognition and enforcement of foreign judgments in that it does not recognize and enforce a foreign judgment at all unless there is a treaty obligation or 'reciprocity' in practice between China and the concerned foreign state.[175] Consequently, China basically has quite stark a rule on parallel proceedings arising out of international litigation i.e. a Chinese court can still exercise jurisdiction over a case even if the

[171]Cf. the situations in other countries, see Fawcett (2005, pp. 1, 57–58).

[172]E.g. see *Standard Chartered Bank (Suzhou) v. Yu Chuntai & Changshu Xingyu Xinxing Construction Materials Ltd.* (2010) No. 52 Su Foreign Commercial Final of Jiangsu High Court; *also see* paragraph 8 of the SPC's 2005 Notice which says '……if the parties have made an arbitration agreement or an exclusive choice of foreign court agreement, Chinese court shall not exercise jurisdiction'.

[173]See supra paras. 266–267; also see paragraph 12 of the SPC's 2005 Notice which says 'If the parties of a foreign-related commercial dispute have made a non-exclusive choice of court agreement, it can be inferred that this agreement does not preclude the jurisdiction of other courts which may have jurisdiction according to the laws. Therefore, if one party files the case with a Chinese court, that Chinese court can exercise jurisdiction and take up the case if only it has jurisdiction according to the relevant provision of CPL'. Cf. the situations in other countries, see Fawcett (2005, pp. 1, 47–51).

[174]See Fawcett (2005, pp. 1, 27–28).

[175]See Articles 281 & 282 of CPL.

same case is being filed with a foreign court; and a foreign *lis pendens* does not have much influence on a Chinese court.[176]

295. This indifferent Chinese attitude towards a foreign *lis pendens* has been seen in the cases examined above.[177] Thus, in applying the doctrine, a foreign *lis pendens* cannot be given 'considerable weight' in China as in many other countries.[178]

296. It is, however, still interesting to see if China would adopt a different approach on a foreign *lis pendens* in the situation where a court of a foreign country is earlier seized and China has concluded a treaty with that foreign country on recognition and enforcement of judgments according to which the judgment to be rendered by the earlier-seized foreign court could be recognized and enforced by China.[179] In contrast with paragraph 306 of the SPC's 1992 Interpretation (now Article 533 of the 2015 Interpretation on CPL), the added wording in paragraph 10 of the SPC's 2005 Notice is worth citing here, which reads:

> [When there are parallel proceedings in a Chinese court and a foreign court], the Chinese court, however, has some discretion to decide whether to exercise its own jurisdiction according to the circumstances of the case...[180]

297. It is submitted that under the situation described above, the wording in paragraph 10 of the SPC's 2005 Notice could sensibly provide a Chinese court leeway to give weight to a foreign *lis pendens* and apply the doctrine to decline its own jurisdiction.

The Applicable Law

298. The factor of the applicable law is often seen as a significant one in the application of *forum non conveniens*.[181] If *lex fori* is the applicable law, the trying court could be exempted from the burden of identifying and applying a usually

---

[176]See Article 533 of the 2015 Interpretation on CPL which says, 'When both a Chinese court and a foreign court have jurisdiction over the same case, if one party is launching the litigation in the foreign court and the other party in the Chinese court, the Chinese court can exercise jurisdiction and take up the case...'; also see paragraph 10 of the SPC's 2005 Notice which says 'In a case where both a Chinese court and a foreign court have jurisdiction, if one party is suing in the foreign court and sues again for the same case in the Chinese court or the other party sues again for the same case in the Chinese court, the jurisdiction of the Chinese court shall not be influenced whether or not the foreign court has already taken up or made a judgment on the same case. The Chinese court, however, has some discretion to decide whether to exercise its own jurisdiction according to the circumstances of the case ...'.

[177]See supra paras. 267, 271.

[178]See Fawcett (2005, pp. 1, 29) and Beaumont (2005, pp. 207, 214–217).

[179]See Fawcett (2005, pp. 1, 36–38). So far China has concluded more than 20 bilateral treaties with different foreign countries on recognition and enforcement of judgments in civil and commercial matters, see infra para. 345.

[180]See supra para. 294.

[181]See Beaumont (2005, pp. 207, 212–214).

unfamiliar foreign law that could otherwise be applicable. When local law is the applicable substantive law for the case, it would, thus, be more difficult for the local court to say it is a forum of *non conveniens* in terms of the expense of proceedings and the accuracy of judgment.[182] Conversely, it would be natural for a local forum to more intend to decline the case for the purpose of avoiding the difficulties respecting an applicable foreign law.

299. To apply the Chinese doctrine, particular attention has been drawn to this factor by Point (6) of paragraph 11 of the SPC's 2005 Notice.[183] This factor has also been underlined in some cases examined earlier.[184] Important as this factor is, it is not dispositive for the application of the Chinese doctrine. It can, however, be predicted that a Chinese court will not easily apply the doctrine to decline a case if Chinese law is the substantive applicable law for the case.

The Identity of the Parties

300. Whereas the factor of the plaintiff's origin did not attract much attention and has not particularly been given some weight in the application of the Chinese doctrine,[185] the defendant's Chinese domicile has been a crucial factor for Chinese courts to dis-apply the doctrine in a series of cases even though those cases do not have many other connections with China.[186] Foreseeably, it would be quite difficult for a Chinese court to apply the doctrine to decline a case if only the defendant in the case is domiciled in China.[187]

301. Historically, China has been very sensitive to judicial sovereignty.[188] In private international law cases, it intended to exercise international jurisdiction as much as possible so that it would not lose any of its 'celebrated' sovereignty.[189] With the British wind of *forum non conveniens* blowing to Hong Kong,[190] China, however, began to apply its own version of *forum non conveniens* to decline international jurisdiction in 1990s at the request of Hong Kong litigants whose

[182] See Tu (2009, p. 154).

[183] See supra para. 273.

[184] E.g. see supra paras. 266–267.

[185] Cf. the situation in the US where in the application of the doctrine of *forum non conveniens*, an American's choice of home forum in the US deserves more deference than a foreign plaintiff's choice of an American forum, see *Piper v. Reyno* 454 US 235, 256 (1981).

[186] See supra paras. 268, 276.

[187] Ibid. Cf. the situation in the UK, see *Harrods (Buenos Aires) Ltd., Re* (1991) 3 WLR 397 (CA).

[188] See Xi (2002, pp. 81, 84–85).

[189] Ibid.

[190] See *The Adhiguna Meranti* [1998] 1 Lloyd's Rep. 384 (Hong Kong CA).

domestic law's introduction of the British doctrine prompted their arguments for the application of the doctrine in Chinese *fora*. Against the background of negotiating a global jurisdiction and judgments convention at The Hague during which *forum non conveniens* became a topical issue,[191] Chinese lawyers further debated seriously on whether such a doctrine could and should formally be adopted in China.[192]

302. Although legislation did not authorize this doctrine, judicial practice and the academia pressed for its birth. Eventually, this doctrine has now been incorporated into the latest 2015 Interpretation on CPL.[193] The acceptance of this doctrine in China is surely a positive step and to be welcomed because it can spare Chinese judicial resources by sending away those far disconnected cases, serve the parties' interests for their convenience of litigation and benefit international litigation order through coordinating adjudicatory activities between Chinese courts and those concerned foreign courts. However, a systematic exploration of the Chinese doctrine demonstrates that it is only a limited version, compared with the British and American one. It could even just be called a *forum non conveniens* substitute but not a real one. Nevertheless, it conforms to the legal tradition and judicial reality in China. Despite the SPC's 2005 Notice (now 2015 Interpretation on CPL) has systematized the doctrine and court cases have identified some factors for the application of the doctrine over the years, more details are to be worked out. Looking to the future, it is submitted that the nature of the Chinese doctrine must be emphasized and the application of the doctrine streamlined with judges being given room to put more flesh on the bone.

[191] See Tu (2009, pp. 8–9).

[192] See Hu (2002, pp. 138, 153).

[193] The doctrine was proposed in Article 51 of the Model Law of Chinese Private International Law that was drafted by the Chinese academia; this model law is on file with the author. See Article 532 of the 2015 Interpretation on CPL that, with very slight changes, essentially and substantively copied paragraph 11 of the SPC's 2005 Notice, which is why the discussion in this part is still mainly based on the latter.

Chapter 13
Service of Documents

303. A foreign-related case in a Chinese court does not necessarily entail international service of documents. According to Chinese law, if a person to be served is domiciled in China, domestic approaches of service can generally be employed.[1] However, even if it is a case in which the person to be served has no domicile within the territory of China, service of documents still can possibly be completed purely within the territory of China. Of course, there are foreign-related cases where service of documents abroad is unavoidable and necessary.

13.1 Cases Where Service of Process Abroad Is Unnecessary

304. First, service of process on a natural person or a corporate or an organization that is not domiciled within China can be effected by serving that natural person or a legal representative or a person mainly in charge of the concerned corporate or organization when that natural person or legal representative or person mainly in charge is in the territory of China.[2] Secondly, service of documents on a non-domiciliary of China can also be effected by serving the Chinese attorney of the person to be served unless it has been expressly declared by the person to be served that his/its legal attorney has no power to accept the served documents on his/its behalf.[3] Moreover, a Chinese court can serve the documents with a foreign corporate or organization through its representative office in China.[4] In addition, upon

[1]See Articles 84–92 of Chinese CPL.

[2]See Article 3 of 2006 Interpretation on Service of Documents; Article 535 of 2015 Interpretation on CPL.

[3]See Article 267 (4) of CPL and Article 4 of 2006 Interpretation on Service of Documents.

[4]See Article 267 (5) of CPL and Article 5 of 2006 Interpretation on Service of Documents.

G. Tu, *Private International Law in China*, DOI 10.1007/978-981-287-993-6_13

the authorization of the foreign person to be served, a Chinese court can serve documents through its branch office or agent in China.[5]

13.2 Cases Where Service of Process Abroad Is Unavoidable

305. If service of documents in a foreign-related case cannot be completed by the above means, service of documents abroad becomes necessary and unavoidable, for which Chinese law has provided alternatives for various situations.

13.2.1 Service of Documents in the Absence of Specific International Treaties

13.2.1.1 Service via Diplomatic Channel

306. In the absence of international treaties specifically signed for service, documents can be transmitted through diplomatic channels based on the principle of reciprocity.[6] In China, the concerned high court at provincial level shall review the request for transmission submitted by courts at city/prefecture level (intermediate courts) and courts at county (district) level within its territory. The concerned high court, if it thinks necessary, will forward the documents to the Ministry of Foreign Affairs which can further seek foreign judicial assistance.[7] If a person to be served abroad is a Chinese national, service of process may be entrusted to the Chinese embassy or consulate stationed in the State of Destination which can directly serve the Chinese national provided no objection from the domestic law of the State of destination.[8]

13.2.1.2 Service via Postal Channel

307. Although direct service of documents by a foreign court through post upon a person in the territory of China is generally not permitted in Chinese law, Chinese courts may serve a person abroad by post if the country of destination does not

---

[5]Ibid.

[6]See Article 267 (2) of CPL. Also see Notice on Certain Matters Relating to the Service of Legal Documents through Diplomatic Channels between the People's Courts and Foreign Courts, which was jointly issued by the Supreme People's Court, the Ministry of Foreign Affairs and the Ministry of Justice on August 14, 1986 (hereinafter, 1986 Notice on Service).

[7]See para. 4 of 1986 Notice on Service.

[8]See Article 267 (3) of CPL. Also see para. 5 of 1986 Notice on Service.

have any objection to this method.[9] Even if the receipt of service is not returned but based on the whole circumstances of the case it is sufficient to conclude that service has been effected, service of process can be deemed as successfully completed after a lapse of three months starting on the date of post.[10]

308. Service of documents by electronic means has been practiced long in some developed countries.[11] According to Chinese Law, documents can also be served upon a person abroad by fax, e-mail, or any other appropriate means provided that the receipt of service can be secured.[12] If a person served by electronic means responds positively, one can have a due receipt for the service and there is no problem. However, If he does not respond, there will be ambiguity on the applicability of service by electronic means including email, fax and social networking tools for it is technically difficult to confirm whether the addressee has actually received the document or not. Future technology may resolve this problem and if so, service by electronic means would certainly be broadly employed.

13.2.1.3 Service by Publication

309. The application of service by publication is severely restricted in both civil law states and common law states to ensure that the defendant's procedural rights are fully protected. Generally speaking, documents will only be served by publication if the address of the defendant cannot be found or ascertainable after diligent search. According to Chinese law, service by publication will be resorted to only when the defendant's address is unknown and all the other possible means have been exhausted but failed to have the defendant duly served.[13] When serving by publication, the content of service shall be published in social media such as internet and newspapers widely circulated both in China and abroad.[14] Service can be deemed as successfully completed after three months starting on the date of publication.[15]

---

[9]See Article 267 (6) of CPL. Also see Article 8 of 2006 Interpretation on Service of Documents; Article 536 of 2015 Interpretation on CPL.

[10]Ibid.

[11]See Conley (1997, pp. 407, 408–410); Legal papers served via Facebook' (BBC News, 16 Dec 2008), http://news.bbc.co.uk/2/hi/asia-pacific/7785004.stm (last visited August 09, 2015).

[12]See Article 267 (7) of Chinese CPL; Article 10 of 2006 Interpretation on Service of Documents.

[13]See Articles 92 and 267 of CPL. It, however, has to be admitted that in practice, some Chinese courts have misapplied or even abused service by publication and made default judgments without serious considerations, in which case the defendants' rights are severely infringed and the reputation of Chinese courts are at stake, generally see Zhao (2009, pp. 57–59).

[14]See Article 138 of 2015 Interpretation on CPL.

[15]See Article 267 (8) of CPL; Articles 534 & 537 of 2015 Interpretation on CPL.

13.2.2 *Service of Documents Under International Treaties*

310. As mentioned above, China has concluded bilateral treaties on judicial assistance including service of documents with more than 30 countries and also been a member of the Hague Service Convention since 1991.[16] Therefore, if the person to be served is in a foreign country which has concluded a bilateral treaty with China or is a Member State of the Hague Service Convention, service of documents can be conducted according to such a treaty or the Hague Service Convention.[17] In the case where a country has concluded a bilateral treaty with China and in the meantime, is also a Member State of the Hague Service Convention, the bilateral treaty generally shall prevail.[18] Nevertheless, it is worth noting that provisions in most bilateral treaties are consistent with China's attitude towards the Hague Service Convention.[19]

13.2.2.1 Service of Documents Under Bilateral Treaties

311. Up to now, there is no bilateral treaty specifically addressing service of documents only signed by China. As a matter of fact, provisions regarding service of documents are often included in treaties on mutual judicial assistance, together with other matters such as taking of evidence, recognition and enforcement of foreign judgments and arbitral awards.[20]

312. The main channel of transmitting judicial documents provided under the bilateral treaties is via the Central Authorities of the two Contracting States. The Central Authority, normally the Ministry of Justice or the Supreme Court, is specified in the agreement at the time of conclusion[21] or confirmed later by the con-

[16]See supra para. 47.

[17]See Article 267 (1) of Chinese CPL; Article 6 of 2006 Interpretation on Service of Documents.

[18]See Article 6 of the 2006 Interpretation on Service of Documents, which corresponds to Article 11 of the Hague Service Convention that says: 'The present Convention shall not prevent two or more Contracting States from agreeing to permit, for the purpose of service of judicial documents, channels of transmission other than those provided for in the preceding Articles and, in particular, direct communication between their respective authorities'.

[19]It will be seen immediately that as under the Hague Service Convention, most such bilateral treaties provide transmission of documents through the Central Authority and permit service of documents via Consular Channel. See infra paras. 311–313.

[20]See supra para. 223.

[21]E.g., see Article 3 of Treaty on Civil and Criminal Judicial Assistance between the People's Republic of China and the Mongolia People's Republic; Article 3 of Treaty on Civil and Commercial Judicial Assistance between the People's Republic of China and the Kingdom of Spain; and Article 8 of Treaty on Civil Judicial Assistance between the People's Republic of China and Republic of Italy.

tracting parties through diplomatic channel.[22] Where judicial assistance from the other party of the treaty is necessary, the Central Authority of the requesting state shall transmit the relevant documents to the Central Authority of the requested state, the latter shall serve the documents according to its domestic law upon the addressee as required under the treaty.[23] Upon the effecting of service, the Requested State shall forward the proof of service to the Central Authority of the Requesting State, which includes the description of the date, place and manner of service and is affixed with the signature or seal of the authority that has served the documents.[24] The Requested State may refuse to provide judicial assistance if such assistance would violate the state sovereignty, security, social order, public interest or basic rules in its domestic legal system.[25] If service cannot be duly conducted, the Requested State shall also inform the Requesting State of the failure of service and advise the reasons for the failure.[26]

313. In addition, service normally can also be conducted through consular channels by the diplomatic or consular officials of the Requesting State stationed in the Requested State,[27] in which case the documents shall only be served upon a national of the Requesting State without any compulsion measures taken or any infringement on the local law of the Requested State.[28]

13.2.2.2 Service of Documents Under the Hague Service Convention

314. Based on the explanatory document for the convention prepared by the Permanent Bureau of the Hague Conference on Private International Law

---

[22]E.g., see Article 3 of Treaty on Civil and Commercial Judicial Assistance between the People's Republic of China and the French Republic, and Article 6 of Treaty on Civil and Criminal Judicial Assistance between the People's Republic of China and the Republic of Poland.

[23]Ibid.

[24]E.g. see Article 9 of Treaty on Civil and Commercial Judicial Assistance between the People's Republic of China and the French Republic; Article 12 of Treaty on Civil Judicial Assistance between the People's Republic of China and Republic of Italy; and Article 15 of Treaty on Civil and Criminal Judicial Assistance between the People's Republic of China and the Mongolia People's Republic.

[25]E.g. see Article 11 of Treaty on Civil and Commercial Judicial Assistance between the People's Republic of China and the French Republic; Article 19 of Treaty on Civil Judicial Assistance between the People's Republic of China and Republic of Italy; Article 5 of Treaty on Civil and Commercial Judicial Assistance between the People's Republic of China and the Kingdom of Spain.

[26]E.g. see Articles 9, 11 of Treaty on Civil and Commercial Judicial Assistance between the People's Republic of China and the French Republic; and Articles 14, 15 of Treaty on Civil and Criminal Judicial Assistance between the People's Republic of China and the Republic of Poland.

[27]E.g. see Article 7 of Treaty on Civil and Commercial Judicial Assistance between the People's Republic of China and the French Republic; Article 7 of Treaty on Civil and Commercial Judicial Assistance between the People's Republic of China and the Kingdom of Spain; and Article 13 of Treaty on Civil Judicial Assistance between the People's Republic of China and Republic of Italy.

[28]Ibid.

(HCCH), the Hague Service Convention only applies in circumstances where the address of the person to be served is known.[29] In addition, the Hague Service Convention is non-mandatory but exclusive in nature, which means in civil or commercial matters, where a document must be transmitted for service abroad, it shall only be transmitted via the channels stipulated or permitted by the Hague Service Convention among the Member States, even if relevant domestic legislations may have provided other means of service of documents abroad.[30]

1. Main Channel of Transmission

315. The main channel of transmitting documents between the Contracting States under the Hague Service Convention is through the Central Authorities,[31] which means the competent authority of the State where the documents originate (hereinafter, State of Origin) shall forward request for serving documents to the Central Authority of the State where the documents are to be served (hereinafter, State of Destination), thereafter the State of Destination shall arrange service of documents accordingly.[32] In China, the Ministry of Justice is designated as the Central Authority and also the main authority competent to forward the request i.e. Forwarding Authority. In addition, the Supreme People's Court and five high courts at provincial level respectively located in Beijing, Shanghai, Jiangsu, Zhejiang and Guangdong can also directly forward request for service of documents to the Central Authority of other Contracting States.[33]

2. Alternative Channels of Transmission

316. According to the Convention, service of documents may be conducted by the direct diplomatic or consular channel although a Contracting State can make a reservation for the channel.[34] Indeed, China has declared that documents can only be served by diplomatic or consular agents of another Contracting State upon a national of that state within the territory of China.[35] Based on the Convention,

---

[29]See paras. 79 and 80 of *Practical Handbook on the Operation of the Hague Service Convention*, HCCH Publications, 2006, (hereinafter, Practical Handbook).

[30]See paras. 26–45 of Practical Handbook.

[31]See Articles 2–6 of Hague Service Convention. Also see para. 82 of Practical Handbook.

[32]See Articles 3, 5 of Hague Service Convention.

[33]See the table indicating the Central Authority and Forwarding Authorities in China for the purpose of the Hague Service Convention, which can be found at the website of HCCH for Service Section.

[34]See Article 8 of the Hague Service Convention, which says: 'Each Contracting State shall be free to effect service of judicial documents upon persons abroad, without application of any compulsion, directly through its diplomatic or consular agents. Any State may declare that it is opposed to such service within its territory, unless the document is to be served upon a national of the State in which the documents originate'.

[35]See Declarations made by China to the Hague Service Convention, which can be found at the website of HCCH for Service Section.

documents may also be transmitted through indirect diplomatic channel,[36] under which the Supreme People's Court can transmit the relevant documents to the Chinese embassy stationed in the State of Destination, the latter can then forward the documents to the Central Authority of that state.[37] There are three other alternative channels of transmission stipulated in Article 10 of Hague Service Convention, i.e. direct service of documents through postal channel; direct service of documents by judicial officers, officials or other competent persons of the State of Origin through the judicial officers, officials or other competent persons of the State of Destination; and direct service of documents by any person interested in a judicial proceeding through the judicial officers, officials or other competent persons of the State of Destination.[38] Though China has made reservation for service of documents via these channels within the territory of China, the reservation does not prohibit Chinese courts from serving documents through these channels upon persons in the territory of other Member States.[39] This is especially true in the case of service of documents via the postal channel, where Member States accepting service by postal channels do not necessarily assert 'reciprocity' against other Member States that have made reservation.[40] However, it has been proven in practice that transmission channels under Article 10 are not deemed by Chinese authorities as applicable when serving documents to other Member States of the Hague Service Convention.[41] Nonetheless, it's worth noting that since China did not expressly give up the freedom to directly serve judicial documents by these channels abroad, it is entirely possible that China would serve documents abroad via such means in future.[42]

3. Derogatory Channels of Transmission

317. Still, documents can be transmitted through the derogatory channels which are not defined and yet permissible by the Hague Service Convention. Contracting States of the Convention may agree upon methods of transmission other than those

---

[36]See Article 9 of the Hague Service Convention. Also see Articles 8, 9 of Measures for Implementation with Regards to Enforcement of the Hague Service Convention jointly issued by the SPC, Ministry of Justice and Ministry of Foreign Affairs on September 19, 1992 (hereinafter, 1992 Measures Implementing the Hague Service Convention).

[37]See Article 9 of 1992 Measures Implementing the Hague Service Convention.

[38]See Article 10 of Hague Service Convention.

[39]See Declarations made by China to the Hague Service Convention, which can be found at the website of HCCH for Service Section.

[40]See para. 79 of Conclusions and Recommendations Adopted by the Special Commission on the Practical Operation of The Hague Apostille, Evidence and Service Conventions published in 2003 on the website of the HCCH (hereinafter, 2003 Conclusions and Recommendations). Also see paras. 206–210 of Practical Handbook.

[41]See Articles 8, 9 of 1992 Measures Implementing the Hague Service Convention. Also see He (2005, pp. 126, 137).

[42]Under the Hague Service Convention, it is possible that a Member State prohibits service via postal channels within its territory by other member states but serves documents abroad by postal channels itself. This approach is actually adopted by Switzerland. See para. 209 of Practical Handbook.

provided in the Convention, in particular, direct communication between their respective authorities.[43] Thus, China is free to conclude further bilateral treaties with other Contracting States.[44] Additionally, other means of transmission provided in CPL and relevant Judicial Interpretations, including diplomatic channel, postal channel and service by publication, can also be resorted to as long as the internal law of the State of Destination has no objection to them.[45] In this case, what the domestic law of the State of Destination says is crucial. To the contrary, service of judicial documents issued by foreign courts within the territory of China is relatively more restricted in general. Documents can only be transmitted through diplomatic or consular channel if no available channels provided in applicable treaties or convention.[46] Direct service such as service through post channel or by judicial officers of a foreign state is generally not permitted in the territory of China.[47]

---

[43]See Articles 11, 24 of Hague Service Convention.

[44]See supra paras. 310–313.

[45]See Article 19 of Hague Service Convention.

[46]See Article 277 of CPL.

[47]Ibid.

Chapter 14
Taking of Evidence

318. Like in most civil law jurisdictions, taking of evidence is considered as the exercising of public judicial power in China.[1] Evidence can only be taken through the diplomatic channel or under specific international treaties and unauthorized taking of evidence by a foreign individual or authority within the territory of China is strictly forbidden.[2]

14.1 Taking of Evidence in the Absence of Specific International Treaties

319. Evidence can only be taken through diplomatic/consular channels based on the principle of reciprocity if there is no relevant treaty applicable between China and the concerned foreign State.[3] When evidence is to be taken in China for the use of foreign proceedings, the embassy of State of Origin stationed in China shall transmit documents requesting judicial assistance to the Ministry of Foreign Affairs of PRC, which will then forward the request to the concerned high court at provincial level. The concerned high court will then execute the request according

[1]See Betti (1986, pp. 109, 119).

[2]See Article 277 of CPL, which says:

> Judicial assistance shall be requested and provided through the channels prescribed in an international treaty concluded or acceded to by the People's Republic of China; or in the absence of such a treaty, shall be requested and provided through diplomatic channels;
>
> A foreign embassy or consulate to the People's Republic of China may serve process on and investigate and collect evidence from its citizens but shall not violate the laws of the People's Republic of China and shall not take compulsion measures;
>
> Except for the circumstances in the preceding paragraph, no foreign authority or individual shall, without permission from the competent authorities of the People's Republic of China, serve process or conduct investigation and collection of evidence within the territory of the People's Republic of China.

[3]See Article 277 of CPL.

G. Tu, *Private International Law in China*, DOI 10.1007/978-981-287-993-6_14

to Chinese law or follow a special method required by the foreign requesting State, provided that such method is compatible with domestic Chinese law.[4] Nevertheless, Chinese courts can refuse to execute a request if the execution would infringe upon the sovereignty, security or public interest of PRC.[5]

320. In the case where evidence is to be taken abroad for the use of Chinese foreign-related civil proceedings, it is the concerned high court at provincial level that will review the request for transmission submitted by its subordinate intermediate courts or courts at county (district) level and, if it thinks necessary, forward the document of request to the Ministry of Foreign Affairs, which will transmit the request to the Ministry of Foreign Affairs of the concerned foreign State where the request of evidence-taking can be executed. In addition, evidence can be taken upon a Chinese national directly by the Chinese embassy or consulate stationed in a concerned foreign State as long as its local law allows.[6]

14.2 Taking of Evidence via International Treaties

321. China has concluded bilateral treaties for taking of evidence with over 20 States.[7] Moreover, China has been a party of the Hague Convention on the Taking of Evidence Abroad in Civil and Commercial Matters (hereinafter, Hague Evidence Convention) since 1997 and this Convention has played an important role in cross-border taking of evidence between China and its other Contracting States.[8]

14.2.1 Taking of Evidence Under Bilateral Treaties

322. As mentioned, the issue of taking of evidence is usually addressed together with other issues of international judicial assistance such as service of documents and recognition and enforcement of foreign judgments and arbitral awards in the bilateral treaties China has concluded with other countries.[9] For the purpose of taking of evidence, generally speaking, States can request judicial assistance from

[4]See Article 279 of CPL.

[5]See Article 276 of CPL.

[6]Similarly, without any compulsion measure taken upon the witness or any infringement upon the sovereignty and security of China, the embassy or consular of a foreign State is also allowed to directly take evidence from its national in the territory of China. See Article 277 of CPL.

[7]See supra para. 223.

[8]Ibid.

[9]See supra para. 223.

each other on questioning parties, witnesses and experts,[10] inspection,[11] carrying out forensic appraisal[12] and collecting other forms of evidence permitted under the Executing State.[13] Such requests shall be clearly indicated in the Letter of Request and forwarded by the Central Authority of the Requesting State to the Central Authority of the Requested State where the request is to be executed.[14] In China, it is usually the Ministry of Justice or the Supreme People's Court that is designated as the Central Authority.[15]

323. The Requested State shall execute the Letter of Request according to its domestic law and can take compulsion measures when it is deemed appropriate under the local law.[16] If the Requesting State requests the Letter of Request to be executed via a special method or procedure, the Requested State may follow such a method or procedure unless to do so is incompatible with its domestic law.[17] Without any compulsion measure being taken and in compliance with the local law, one Contracting State may also entrust its embassy or consular agent locally stationed in the other Contracting State to take evidence from its nationals in that other State.[18]

---

[10]E.g. see Article 10 of Treaty on Civil and Commercial Judicial Assistance between the People's Republic of China and the Kingdom of Spain; Article 12 of Treaty on Civil and Commercial Judicial Assistance between the People's Republic of China and the French Republic.

[11]E.g. see Article 10 of Treaty on Civil and Commercial Judicial Assistance between the People's Republic of China and the Kingdom of Spain; Article 12 of Treaty on Civil and Commercial Judicial Assistance between the People's Republic of China and the French Republic; and Article 13 of Treaty on Civil and Criminal Judicial Assistance between the People's Republic of China and the Republic of Poland.

[12]E.g. see Article 12 of Treaty on Civil and Commercial Judicial Assistance between the People's Republic of China and the French Republic; Article 13 of Treaty on Civil and Criminal Judicial Assistance between the People's Republic of China and the Republic of Poland; and Article 8 of Treaty on Civil Judicial Assistance between the People's Republic of China and Republic of Italy.

[13]E.g. see Article 13 of Treaty on Civil and Criminal Judicial Assistance between the People's Republic of China and the Republic of Poland; Article 10 of Treaty on Civil and Commercial Judicial Assistance between the People's Republic of China and the Kingdom of Spain.

[14]E.g. see Article 3 of Treaty on Civil and Commercial Judicial Assistance between the People's Republic of China and the French Republic; Article 3 of Treaty on Civil and Commercial Judicial Assistance between the People's Republic of China and the Kingdom of Spain; and Article 6 of Treaty on Civil and Criminal Judicial Assistance between the People's Republic of China and the Republic of Poland.

[15]See supra para. 315.

[16]E.g. see Article 12 of Treaty on Civil and Commercial Judicial Assistance between the People's Republic of China and the Kingdom of Spain; Article 14 of Treaty on Civil and Commercial Judicial Assistance between the People's Republic of China and the French Republic.

[17]E.g. see Article 12 of Treaty on Civil and Commercial Judicial Assistance between the People's Republic of China and the Kingdom of Spain; Article 11 of Treaty on Civil Judicial Assistance between the People's Republic of China and Republic of Italy.

[18]E.g. see Article 14 of Treaty on Civil and Commercial Judicial Assistance between the People's Republic of China and the French Republic; Article 13 of Treaty on Civil Judicial Assistance between the People's Republic of China and Republic of Italy; and Article 12 of Treaty on Civil and Commercial Judicial Assistance between the People's Republic of China and the Kingdom of Spain.

324. The Requested State may refuse to execute the Letter of Request if providing such assistance would violate the state sovereignty, security, social order, public interest or basic rules in its domestic legal system.[19] If the Letter of Request cannot be executed, the Requested State shall also inform the Requesting State of the failure of execution and advise the reasons for the failure.[20]

14.2.2 Taking of Evidence Under the Hague Evidence Convention

325. As a bridge between the civil law and common law States, the Hague Evidence Convention has made significant contribution to the judicial cooperation among the Contracting States in respect of taking of evidence in civil and commercial matters.[21] However, China's attitude towards the Convention is still quite conservative.[22] Basically, evidence can be taken under the Hague Evidence Convention through transmission and execution of Letters of Request or via diplomatic channel. Taking evidence via modern technology such as video-link is a new phenomenon arising out of the operation of the Convention that is worth noting.

14.2.2.1 Transmission and Execution of Letters of Request

326. Execution of a Letter of Request is the most common form for evidence to be taken abroad under the Convention. According to the Hague Evidence Convention, the competent authority of a Contracting State (hereinafter, State of Origin) may request evidence to be obtained from or other judicial act[23] to be performed by another Contracting State by transmitting a Letter of Request to the Central

[19]E.g. see Article 18 of Treaty on Civil and Commercial Judicial Assistance between the People's Republic of China and the French Republic; Article 19 of Treaty on Civil Judicial Assistance between the People's Republic of China and Republic of Italy; Article 5 of Treaty on Civil and Commercial Judicial Assistance between the People's Republic of China and the Kingdom of Spain.

[20]E.g. see Articles 15, 18 of Treaty on Civil and Commercial Judicial Assistance between the People's Republic of China and the French Republic; and Articles 14, 15 of Treaty on Civil and Criminal Judicial Assistance between the People's Republic of China and the Republic of Poland.

[21]See Betti (1986, pp. 109, 114)

[22]This can be reflected by China's reservation to the whole Chapter II except for Article 15 and its strict limitation on documents for pre-trial discovery. See Declarations made by China to the Hague Evidence Convention, which can be found at the website of HCCH for Evidence Section.

[23]The Convention itself explains that the expression 'other judicial act' does not cover service of judicial documents or issuance of any process by which judgments or orders are executed or enforced, or orders for provisional or protective measures. See Article 1 of Hague Evidence Convention.

Authority of the State where the evidence-taking can be executed (hereinafter, State of Execution).[24] China has designated the Ministry of Justice as the Central Authority and the Supreme People's Court, five high courts respectively located in Beijing, Shanghai, Jiangsu, Zhejiang and Guangdong, together with the Ministry of Justice as the authorities competent to forward a Letter of Request to the Central Authorities of other Contracting States,[25] which is identical with what has been provided for the Hague Service Convention.[26]

327. The State of Origin may request to obtain evidence for pending judicial proceedings as well as documents to be collected for pre-trail discovery.[27] However, in the latter case, China only accept request for obtaining discovery of the documents clearly enumerated in the Letter of Request and of direct and close connection with the subject matter of the litigation.[28]

14.2.2.2 Taking of Evidence via Diplomatic Channel

328. A Contracting State can entrust its diplomatic officer or consular agent to take evidence in another Contracting State where he exercises his function.[29] In this case, evidence can only be taken without any compulsion on the nationals of the State the diplomatic officer or consular agent represents.[30] Taking evidence on a national of a third State through this method is not accepted by China according to its declaration to the Convention.[31] Meanwhile, China has also made reservation to taking evidence by commissioners appointed by the Contracting State where the judicial proceedings are commenced or contemplated.[32]

---

[24]See Article 1 of Hague Evidence Convention.

[25]The designated Central Authority of China for the purpose of the Hague Evidence Convention can be found at the website of HCCH for Evidence Section. In 2003, the Supreme People's Court issued a Notice designating five high courts of Beijing, Shanghai, Guangdong, Zhejiang and Jiangsu as competent authorities to directly forward a Letter of Request to Central Authorities of other Contracting States. However, it is worth noting that this authorization cannot be reflected on the website of HCCH. See Notice of the Supreme People's Court on Assigning the High People's Courts of Beijing Municipality, Shanghai Municipality, Guangdong, Zhejiang, and Jiangsu Provinces to Directly Put Forward and Transfer Judicial Assistance Requests and Relevant Documents, which was issued by the Supreme People's Court on September 23, 2003.

[26]See supra para. 315.

[27]See Articles 1 & 23 of the Hague Evidence Convention.

[28]See Declarations made by China to Hague Evidence Convention, which can be found at the website of HCCH for Evidence Section.

[29]See Article 15 of Hague Evidence Convention.

[30]Ibid.

[31]See Article 16 of Hague Evidence Convention. Also see Declarations made by China to Hague Evidence Convention, which can be found at the website of HCCH for Evidence Section.

[32]See Article 17 of Hague Evidence Convention. Also see Declarations made by China to Hague Evidence Convention, which can be found at the website of HCCH for Evidence Section.

14.2.2.3 Taking of Evidence via Modern Technology

329. The taking of evidence by video-link technology has been an important topic for the Permanent Bureau of HCCH and Special Commission of the Hague Evidence Convention in the past years.[33] The use of video-link technology may considerably facilitate the evidence taking process under Hague Evidence Convention. Compared with the traditional approaches such as evidence taken and presented in written and recorded audio-visual forms, instant video-link transmission may enable the judge and other qualified questioners to respond immediately to the witness' conducts and answers so that they can make new and further detailed inquiries into the case.[34] In this sense, evidence taken through instant video transmission can be given nearly the same effect as where the witness is physically present in the court trial. In addition, taking evidence by this way may also significantly reduce the expense and avoid many logistical difficulties of arranging the witnesses.[35]

330. Based on the explanatory documents released by the Permanent Bureau, taking of evidence by instant video-link technology can be deemed as a 'special method or procedure' which can be requested by the Central Authority of the State of Origin.[36] The State of Execution shall follow the request unless it is 'incompatible with the internal law of the State of execution; or… impossible of performance by reason of either… internal practice and procedure; or… practical difficulties'.[37] It is also emphasized that the aforesaid exceptions shall be interpreted restrictively in order to permit the use of modern information technology to the greatest extent possible.[38] It has been further explained that, 'to be "incompatible" with the internal law of the State of Execution does not mean "different" from the internal law. It means that there must be some constitutional inhibition or some absolute statutory prohibition'.[39] Additionally, '[provided that] a State has video-link facilities available in its court rooms, it cannot be said that the taking of evidence pursuant by video-link to a request for a special method under Article 9(2) is inconsistent with the law of the Requested State'.[40]

---

[33]See para. 1 of Preliminary Document No 6 of December 2008 for the attention of the Special Commission of February 2009 on the practical operation of the Hague Apostille, Service, Evidence and Access to Justice Conventions, 'The Taking of Evidence By Video-Link Under The Hague Evidence Convention' (hereinafter, Prel. Doc. No 6), drawn up by the Permanent Bureau and can be found at the website of the HCCH.

[34]See Friedman (2002, pp. 695, 702).

[35]See para. 3 of Prel. Doc. No 6.

[36]See para. 20 of Prel. Doc. No 6.

[37]Ibid.

[38]See para. 43 of 2003 Conclusions and Recommendations.

[39]See para. 22 of Prel. Doc. No 6.

[40]Ibid, para. 23.

331. China remained silent on the relevant questions regarding taking of evidence by video-link in the questionnaire designed by the Permanent Bureau of HCCH for the practical operation of Hague Evidence Convention.[41] In fact, taking evidence through video-link by foreign courts on Chinese soil or by Chinese courts abroad could seldom be seen in practice.[42] However, taking of evidence through modern technology such as audio and/or video transmission has been permitted in Chinese courts since the SPC Evidence Provisions were publicized as early as in 2002[43] and has been formally accepted by Chinese CPL in 2012.[44] When a witness cannot attend the court trial for reasons of illness, inconvenient transportation resulting from geographical distance, *force majeure* caused by natural disasters or other justifiable reasons, the court may allow the witness to give evidence via audio and/or video transmission technology such as video-conference and/or teleconference, without physical presence at the court.[45] Given this, it can be fully confirmed that taking evidence by video-link is consistent with the local law and practice of China and thus a Letter of Request requesting evidence to be taken by video-link can be executed by Chinese authorities. On the other hand, China itself can also request the Central Authority of a Contracting State of the Hague Evidence Convention to allow evidence-taking by video-link, as long as such request is compatible with the local law of that state.[46]

---

[41]See the questionnaires and responses received by the Permanent Bureau of HCCH, which can be found on the website of HCCH for Evidence Section.

[42]See Qiao (2010, pp. 145, 159).

[43]See Article 56 of Some Provisions of the Supreme People's Court on Evidence in Civil Procedures that has entered into force since April 1, 2002 (hereinafter, SPC Evidence Provisions), which says: 'The situation referred to by "the witness cannot appear in court due to real difficulties" mentioned in Article 70 [now 73] of the Civil Procedure Law shall include any of the following circumstances… In any of the circumstances as mentioned in the preceding paragraph, the witness may, upon the approval of the People's court, provide evidence by way of submitting a written testimony or audio-visual materials or by means of two-way audio-visual transmission technology'.

[44]See Article 73 of CPL, which is essentially modeled on Article 56 of SPC Evidence Provisions.

[45]See Article 73 of CPL.

[46]See Article 9 of Hague Evidence Convention.

Chapter 15
Recognition and Enforcement of Foreign Judgments

332. As a State with a long history of planned economy and sensitive to national interests and sovereignty, China has been cautious about recognition and enforcement of foreign judgments so as to prevent resources flowing out of the State.[1] This could be reflected by the fact that before CPL was formally enacted in 1991, a foreign judgment could only be recognized and enforced in China through entrustment from the rendering foreign court based on an international treaty or the principle of reciprocity.[2] The requirement of entrustment precluded private parties from initiating the process of recognition and enforcement of a foreign judgment and it was once extremely difficult for a foreign judgment to be recognized and enforced in China.[3]

333. The current framework for recognition and enforcement of foreign judgments in China was first established by the CPL in 1991 and later on re-confirmed in a series of Amendments of the CPL.[4] According to the current rules in the CPL, direct application made by private parties to Chinese courts for recognition and enforcement of a foreign judgment is acceptable.[5] A request for

[1]See Reyes (1997, pp. 241, 266).

[2]See Article 204 of Civil Procedure Law of the People's Republic of China (Provisional), which says: 'The People's Court of the People's Republic of China shall examine the ascertained judgment or decision which a foreign court has rendered and entrusted to the People's Court for enforcement in accordance with the international treaties which China has concluded or to which China is a party or according to the principle of reciprocity. Where it is found to be not in contravention of the basic principles of the laws of the People's Republic of China or China's national and social interests, the People's Court shall acknowledge its effect by a ruling and enforce it according to the procedure specified by this Law. Otherwise, it shall be returned to the foreign court'; supra paras. 218–219.

[3]See Reyes (1997, pp. 241, 250–251).

[4]See supra paras. 218–219.

[5]See Article 281 of CPL, which says: 'If a legally effective judgment or ruling made by a foreign court requires recognition and execution by a People's Court of the People's Republic of China, the party concerned may directly apply for recognition and execution to the competent Intermediate People's Court of the People's Republic of China. Alternatively, the foreign court may, pursuant to the provisions of an international treaty concluded between or acceded to by the foreign state and the People's Republic of China, or in accordance with the principle of reciprocity, request the People's Court to recognize and execute the judgment or ruling'.

G. Tu, *Private International Law in China*, DOI 10.1007/978-981-287-993-6_15

recognition and enforcement of a foreign judgment can also be made by the foreign court rendering the judgment under the means specified in an international treaty concluded between the two States or based on the principle of 'reciprocity'.[6] Upon receipt of the application or request, Chinese courts are required to examine the foreign judgment according to the international treaty or principle of 'reciprocity' between China and the concerned foreign State.[7] Theoretically, in the absence of an international treaty or 'reciprocity' in practice, a foreign court may also request for recognition and enforcement of its judgment through the diplomatic channel.[8] It, however, has been proven in practice that Chinese courts have unanimously rejected to grant the order for recognition and enforcement of foreign judgments once it is confirmed that there is no treaty obligation or reciprocity between China and the concerned foreign State.[9]

15.1 Recognition and Enforcement of Foreign Judgments Under the Principle of 'Reciprocity'

334. As mentioned, a foreign judgment may be recognized and enforced by a Chinese court if 'reciprocity' exists in practice between China and the foreign State where the judgment is rendered.[10] However, Chinese courts usually decide whether reciprocity exists and if so, whether further requirements for recognition and enforcement can be satisfied according to Chinese law unilaterally.

15.1.1 The Question for Existence of 'Reciprocity'

335. Neither Chinese CPL nor the SPC's 2015 Interpretation on CPL has explained what may constitute 'reciprocity' under Chinese law. What's more, so far none of Chinese courts has actually granted recognition and enforcement for a foreign judgment directly based on the principle of 'reciprocity', as least according to the cases available to the public.

---

[6]Ibid.

[7]See Article 282 of CPL.

[8]See Article 549 of 2015 Interpretation on CPL, which says: 'Where a court of a country with which the PRC has no judicial assistance agreement or reciprocal relations requests judicial assistance directly from a court of the PRC without going through diplomatic channels, the Chinese court shall refuse the request and explain the grounds for such refusal.' Also see Zhang (2002, pp. 59, 87).

[9]See Tu (2011, pp. 341, 362). Also see Zhang (2013, pp. 143, 152–156). However, there is one exception that without a treaty or reciprocity in practice, a Chinese court is ready to recognize a divorce judgment of a foreign court that does not touching upon property, see Article 544 of 2015 Interpretation on CPL.

[10]See Article 281 of CPL.

336. Since the SPC issued its reply on *Gomi Akira Case*, in which it supported the High Court of Liaoning Province to reject the application for recognition and enforcement of a Japanese judgment as 'there is neither international treaty… nor relevant reciprocal relationship' between China and Japan, Chinese courts have shown a high degree of consensus in giving reasons for rejection.[11] When a relevant international treaty is absent, the courts unanimously resorted to 'lack of reciprocity' as reason for rejecting recognition and enforcement of foreign judgments.[12] However, it has been reflected in practice that Chinese courts would consider there is 'reciprocity' when a court of the concerned foreign State has once recognized and/or enforced a Chinese court judgment.[13]

337. There was no reported case where a Chinese judgment was recognized in a foreign State until the Court of Appeal of Berlin recognized a Chinese judgment in *German Zublin International Co. Ltd* versus *Wuxi Walker General Engineering Rubber Co., Ltd.* (hereinafter, *Zublin* Case) in 2006.[14] Chinese scholars were once encouraged by the step taken by the German court and believed that 'reciprocity' should be deemed established between China and Germany from then on.[15] Their presumption was indirectly proved to be right four years later in a case launched by a judgment creditor in Beijing High Court for recognition and enforcement of a German judgment, namely *Hukla Matratzen GmbH* vesus *Beijing Hukla Ltd* (hereinafter, *Hukla* Case).[16] The German applicant, citing the *Zublin* Case, argued that 'reciprocity' exists between Germany and China.[17] Cautious as it has always been, when asked by the Beijing High Court, the SPC did not expressly say whether there is 'reciprocity' between the two States. Instead, it instructed that Beijing High Court shall refuse to grant recognition because the German judgment was rendered without the defendant being properly served within China under the Hague Service Convention.[18] However, it seems that the SPC's silence on the

[11]See Reply Issued by the Supreme People's Court on Whether Japanese Judgment Containing Credit and Debt Relationship Shall Be Recognized and Enforced by Chinese Courts [1995] Min Ta Zi No. 17.

[12]E.g. see Application by Awabiya Co., Ltd for Recognition and Enforcement of Judgment in China (2001) Hu Yi Zhong Jing Chuzi No. 267; Wang Qingfang's Application for the Recognition of An American Adoption Judgment to the No. 2 Intermediate People's Court of Beijing Municipality (2006) Er Zhong Min Tezi No. 10319; Application by Russian National Symphony Orchestra & Altamont Co. Ltd for the Recognition and Enforcement of English Judgments to the No. 2 Intermediate People's Court of Beijing Municipality (2004) Er Zhong Min Tezi No. 928.

[13]See Zhang (2013, pp. 143, 170); also see Yuan (2004, pp. 757, 764).

[14]See *German Zublin International Co. Ltd* versus *Wuxi Walker General Engineering Rubber Co., Ltd*, 18 May 2006, document number: 20 S ch 13/04.

[15]E.g. see Ma (2007, pp. 150, 154).

[16]See *Hukla Matratzen GmbH* vesus *Beijing Hukla Ltd*, the No. 2 Intermediate People's Court of Beijing Municipality (2010) Er Zhong Min Te Zi No. 13890.

[17]See Reply Issued by the SPC on Recognition (and Enforcement) of Judgment No. 20460/07 Rendered by Court of Offenburg, Germany (2010) Min Si Ta Zi No. 81.

[18]Ibid.

issue of reciprocity in this case is actually an implicit confirmation on the existence of reciprocity for Chinese courts tend to refuse a foreign judgment immediately in the absence of an international treaty and reciprocity, usually without further looking into other requirements stipulated in CPL.[19] A further examination on the requirement of due service other than the existence of a treaty and 'reciprocity', therefore, may indicate that the necessity of 'reciprocity' has already been satisfied in the eyes of the SPC.

338. In addition to the German court, a California court of the United States also expressed its readiness in building up reciprocal relationship with China by granting recognition of Chinese judgments concerning damage and compensation in tort.[20] It could be optimistically predicted that Chinese courts will confirm the existence of 'reciprocity' between China and the State of California when an applicant seeks recognition and enforcement of a California judgment in China in the future.

15.1.2 Further Requirements Under the Principle of 'Reciprocity'

339. In contrast with the international treaties which clearly list requirements for recognition and enforcement, Chinese CPL is rather vague in prescribing conditions where Chinese courts may grant recognition and enforcement under the principle of 'reciprocity'.[21] Article 282 of CPL, which is the fundamental provision for this issue, reads as follows:

> In the case of an application or request for recognition and enforcement of a legally effective judgment or written order of a foreign court, the People's Court shall, after examining it in accordance with the international treaties concluded or acceded to by the People's Republic of China or with the principle of reciprocity and arriving at the conclusion that it does not contradict the basic principles of the People's Republic of China nor violates State sovereignty, security and social and public interests of the country, recognize the validity of the judgment or written order and, if requested, issue a writ of execution to enforce it in accordance with the relevant provisions of this Law; if the application or request contradicts the basic principles of the law of the People's Republic of China or violates State sovereignty, security and socio-public interests of the country, the people's court should not recognize and enforce it.[22]

340. Accordingly, the first requirement for a foreign judgment to be recognized and enforced in China is that the foreign judgment has to be 'legally effective'.

---

[19]See Zhang (2013, pp. 143, 166).

[20]See *Hubei Gezhouba Sanlian Industrial Co. Ltd.* versus. *Robinson Helicopter Co., Inc.*, 2009 WL 2190187 (C.D.Cal. 22 July 2009) (NO. 2:06-CV-01798-FMCSSX); and *Hubei Gezhouba Sanlian Indus., Co., Ltd.* versus *Robinson Helicopter Co.*, Inc., 425 Fed. Appx. 580 (9th Cir. (Cal.) 29 March 2011).

[21]See infra paras. 345–347.

[22]See Article 282 of CPL.

It might be deducible from the bilateral treaties China has entered into that the judgment shall be effective under the law of the foreign State, even though Article 282 does not attempt to clarify this issue.[23] Another prerequisite for recognition and enforcement of a foreign judgment is that it does not contradict with the basic principles of law and State sovereignty, security and social and public interests of China.[24] Still, there is neither interpretation on the concept of basic principles of law nor the concept of State sovereignty, security and social and public interests of China.[25]

341. An examination on the bilateral treaties to which China is a party might be helpful to provide some further useful guidance to litigants. According to those treaties, recognition and enforcement will not be granted provided that the foreign judgment was made by an incompetent foreign court according to domestic law of China or the foreign State, or relevant provision included in the treaty.[26] It is, therefore, inferable that for a foreign judgment to be recognized and enforced in China under the principle of 'reciprocity', the court rendering the judgment must have legitimate jurisdiction, especially shall not offend Chinese exclusive jurisdiction.

342. Due service to the defendant under Chinese law and relevant international treaty is also considered as a basic requirement in China for recognition and enforcement of a foreign judgment and has actually been frequently resorted to by Chinese Courts to reject foreign judgments in practice.[27] In Reply issued by the SPC for the *Hukla* Case, the SPC indicated that the German court's service of process by post to the defendant in China was not allowed by Chinese law and hence the judgment shall not be recognized and enforced in China.[28]

343. In addition, it is also possible that Chinese courts will refuse a foreign judgment if a defendant lacking legal capacity was not properly represented by a guardian,[29] or parallel proceedings has already been initiated in China or a judgment for the same case from a local court or a third country has already been made or recognized.[30] Of course, some commonly-accepted standards shall also be taken into consideration, such as whether the judgment is rendered in accordance with due process.[31]

---

[23]See infra para. 347.

[24]See Article 282 of CPL.

[25]It is submitted by the author that the two concepts may overlap with each other. In fact, serious divergence with Chinese law may also constitute violation to public order, and legal activities infringing public order of China are often forbidden under Chinese law. A more detailed discussion on public order of China may be found in Xiao and Huo (2005, pp. 653–678).

[26]See infra para. 347.

[27]Lack of due service to the defendant is a popular reason used by Chinese courts in rejecting recognition and enforcement of a foreign judgment and it only comes after the 'lack of international treaty and reciprocity'. Generally see Zhang (2013, p. 143).

[28]See supra para. 337.

[29]See infra para. 347.

[30]See infra para. 347.

[31]See Reyes (1997, pp. 241, 259).

344. It is submitted that a mature system on recognition and enforcement of foreign judgments in Chinese domestic law would be built up on the above analysis in the future.

15.2 Recognition and Enforcement of Foreign Judgments Under Bilateral Treaties

345. Up to now, China has not entered into any multi-lateral convention comprehensively regulating mutual recognition and enforcement of judgments. However, it has concluded bilateral treaties with over 20 States on mutual judicial assistance covering recognition and enforcement of court judgments.[32] Generally speaking, the scope of these treaties covers court judgments including court settlements in civil and commercial proceedings and judgments in civil and commercial proceedings incidentally attached to criminal proceedings.[33] Some treaties, however, does not apply for recognition and enforcement of judgments on bankruptcy and liquidation,[34] wills and succession,[35] social security,[36] and provisional and protective measures other than on matters of alimony.[37]

346. Some treaties provide that request for recognition and enforcement can only be submitted to competent courts directly by the parties[38] while others also

[32]See supra para. 47.

[33]E.g. see Article 19 of Treaty on Civil and Commercial Judicial Assistance between the People's Republic of China and the French Republic; Article 16 of Treaty on Civil and Criminal Judicial Assistance between the People's Republic of China and the Republic of Poland; and Article 20 of Treaty on Civil Judicial Assistance between the People's Republic of China and Republic of Italy.

[34]E.g. see Article 17 (1) of Treaty on Civil and Commercial Judicial Assistance between the People's Republic of China and the Kingdom of Spain; Article 21 of Treaty on Judicial Assistance in Civil and Commercial Matters between the People's Republic of China and the Republic of Peru; and Article 19 (3) of Treaty on Judicial Assistance in Civil and Criminal Matters between the People's Republic of China and the Republic of Tunisia.

[35]E.g. see Article 21 of Treaty on Judicial Assistance in Civil and Commercial Matters between the People's Republic of China and the Republic of Peru; and Article 19 (3) of Treaty on Judicial Assistance in Civil and Criminal Matters between the People's Republic of China and the Republic of Tunisia.

[36]Ibid.

[37]Ibid.

[38]E.g. see Article 20 of Treaty on Civil and Commercial Judicial Assistance between the People's Republic of China and the French Republic; Article 19 of Treaty on Civil and Commercial Judicial Assistance between the People's Republic of China and the Kingdom of Spain; and Article 20 (1) of Treaty on Judicial Assistance in Civil and Criminal Matters between the People's Republic of China and the Republic of Tunisia.

allow request to be transmitted through Central Authorities of the two States.[39] In the latter case, the court rendering the judgment shall submit the request to the Central Authority of its home State which will transmit the request to the Central Authority of the State where the judgment is to be executed and the latter will then further forward the request to the competent courts in its territory.[40]

347. Upon acceptance of the request submitted by the parties or transferred through Central Authorities, the competent court, usually the court where the judgment debtor is domiciled or the property at issue is located[41] shall review the request according to the applicable treaty and its domestic law without looking into the substantive issues of the case.[42] Most treaties have provided clear and detailed instructions for courts to review the request. Generally speaking, for a foreign judgment to be recognized and enforced, the judgment shall be final, effective and executable under the law of the rendering court[43]; the foreign court rendering the judgment shall have jurisdiction over the case according to its domestic law,[44] or the law of the State executing the judgment,[45] or a provision specified in the treaty[46]; based on the domestic law of the State where the judgment is rendered, the defendant has been given adequate notice for the proceedings and was

[39]E.g. see Article 18 of Treaty on Civil and Criminal Judicial Assistance between the People's Republic of China and the Republic of Poland; Article 22 (1) of Treaty on Judicial Assistance in Civil and Criminal Matters between the People's Republic of China and the Republic of Cuba; and Article 16 of Treaty on Civil and Commercial Judicial Assistance between the People's Republic of China and the Argentine Republic.

[40]Ibid.

[41]See Article 224 of CPL; also see Reyes (1997, pp. 241, 257).

[42]E.g. see Article 23 (2) of Treaty on Civil and Commercial Judicial Assistance between the People's Republic of China and the French Republic; Article 19 (2) of Treaty on Civil and Commercial Judicial Assistance between the People's Republic of China and the Argentine Republic.

[43]E.g. see Article 22 (3) of Treaty on Civil and Commercial Judicial Assistance between the People's Republic of China and the French Republic; Article 22 (3) of Treaty on Civil and Commercial Judicial Assistance between the People's Republic of China and the Kingdom of Spain; and Article 18 (1) of Treaty on Civil and Commercial Judicial Assistance between the People's Republic of China and the Argentine Republic.

[44]E.g. see Article 22 (1) of Treaty on Civil and Commercial Judicial Assistance between the People's Republic of China and the French Republic.

[45]E.g. see Article 25 (1) of Treaty on Judicial Assistance in Civil and Criminal Matters between the People's Republic of China and the Republic of Cuba; Article 20 (1) of Treaty on Civil and Criminal Judicial Assistance between the People's Republic of China and the Republic of Poland.

[46]E.g. see Articles 21, 22 (1) of Treaty on Civil and Commercial Judicial Assistance between the People's Republic of China and the Kingdom of Spain; Articles 22 (2), 23 of Treaty on Judicial Assistance in Civil and Criminal Matters between the People's Republic of China and the Republic of Tunisia.

properly represented by a guardian if the defendant lacks legal capacity.[47] On the other side, a foreign judgment cannot be recognized provided that judicial proceedings with regard to the same cause of action between the same parties are pending in or have been given a judgment by a local court or a local court has recognized an effective judgment for the same case rendered by a third State.[48] In addition, recognition and enforcement of a foreign judgment can also be rejected if infringement on State sovereignty, basic principles of local law, local security and public policy could occur.[49]

[47]E.g. see Article 22 (4) of Treaty on Civil and Commercial Judicial Assistance between the People's Republic of China and the French Republic; Article 18 (3) of Treaty on Civil and Commercial Judicial Assistance between the People's Republic of China and the Argentine Republic; and Article 22 (4) of Treaty on Civil and Commercial Judicial Assistance between the People's Republic of China and the Kingdom of Spain.

[48]E.g. see Article 22 (6) of Treaty on Civil and Commercial Judicial Assistance between the People's Republic of China and the French Republic; Article 18 (4) of Treaty on Civil and Commercial Judicial Assistance between the People's Republic of China and the Argentine Republic; and Article 22 (6) of Treaty on Civil and Commercial Judicial Assistance between the People's Republic of China and the Kingdom of Spain.

[49]E.g. see Article 22 (5) of Treaty on Civil and Commercial Judicial Assistance between the People's Republic of China and the French Republic; Article 20 (6) of Treaty on Civil and Criminal Judicial Assistance between the People's Republic of China and the Republic of Poland.

Chapter 16
International Arbitration

16.1 Chinese Law and Practice on International Arbitration

16.1.1 Before 1995

348. In ancient China, people normally had their disputes resolved through alternative dispute resolution mechanism such as mediation or conciliation presided by their trustworthy elders, due to the Confucianism which emphasized the ideal of a peaceful society. As litigation was generally dis-favoured, arbitration was generally not developed partly because of its semi-judicial nature and partly because of the underdeveloped commerce.[1]

349. After the founding of the People's Republic of China, from 1949 to late 1970s, China implemented the policy of a highly centralized and planned economy, under which administrative powers controlled almost all aspects of societal activities. During this period, although many disputes were settled by arbitration instead of litigation, this kind of arbitration was regulated and conducted by administrative authorities who were governmental officers rather than impartial arbitrators from the general public. Therefore, it was called 'administrative arbitration'.[2]

350. Being still administrative as its domestic arbitration, the modern concept of arbitration was, however, accepted by China to resolve international commercial disputes.[3] International commercial arbitration was developed to meet the practical demand of resolving private disputes arising out of the trade agreements between China and other socialist countries since 1950s.[4] For that purpose, two arbitration institutions were specifically created i.e. Foreign Trade Arbitration Commission (now, China International Economic and Trade Arbitration Commission) and Maritime Arbitration Commission (now, China Maritime Arbitration Commission).

---

[1]See Wunschheim (2011, pp. 29–30), Feinerman (1995, p. 5 et seq).

[2]See Wunschheim (2011, pp. 29–30), Feinerman (1995, p. 5 et seq).

[3]See Wunschheim (2011, p. 30).

[4]See Tao (2012, p. 8).

G. Tu, *Private International Law in China*, DOI 10.1007/978-981-287-993-6_16

These two institutions were the only competent authority for foreign-related arbitration at the time and in the meantime, they were not entitled to arbitrate any domestic dispute.[5] Given that China's interaction with the outer world at that time was very limited, according to statistics, the Foreign Trade Arbitration Commission had only dealt with 20 cases from 1956 to 1966 and 7 cases from 1967 to 1976, most of which were disputes between a Chinese party and another party from other socialist countries.[6]

351. With the opening-up policy being adopted in 1978, China was geared up to the global market.[7] More and more disputes between Chinese and foreign private parties began to be referred to arbitration. To keep pace with the reality, China adopted a series of laws in which one could find provisions concerning arbitration. Before 1995, there were 14 laws, more than 80 administrative regulations and nearly 200 local regulations containing provisions regulating arbitration.[8] To modernize its arbitration regime and streamline its arbitration rules, China eventually promulgated its arbitration law i.e. Chinese Arbitration Law (CAL) that has come into effect since 1 September 1995.[9]

16.1.2 1995–Up to Now

352. Undoubtedly, the Chinese Arbitration Law (CAL) is the most important legal source for both domestic and international arbitration in China. It was drafted with reference to international practices, especially the 1985 UNCITRAL Model Law and 1958 New York Convention.[10] In the law, there is a Chapter (VII) specifically devoted to international commercial arbitration titled 'Special Provisions concerning Foreign-Related Arbitration' containing provisions only applicable to foreign-related arbitration. However, provisions in other Chapters are also applicable to international arbitration where there is no relevant provision available in Chapter VII.[11] Although there are still differences between the 1985 UNCITRAL Model Law and CAL, the general framework and basic ideas in the former have been accepted by the latter.[12]

---

[5]Ibid, p. 9.

[6]See Song et al. (2003, p. 169 et seq), Chen (1991, pp. 457, 458).

[7]See supra para. 3.

[8]See The Legislative Affairs Commission of the Standing Committee of the National People's Congress of the PRC (ed.), *Arbitration Laws of China* (London: Sweet & Maxwell, 1997), p. 21; Civil Law Office of the Commission of Legislative Affairs of the Standing Committee of the National People's Congress and Secretariat of China International Economic and Trade Arbitration Commission, *The Complete Works on Arbitration Law of the People's Republic of China* (Beijing: Law Press, 1995, p. 59).

[9]This law was adopted by the Standing Committee of the National People's Congress on 31 August 1994.

[10]See Wunschheim (2011, p. 34).

[11]See Article 65 of Chinese Arbitration Law.

[12]See Zhao and Kloppenberg (2005–2006, pp. 421, 428–429).

In particular, Article 14 of CAL clearly declares the principle of independence of arbitration institutions, stating that arbitration institutions are independent from and are neither subject to nor affiliated to any administrative organ.[13] This Article has totally thrown off the previous administrative nature of Chinese arbitration.

353. There are, however, two points that are particularly worth noting under this new law i.e. predominance of institutional arbitration and distinction between domestic and international arbitration:

(1) Ad hoc arbitration is an important alternative mode to institutional arbitration. Although no provision in CAL expressly prohibits ad hoc arbitration, CAL has only touched upon institutional arbitration. In accordance with Articles 16 (2) and 18 of the CAL, an arbitration agreement without a clear designation of a specific arbitration institution will be rendered invalid.[14] It was thus argued that ad hoc arbitration is not possible in China.[15] China is said to be an 'absolute institutional arbitration country'.[16] However, in order to faithfully perform the treaty obligation under the New York Convention, China does recognize the validity of an ad hoc arbitration agreement concluded in any other Member State of the Convention.[17] This raises the problem of unequal treatment of foreign and domestic arbitration agreements.

(2) After CAL, domestic arbitration institutions can hear foreign-related cases if only the parties agree so and the arbitration institutions which previously dealt with international cases only have also extended their jurisdiction to handle domestic disputes. This breakthrough 'further distances arbitration from governmental intervention and weakens the quasi-governmental image of China arbitration institutions'.[18] Although the distinction between domestic arbitration and foreign-related arbitration handled by two parallel systems of institutions has been melted down with the adoption of CAL, there are still differences between international arbitration and domestic arbitration reflected in legislations and practice. Chapter VII of CAL is specifically designed to provide special rules for foreign-related arbitration. As stated above, from the very beginning of the development of arbitration in China, 'foreign-related' arbitration was differentiated to be regulated by a separate system from the pure domestic arbitration.[19] This distinction will still maintain for a while although it is diminishing.

---

[13]See Article 14 of CAL.

[14]See Articles 16 (2) and 18 of CAL.

[15]See Tao (2012, pp. 76–77).

[16]See Hu (1999, pp. 1, 30), Aglionby (2007, pp. 673, 675).

[17]See Art. 2 of the New York Convention; the Supreme People's Court's Reply given on 20 October 1995 on the Validity of the Arbitration Clause contained in the bill of lading in the case of *Productive Materials Corporation of Fujian Province versus Jinge Shipping Ltd. Co.* regarding international maritime transportation.

[18]See Tao (2012, p. 12).

[19]See supra para. 350.

354. As to the practice of international arbitration in China during this period, the business of China International Economic and Trade Arbitration Commission (CIETAC) and China Maritime Arbitration Commission (CMAC), the two main institutions dealing with foreign-related arbitration cases, has prospered not only in terms of the number of cases but also the types of disputes. Take CIETAC as an example, compared with 87 cases decided in 1988,[20] it decided over 200 annually from the beginning of 1990s and incrementally up to 1051 in 2007.[21] And CMAC has settled over 1000 maritime affairs and commercial arbitration cases over the past decade.[22] Most of the disputes were about sales contracts and roughly half of them were petitioned by foreigners or foreign companies.[23]

355. As demonstrated, although there are improvements still to be made, China has long been endeavoring to improve international commercial arbitration within its territory and indeed has gained great success over the past decades.[24]

16.2 Recognition and Enforcement of Foreign Arbitral Awards in China

356. Like a foreign judgment, a foreign arbitral award can be recognized and enforced in China only on the principle of 'reciprocity' if there is no applicable international treaty concluded between China and the concerned foreign State for the purpose of enhancing the free movement of arbitral awards.[25] As said, China has concluded quite a few bilateral treaties for international judicial assistance covering mutual recognition and enforcement of arbitral awards.[26] However, most corresponding foreign States for those bilateral treaties are, in the meantime, Member States of the 1958 New York Convention on recognition and enforcement of foreign arbitral awards. Of course, those bilateral treaties shall prevail if interested parties can enjoy more preferential rights under them.[27] The fact is that in

[20]See Chen (1991, pp. 457, 476–477).

[21]See statistics publicized on the CIETAC official website i.e. http://www.cietac.org/index.cms (last accessed on 12 August 2015).

[22]See statistics publicized on the CMAC official website i.e. http://www.cmac-sh.org/en/home.asp (last accessed on 12 August 2015).

[23]See Chen (1991, pp. 457, 477).

[24]See Shaojie (1995, p. 16).

[25]See Article 283 of Chinese CPL; supra para. 333.

[26]See supra para. 223.

[27]See Article VII (1) of the New York Convention, which says: 'The provisions of the present Convention shall not affect the validity of multilateral or bilateral agreements concerning the recognition and enforcement of arbitral awards entered into by the Contracting States nor deprive any interested party of any right he may have to avail himself of an arbitral award in the manner and to the extent allowed by the law or the treaties of the country where such award is sought to be relied upon'.

most of those bilateral treaties, as far as mutual recognition and enforcement of arbitral awards is concerned, there is a provision that simply refers to the New York Convention.[28] Therefore, Chinese practice under the New York Convention is particularly worth noting.

357. As mentioned, China acceded to the New York Convention on 2 December 1986 and it has entered into force in China since 22 April 1987 by virtue of Decision of the Standing Committee of the National People's Congress on China Joining the Convention on the Recognition and Enforcement of Foreign Awards (SCNPC Decision on Foreign Arbitral Award).[29] To effectively implement this Convention, just before its entry into force, on 10 April 1987, the Supreme People's Court also issued a Notice, commanding that all the People's Courts should comply with the rules in the Convention even if there exists a conflict between the Convention and Chinese domestic law.[30] Moreover, after the Chinese Arbitration Law came into force in 1995, the Supreme People's Court has issued a series of Interpretations concerning recognition and enforcement of foreign-related arbitral awards, which, in a purposeful and flexible manner, make the application of Chinese Arbitration Law close to international standards and these Interpretations are particularly helpful for applying the New York Convention in China.[31] The Supreme People's Court has also demonstrated its positions, through a substantial amount of 'Responses' to inquiries from lower courts, towards various concrete issues such as 'arbitrability', 'validity of arbitration agreement', 'enforceability of foreign award' and 'public policy'.[32]

358. The most salient feature of the Chinese mechanism to apply the New York Convention is probably the 'Mandatory Report for Refusal' system, according to which if a Chinese court decides to deny recognition of a foreign arbitral award,

---

[28]This is the case in the bilateral treaties China has signed with Belgium, Brazil, Bulgaria, Cuba, Cyprus, Egypt, France, Greece, Italy, Kyrgyzstan, Laos, Lithuania, Morocco, Poland, Romania, Russia, Singapore, South Korea, Spain, Thailand, Tunisia, Ukraine, Uzbekistan, Vietnam, and Kuwait. However, a set of rules for mutual recognition and enforcement of arbitral awards that are different from those in the New York Convention have been provided in the bilateral treaties China has signed with Turkey, Mongolia and Kazakhstan.

[29]See supra para. 46.

[30]See Article 1 of Notice on the Implementation of China's Accession to the Convention on the Recognition and Enforcement of Foreign Arbitral Awards (SPC Notice on Foreign Arbitral Award).

[31]For a list of some of the most important Interpretations, see Tao (2012, pp. 19–20).

[32]E.g. see Letter of Reply of the SPC on 2 June 2006 to the Request for Instructions on the Petition of Hanjin Co., Ltd for Recognizing and Executing the Arbitral Award Made in Great Britain to the Higher People's Court of Guangdong (2005) the 4th Civil Division of the SPC No. 53; Letter of Reply of the SPC on 27 February 2008 to the Petition of the Marshall Islands First Investment Company for Recognizing and Enforcing the Arbitral Awards of the London Temporary Arbitration Tribunal to the Higher People's Court of Fujian (2007) the 4th Civil Division of the SPC No. 35; Letter of Reply of the SPC on 2 June 2008 to the Request for Instructions on Not Recognizing and Executing the Arbitral Awards of the International Court of Arbitration of International Chamber of Commerce to the Higher People's Court of Shandong (2008) the 4th Civil Division of the SPC No. 11.

the court itself must report to its immediate higher court for approval until to the SPC and only with the approval of the SPC, can a foreign arbitral award be refused for recognition under the New York Convention in China; Contrarily, if a Chinese court decides to recognize and enforce a foreign arbitral award, the Chinese court can make the decision itself and does not need to report to higher courts for approval.[33] According to statistics, during the period from 2002 to 2006, there were 9 cases reported to the Supreme People's Court under this system and only 5 of them approved for refusal.[34] This 'Mandatory Report for Refusal' system, obviously, can ensure the New York Convention to be strictly implemented in China and promote the Chinese image for foreign arbitral awards but it can unduly lengthen the recognition process and the uneven treatment for recognition and non-recognition is also doubtful.

359. Indeed, in the past decades, China has recognized and enforced most foreign arbitral awards under the New York Convention. According to a survey conducted by the Supreme People's Court, only 5 out of 74 foreign arbitral awards were denied for recognition and enforcement.[35] In recent years, given the 'Mandatory Report for Refusal' system, it is seemingly a tendency in China that more and more unreasonable barriers have been removed to faithfully and strictly implement the Convention.[36]

360. Nevertheless, along with the accession to the New York Convention, China made two reservations: one is the 'reciprocity' reservation, according to which China only recognizes and enforces arbitral awards rendered in another Contracting State to the Convention[37]; another is the 'commercial' reservation according to which the Convention is applicable in China only if the disputes arise out of legal relationships that can be viewed as 'commercial' in the eyes of Chinese law.[38]

[33]See Article 2 of Notice of the Supreme People's Court on the Handling of Issues Concerning Foreign-related Arbitration and Foreign Arbitration by People' Courts issued on 28 August 1995.

[34]See 'Chinese Courts Strictly Implement the Convention to Recognize and Enforce Foreign Arbitral Awards', Legal Daily, 15 Dec. 2008, available at http://www.legaldaily.com.cn/bm/2008-12/15/content_1001345.html (last accessed on 12 August 2015).

[35]See Yang (2009, p. 304 et seq).

[36]See Xia (2011, p. 20).

[37]See Article I (3) of New York Convention.

[38]Ibid; SCNPC Decision on Foreign Arbitral Award and SPC Notice on Foreign Arbitral Award.

Bibliography

Books

Basedow J (2010) Foundations of private international law in intellectual property. In: Basedow J, Kono T, Metzger A (eds) Intellectual property in the global arena—jurisdiction, applicable law and the recognition of judgments in Europe, Japan and the US. Mohr Siebeck, Germany

Chen L (2003) China's interregional judicial assistance under one country, two systems. Fudan University Press, Shanghai

Chen W (2012) Chinese civil procedure and the conflict of laws. Tsinghua University Press, Beijing

Cheshire GC, North PM, Fawcett JJ (2008) Private international law, 14th edn. Oxford University Press, Oxford

Chiu H, Jao YC, Wu Y (1987) The future of Hong Kong: toward 1997 and beyond. Praeger, Westport

Chow D (2003) The legal system of the People's Republic of China in a Nutshell. West Group, Eagan

De Miguel Asensio PA (2008) Applicable law in the absence of choice to contracts relating to intellectual or industrial property rights. In: Bonomi A, Volken P (eds) Yearbook of private international law. Sellier European Law Publishers, Munich

Dicey AV, Morris JHC, Collins L (2000) The conflict of laws, 13th edn. Sweet & Maxwell, London

Dicey AV, John HCM, Lawrence C (2006) The conflict of laws, 14th edn. Sweet & Maxwell, London

Ding W, Zhidong C (2005) Conflict of laws. Law Press, Beijing

Fawcett JJ (2005) General report. In: Fawcett JJ (ed) Declining jurisdiction in private international law. Oxford University Press, Oxford

Fawcett JJ, Torremans P (1998) Intellectual property and private international law. Oxford University Press, Oxford

Feinerman JV (1995) The history and development of China's dispute resolution system. In: Chris H (ed) Dispute resolution in China—a practical guide to litigation and arbitration in China. Asia Law & Practice Ltd., Hong Kong, p 5

Feng X (2006) China's interregional private law theory. The People's Court Press, Beijing

Folsom RH, Minan JH, Otto LA (1992) Law and politics in the People's Republic of China in a Nutshell. Western Publishing Company, Saint Paul (USA)

Geeroms S (2004) Foreign law in civil litigation. Oxford University Press, England

Han D (1997) New private international law. Wuhan University Press, Wuhan

Han D (2000) Private international law. Beijing University Press, Beijing

G. Tu, *Private International Law in China*, DOI 10.1007/978-981-287-993-6

Han D (2003) Private international law. Wuhan University Press, Wuhan
Han D (2005) Private international law. Beijing University Press, Beijing
He Q (2006) The applicable law on three kinds of foreign investment contracts. Wuhan University Press, Wuhan
He Q (2009) Recent developments with regard to choice of law in Tort in China. In: Bonomi A, Volken P (eds) Yearbook of private international law. European Law Publishers, Munich
Hu Z (1999) Chinese perspectives on international jurisdiction and the enforcement of judgments in contractual matters: a comparative study of the relevant provisions of Chinese, Swiss, and US law, of the European conventions and of other international treaties. Schulthess Polygraphischer Verlag, Switzerland
Huang J (2001) Interregional legal studies in China. Law Press, Beijing
Huang J (2005) Private international law, 2nd edn. Law Press, Beijing
Huang J, Guo H (1997) General part of private international law in Macau. Macau Foundation, Macau
Huang J, Jisheng H, Kai X (2004) Private international law: cases and data. Law Press, Beijing
Huo Z (2010) Private international law in China. Law Press, Beijing
Johnston G (2005) The conflict of laws in Hong Kong. Sweet & Maxwell Asia, Hong Kong
Lein E (2008) The new Rome I/Rome II/Brussels I synergy. In: Bonomi A, Volken P (eds) Yearbook of private international law. Sellier European Law Publisher, Munich
Li S (2000) Private international law. Beijing University Press, Beijing
Li S (2007) The general theory of private international law in China. Law Press, Beijing
Liu J (1994) Courses on Chinese civil procedure law. Beijing University Press, Beijing
MacFarquhar R, Fairbank JK (eds) (1987) The People's Republic, Part 1: emergence of revolutionary China, 1949–1965, vol 14. In: Denis T, Fairbank JK (eds) The Cambridge history of China. Cambridge University Press, Cambridge
Okuda Y (2008) A short look at Rome I on contract conflicts from A Japanese perspective. In: Bonomi A, Volken P (eds) Yearbook of private international law, vol 30. Sellier European Law Publisher, Munich
Peerenboom R (2002) China's long march toward rule of law. Cambridge University Press, Cambridge
Shen J (1999) The research on inter-regional conflict of laws of China. China University of Political Science and Law Press, Beijing
Symeonides SC (2000) General report. In: Symeonides SC (ed) Private international law at the end of the 20th century: progress or regress. Kluwer Law International, The Hague
Symeonides SC (2008) American private international law. Kluwer Law International, Alphen aan den Rijn
Tao J (2012) Arbitration law and practice in China, 3rd edn. Kluwer Law International, The Hague
Tu G (2009) A study on a global jurisdiction and judgments convention. Sweet & Maxwell, Hong Kong
Tu G (2013) Private international law in Macau. China Social Science Academic Press/Macau Foundation
von Mehren AT (2002) Theory and practice of adjudicatory authority in private international law: a comparative study of the doctrine, policies and practices of common-and civil-law systems. In: Collected courses of the Hague Academy of International Law, vol 295
Wunschheim C von (2011) Enforcement of commercial arbitral awards in China. West/Thomson Reuters, St. Paul, MN
Wang F (2010) Internet jurisdiction and choice of law: legal practices in the EU, US and China. Cambridge University Press, Cambridge
Xiao Y (2005) General theories on private international law. Law Press, Beijing
Xiao J (2006) A Study on inter-regional judicial assistance within China. Chinese People's National Security University Press, Beijing
Xiao Y (2007) Theories on private international law, 2nd edn. Law Press, Beijing

Xiao Y (2011) A milestone for the legislation of private international law in China. Legal Forum 2
Xie S (2007) The conflict of the laws of the Pearl River Delta area, Hong Kong and Macau and their coordination. Social Science Academic Press, Beijing
Ye Z (2004) Civil procedure law in the People's Republic of China. Law Press, Beijing
Zhang Q (2004) An introduction to constitutional law. Law Press, Beijing
Zhang W (2007) Jurisprudence, 3rd edn. Law Press, Beijing
Zhao X (2007) Private international law, 4th edn. China University of Political Science & Law Press, Beijing

Articles

Aglionby A (2007) Arbitration outside China: the alternatives. J Intl Arb 24:673
Atrill S (2004) Choice of law in contract: the missing pieces of the article 4 Jigsaw? ICLQ 53:549
Avino GR (2003) China's judiciary: an instrument of democratic change. Penn State Intl L Rev 22:380
Betti JM (1986) Reconciling American and civil law concerns in taking evidence abroad: a re-evaluation of the compromise from the Hague. ASILS Intl LJ 109, 119
Bies J (2000) Conditioning Forum Non Conveniens. U Chi L Rev 67:489
Bonomi A (2008) The Rome I regulation on the law applicable to contractual obligations: some general remarks. In: Bonomi A, Volken P (eds) Yearbook of private international law. Sellier European Law Publisher, Munich, pp 165, 170–171
Briggs A (1987) Forum non conveniens-the Last Word?' LMCLQ 1
Carruthers JM (2005) Damages in the conflict of laws—the substance and procedure spectrum: Harding v Wealands. J Priv Int L 1:323
Chang D (1988) Towards a jurisprudence of a third kind-one country, two systems. Case W Res J Intl L 20:99
Chen H (1991) China and its arbitration system in foreign trade. U Detroit L Rev 68:457
Chen R (1997–1998) A boat on a troubled strait: the interregional private law of the Republic of China on Taiwan. Wisconsin Intl L J 16:599
Chen W (2008) The conflict of laws in the context of the CISG: a Chinese perspective. Pace Intl L Rev 20:115–116, 118–119, 123–124
Chen L (2010) The historical development of the civil law tradition in China: a private law perspective. Legal Hist Rev 78:159
Chi S (1995) Arbitration mechanism to be updated in China. Intl Bus Law 23:16
Chong A (2006) The public policy and mandatory rules of third countries in international contracts. J Priv Intl L 2:27, 30
Claker DC (1996) Power and politics in the Chinese court system: the enforcement of civil judgments. Col J Asian L 10:6
Conley F (1997) Service with a smiley: the effect of e-mail and other electronic communication on service of process. Temp Intl Comp L J 11:407, 408–410
Corwin DM (1987) China's choices: the 1984 Sino-British joint declaration and its aftermath. Law & Pol Intl Bus 19:505
D'Oliveira HUJ (1977) Characteristic obligation in the draft EEC obligation convention. Am J Comp L 25:303, 304–308
Davis MC (1988) Where two legal systems collide: an American constitutional scholar in Hong Kong. Case W Res J Intl L 20:145
Edmonds RL, Yee HS (1999) Macau: from Portuguese autonomous territory to Chinese special administrative region. China Q 160:801
Edwin P (1998) Exclusive jurisdiction agreements: purity and pragmatism in the conflicts of laws. LMCLQ 182:182–183

Fawcett JJ (2001) Non-exclusive jurisdiction agreements in private international law. LMCLQ 234:234–235

Fentiman R (2002) Commercial expectations and the Rome convention. CLJ 61:50

Finder S (1993) The supreme people's court of the People's Republic of China. J Chinese L 7:180

Fiorini A (2005) The codification of private international law: the Belgium experience. ICLQ 54:499

Forsyth C (2006) Mind the gap part II: the South African supreme court of appeal and characterization. J Priv Intl L 2:425, 430–431

Garnett R, Richardson M (2009) Libel tourism or just redress? Reconciling the (English) right to reputation with the (American) right to free speech in cross-border libel cases. J Priv Intl L 5:471

Guo Y, Xu J (2008) A statistical analysis of judicial practice on foreign-related cases in civil and commercial matters in China. Chin Yb Comp Priv Intl L 11:122

Hansell HJ et al (1986) The Hong Kong accord as a model for dealing with other disputed territories. Am Soc Intl L 80:348

He Q (2005) Dilemma and choice confronted by China in service of documents abroad. CASS J L 126

He Q (2010) China's private international law (1978–2008). Front L China 5:118

He Q (2013) Reconstruction of *Lex Personalis* in China. ICLQ 62:137

Heye W (2003–2004) Forum selection for international dispute resolution in China-Chinese courts vs. CIETAC. Hastings Intl & Comp L Rev 27:546

Hill J (2004) Choice of law in contract under the Rome convention: the approach of the UK Courts. ICLQ 53: 325, 327–332, 334–336, 346–347

Hsia T, Zeldin WI (1987) Recent legal developments in the People's Republic of China. Harvard Intl LJ 28:258

Hu Z (2002) A comparative study on the doctrine of forum non conveniens. CASS J L 138, 153

Huang J (1998) The structure of China's conflicts law: new developments of the rules on special commercial law. NILR 45:188

Huang J (2010) Interregional recognition and enforcement of civil and commercial judgments: lessons for China from US and EU laws. J Priv Intl L 6:109

Huang J (2011) The formulation and improvement of China's conflicts code. Tribune Pol Sci L 3:12

Huang J, Qian AX (1995) One country, two systems, three law families, and four legal regions: the emerging inter-regional conflicts of laws in China. Duke J Comp & Intl L 5:289

Huang J, Hu W, Wang Q (2008) Annual survey of judicial practice in Chinese private international law in 2007. Chin Yb Comp Priv Intl L 11:436

Huang J, Hu W, Du H (2009) Annual survey of judicial practice in chinese private international law in 2008. Chin Yb Comp Priv Intl L 12:425

Hung MS (2008) Obstacles to self-actualization in Chinese legal practice. Santa Clara L Rev 48:223

Huo Z (2011) An imperfect improvement: the new conflict of laws act of the People's Republic of China. ICLQ 60:1065

Juenger FK (1995) Appendix A: letter from Friedrich Juenger to Harry C. Sigman, Esq., June 23, 1994. Vanderbilt J Transnatl L 28:445, 449

Juenger FK (1997) Contract choice of law in the Americas. Am J Comp L 45:195–196, 199, 200, 204–206

Kong Q, Minfei H (2002) Chinese practice of private international law. Melb J Intl L 3:414

Konstantinos DK (1987) A civilian lawyer looks at common law procedure. Louisiana L Rev 47:493, 494

Lando O, Nielsen PA (2007) The Rome I proposal. J Priv Intl L 3:29, 30–34

Lee C, Lu A (2005) Ignored no more: Renvoi and international torts litigated in Australia. J Priv Intl L 1:35, 66

Li H (1999) Enforcement of the international commercial arbitration award in the PRC. J Int Arb 16:1

Liu N (1989–1990) Ignored source of Chinese law: the Gazette of Supreme People's Court. Conn J Intl L 5:278

Liu N (1991) Legal precedents with Chinese characteristics: published cases in the gazette of the Supreme People's Court. J Chin L 5:118

Lorenzen EG (1921) Validity and effects of contracts in the conflict of laws. Yale L J 30:565, 573

Lubman S (2000) Bird in a cage: Chinese law reform after twenty years. Northwest J Intl L & Bus 20:396

Luke FM (2000) Imminent threat of China's intervention in Macau's autonomy: using Hong Kong's past to secure Macau's future. Am U Intl L Rev 15:717

Ma L (2007) The first case that Chinese judgment being recognized by a German Court. Study L & Bus 150:154

Mills A (2008) The dimensions of public policy in private international law. J Priv Intl L 4:201–202

Palumbo PH (1990–1991) Analysis of the Sino-British joint declaration and the basic law of Hong Kong: what do they guarantee the people of Hong Kong after 1997. Conn J Intl L 6: 667

Panagopoulos G (2005) Substance and procedure in private international law. J Priv Intl L 1:69

Nygh P (1995) The reasonable expectations of the parties as a guide to the choice of law in contract and in Tort. Collect Courses Hague Acad Intl L 251: 269, 309

Qiao X (2010) Information technology and taking of evidence abroad: problems, rules and practices. Wuhan U Intl L Rev 11:145

Reyes RE (1997) The enforcement of foreign court judgments in the People's Republic of China: what the American Lawyer needs to know. Brooklyn J Intl L 23: 241

Shi S, Teng M (2003) The current status of the doctrine of *forum non conveniens* in China. Natl Judges Coll L J 7:60, 61

Song L, Jian Z, Hong L (2003) Approaches to the revision of the 1994 arbitration act of the People's Republic of China. J Intl Arb 20

Struycken AVM (1978) The rules of jurisdiction in the EEC convention on jurisdiction and the enforcement of judgments in civil and commercial matters. NILR 25:356–357

Symeonides SC (2008a) Rome II and Tort conflicts: a missed opportunity. Am J Comp L 56:173, 188

Symeonides SC (2008b) The American revolution and the European evolution in choice of law: reciprocal lessons. Tul L Rev 82:1741, 1747, 1752, 1760

Tetley W (2000) Mixed jurisdictions: common law v. civil law (codified and un-codified). Louisiana L Rev 60:677, 705

Tong R, Zhang X, Guan T (1988) Retrospect and prospect of Chinese civil law. Legal Stud Res 6:20

Tu G (2007) The Hague choice of court convention—a Chinese perspective. Am J Comp L 55:204–205, 347

Tu G (2011) Forum non conveniens in the People's Republic of China. Chin J Intl L 11:341, 343–344

Tu G (2013) The arrangement on mutual recognition and enforcement of judgments in civil and commercial matters between mainland China and Macau special administrative region: inherent problems, six years' experience and the way forward. HKLJ 43:349

Tu G, Muchi X (2011) Contractual conflicts in the People's Republic of China: the applicable law in the absence of choice. J Priv Intl L 7:179

Tu G, Li X (2013) The second amendment of Chinese civil procedure law: a note from the perspective of international civil litigation. HKLJ 43:633–658

Turkel LJ (1986–1987) One country, two systems: Hong Kong's paradox of politics and business. NY Sch J Intl Comp L 8:471

Wang Z (2006) The Roman law tradition and its future development in China. Front L China 1:72, 77, 78

Wong SK (1999, Nov) Mutual enforcement of arbitral awards between the mainland and the HKSAR. HKL 67–70
Wu Y (2005) The authoritative level of the legal interpretations and applicable rules of conflict. People's Procuratorate Monthly 7:60
Wu C-H (2010) Mutual recognition of arbitral awards among Taiwan, China, Hong Kong and Macau: Regulatory Framework and Judicial Development. Contemp Asia Arb J 3:65
Xi X (2002) A few thoughts on the doctrine of *forum non conveniens*. CASS J L (2002): 81, 85
Xia X (2011) Implementation of the New York convention in China. Intl Com Arb Brief 1:20
Xiao Y (2000) Comments on the judgment on the right of abode by Hong Kong CFA. Am J Comp L 48:471
Xiao Y (2002) The conflict of laws between mainland China and the Hong Kong special administrative region: the choice of coordination models. Yrbk Priv Intl L 4:182
Xiao Y, Du T (1998) The study of coordination models of inter-regional conflict of laws in multiple-legal systems countries. Chin Yb Priv Intl L & Comp L 1:358
Xiao Y, Huo Z (2005) *Ordre public* in China's private international law. Am J Comp L 53:653
Xiao Y, Long W (2009) Enforcement of international arbitration agreements in Chinese Courts. Arb Intl 25:569
Xu G (1989) Contract in Chinese private international law. ICLQ 38:648, 651–652
Xu H (2008) A review of China's participation in the Hague conference on private international law in the past two decades. Wuhan U Intl L Rev 2:407
Yan Q, Wang Y (1984) A brief introduction to the convention on agency in the international sale of goods. Issues Intl Trade 6
Yang Z (1986) The historical conditions and significance of the birth of the <General Principle of Civil Law>. Tribune Pol Sci L 3:8
Yang H (2009) Report on the judicial review of international arbitration in Chinese courts. Intl L Rev Wuhan U 7:304 et seq
Yu S, Xiao Y, Wang B (2009) Closest connection doctrine in the conflict of laws in China. Chin J Intl L 8:423
Yuan AA (2004) Enforcing and collecting money judgments in China from a U.S. judgment creditor's perspective'. Geo Wash Intl L Rev 36 (2004): 757
Zhang Z (1997) Studies about the Chinese legal interpretation system. Soc Sci China 2:102–103
Zhang S (1998) Exploration on the conflict of laws and application of laws among different legal territories in China. Chin Yb Priv Intl L, & Comp L 1:364
Zhang S (1999) The history and current situation of the development of private international law in China. Jurists Rev 5:30
Zhang M (2002) International civil litigation in China: a practical analysis of the Chinese judicial system. Boston Coll Intl & Comp L Rev 25: 59, 87
Zhang M (2006a) Choice of law in contracts: a Chinese approach. Northwest J Intl L & Bus 26:289
Zhang M (2006b) Party autonomy and beyond: an international perspective of contractual choice of law. Emory Intl L Rev 20: 522–524, 551–553
Zhang W (2011) The amendment of civil procedure law to meet current demands. People's Cong China 22:25–27
Zhang M (2011–2012) Codified choice of law in China: rules, processes and theoretic underpinnings. NC J Intl L & Com Reg 37:83
Zhang W (2013) Recognition and enforcement of foreign judgments in China: a call for special attention to both the "due service requirement" and the "principle of reciprocity. Chin J Comp L 12:143
Zhang Y, McLean JS (1987) China's foreign economic contract law: its significance and analysis. Northwest J Intl L & Bus 8:120
Zhang X, Smart P (2006) Development of regional conflict of laws: on the arrangement of mutual recognition and enforcement of judgments in civil and commercial matters between mainland China and Hong Kong SAR. HKLJ 36:568

Zhao Y (2009) The practical dilemma of service by publication in civil proceedings and choice of path in realization of its internal value. J L Appl 57–59

Zhao X, Kloppenberg LA (2005–2006) Reforming Chinese arbitration law and practices in the global economy. U Dayton L Rev 31:421

Zhong J, Yu G (2004) Establishing the truth on facts: has the Chinese civil process achieved this goal. J Transnatl L Pol'y 13:398

Zhu G (2002) Inter-regional conflict of laws under "one country, two systems": revisiting chinese legal theories and Chinese and Hong Kong law, with special reference to judicial assistance. HKLJ 32:637

Zhu W (2007) China's codification of the conflict of laws: publication of a draft text. J Priv Intl L 3:283, 295

Index

G. Tu, *Private International Law in China*, DOI 10.1007/978-981-287-993-6

GPSR Compliance
The European Union's (EU) General Product Safety Regulation (GPSR) is a set of rules that requires consumer products to be safe and our obligations to ensure this.

If you have any concerns about our products, you can contact us on

ProductSafety@springernature.com

In case Publisher is established outside the EU, the EU authorized representative is:

Springer Nature Customer Service Center GmbH
Europaplatz 3
69115 Heidelberg, Germany

www.ingramcontent.com/pod-product-compliance
Lightning Source LLC
LaVergne TN
LVHW052324200926
848481LV00002B/662
* 9 7 8 9 8 1 1 0 0 6 7 5 3 *